What the River Knows

Wayne

Fields

The University of Chicago Press

Chicago and London

What the River Knows

An Angler in Midstream

The University of Chicago Press, Chicago 60637
The University of Chicago Press, Ltd., London

Copyright © 1990 by Wayne Fields

ISBN 0-226-24857-7 (pbk.)

Library of Congress Cataloging-in-Publication Data

Fields, Wayne.
    What the river knows : an angler in midstream / Wayne
Fields.
        p.   cm.
    Originally published: New York : Poseidon Press, 1990.
    1. Trout fishing—Michigan—Cook's Run—Anecdotes.
    2. Fly fishing—Michigan—Cook's Run—Anecdotes.
    3. Fields, Wayne—Anecdotes.   I. Title.
    [SH688   .U6F54   1996]
    799.1'755—dc20   95-50348
                                                          CIP

⊗ The paper used in this publication meets the minimum
requirements of the American National Standard for Information
Sciences—Permanence of Paper for Printed Library Materials,
ANSI Z39.48–1984.

For my family and all the others who have helped me through the deeper waters— some of whom are named in this book, many of whom are not

July 29
Prologue

Late July signals the beginning of the end. There is, of course, a full month remaining, nearly as much time as what has already passed, but August is the last month and, in northern latitudes, brings the surest signs of closure: the reddening of the maples, the clustering of ducks preparing for flight south, the frantic feeding of bears as the last berries ripen, the final noisy training of young loons. Regardless of the number of weeks remaining on the calendar, with the last days of July come the first thoughts of leave-taking, the painful reacceptance of time's triumph.

This summer has been subdued. We came north as we have done for fifteen years, driving through Illinois and the length of Wisconsin to the Upper Peninsula of Michigan. This time Sarah, our oldest child, did not come with us. Sixteen, she had gone on a trip to Rhode Island and did not catch up with us until three weeks ago. A small change, admittedly, but one which hinted at things to come, things that a year ago still seemed far away. And, too, an hour out of Saint Louis, our fourteen-year-old black lab, Smeagol, had some kind of attack. The only veterinarian we could readily find was a half-drunken old man in a filthy building whose normal business was restricted to cattle. He gave the dog a relaxant in a futile effort to restore normal breathing and put him in a pen with a concrete floor. The convulsions grew more violent while the vet, eyes closed, hands trembling in his lap, sat hunched over in a ladderback chair a few feet away. At last Karen, my wife, driven by anger and grief, began calling ahead trying to find assistance in one of the towns up the road until she reached a clinic in Springfield, thirty miles away. With Karen driving as fast as she dared, and Elizabeth, our thirteen-year-old, and Aaron, eleven, crying quietly in the back seat, I tried, in the cargo area of the station wagon, to hold the thrashing dog and prevent his beating against the sides of the car. His entire length repeatedly constricted, folded in the middle, then suddenly thrust out into a straightened position, and, as I tried to absorb the violence with my own body, his head crashed into me again and again, once delivering so strong a blow to my jaw that pain shot up the back of my skull and blurred my vision.

When we reached the Springfield clinic, the veterinarian quieted the convulsions with drugs and gave Smeagol oxygen, but the dog did not awaken. The vet checked and rechecked heart rate and temperature, each time looking at us sympathetically and with an unspoken question in his glance. When we did not respond, he began, hesitantly, to suggest that the animal could not get better, and so at last we went into the waiting room to talk with Elizabeth and Aaron. Back with the doctor and the dog, we told him to get on with it, signed the papers, then caressed Smeagol as the injection was given. Breathing slowed, then stopped.

It is absurd to identify with a dog; nevertheless, I do. We got Smeagol shortly after Elizabeth's birth, and his clumsy antics had provided pleasant distraction during the months of her struggle with heart disease and the long period of uncertainty and, eventually, recovery that followed her surgery. He accepted his pretentious name, borrowed from Tolkien's *Lord of the Rings,* answering with tail-thumping eagerness all the bungled pronunciations the name inspired (we said it Smay–ah–gul), and as a compulsive sniffer, an audible snorter after scents, he lived up to the Anglo-Saxon origin of his identity—the seeker. Then he had out-aged the children. As they moved into adolescence, he became my contemporary: like me, gray around the muzzle; like me, stiffening with age; like me, hard of hearing. In the weeks since his

death I've come to realize how deeply I—and the rest of the
family—have been affected by the loss.

Perhaps that is where all of this begins, that sense of loss and
the related losses, real and anticipated, that go with being forty-
two and a parent. Or perhaps the explanation is simpler. The
fishing has been poor, and in recent days I've gone to the river
rarely and reluctantly—unusual behavior for me, since I have
always fished more for the stream than for the catch. And there
has been ample reward for my efforts this summer: I have found
a pool where two otters play, and once, in late June, a fisher
crossed a beaver dam not more than fifteen feet downstream from
me. Still, for the past five mornings, I have shut off the alarm
clock without getting up.

My lack of enthusiasm may also stem from the fact that Joe,
a neighbor on the lake, and the one who introduced me to
fly-fishing, has rarely gone to the river this summer. In past years
he has gone out daily, and, though we never fish together, we
often share rides, walking into the stream at different locations
or wading in opposite directions once we reach the water. And
we always compare notes even when we go out separately. But
Joe just turned seventy-five, and though he says it is the heat and
the lack of action that keeps him home, I worry that he thinks
himself too old for the tangle of alder, the high water, the
treacherous footing. I worry that he *is* too old. He has always
talked about dying—we began fishing together the summer after
he survived surgery and radiation therapy for cancer—but it used
to be bold, brash talk. This year he is more subdued; he busies
himself with small chores as though tidying up his affairs, repairs
his cabin, sorts his tools. He seems to be preparing his and Vi's
place for someone else.

Of course I do more than fish and not fish during the summer.
I work on the cabin, I prepare for my next year's classes, and I
write, carting books and notes from St. Louis. But our cabin, six
years in the making by our unskilled hands, is finished except for

jobs too insignificant to generate any sense of excitement—
installing light switches in the holes in our walls although our
area has still not been electrified—and jobs too large and too
expensive for our budget—installing a kitchen and a bath. This
was to be the year we started on the plumbing, but the land next
to ours came up for sale, and for the sake of privacy we bought
it, or rather three-fourths of it, and now there is no money for
major projects.

The writing, although I continue at it, has also slowed. All
spring I worked on a book about American literature, wrote
regularly and persistently, but now I cannot finish it. I am a
college teacher and college teachers are supposed to write books,
and my college is less than delighted with the slowness of my
production. I need this book, and I have not been writing it.

My other writing, supposedly more commercial in nature, has
finally started to sell, but the magazine that owns the most
ambitious of my efforts has, for the past five months, been delaying publication, and I have come to doubt that the piece will ever
appear in print.

So it happens that the only job I—we—presently have under
way is the demolition of a collapsing building on our newly
purchased land. Yesterday, while Karen burned boards that had
been riddled by carpenter ants, I tore down the walls of a later
addition to the original log cabin. On a 1-by-6, beneath the
asphalt siding, I found, written in pencil, "Built by D. F. Carlysle
+ Tom Coulter June 22, 1956." I know D. F. Carlysle, a big,
easygoing man, now retired, know his daughter and her family,
and I pictured him building what I was tearing down, his children, the ages of our children, the ages of his grandchildren. The
1-by-6 broke in half where the ant tunnels were thickest, but the
message, untouched by the decay, remained. I looked to where
our cabin soars above the spruce and birch, and with D. F.
Carlysle's message in hand I began thinking about wading Cook's
Run, all of it, from the mouth to the source.

I have always been drawn to streams, and already, as a child, I slipped away to the creek that ran through the hickory and oak timber south of my grandfather's farm. My mother had a terrible fear of rivers and declared the creek officially off limits; but my longing for it was greater than my desire to please her, great as that was, and I would sneak away to sit on the plank bridge and watch the thin, slow water slide beneath me. Here also I came, openly, with my father and uncles to watch on crisp March mornings as they cut firewood and fence posts from the scraggliest trees on the creek bottom. Farther downstream, and in summer, I helped my grandfather tend a cucumber patch that he cultivated on a small island cut by an oxbow in the stream's winding.

And, too, for the better part of a lifetime I have lived within a few miles of the Mississippi, "The River" for those of us who grew up on its floodplain, the great locating presence that gave us, on maps and in mind, a place to be, a kind of string that tied our insignificant farms and towns to places that we took to be more substantial, more important, than those in which we were trying to find ourselves. But "The River," that river, though it continues to run through my life, is not a subject I can take on in anything other than a superficial way. Too long and too deep, unwadeable, unfathomable, it is proper subject perhaps for youth or age, but not for forty-two.

Once, more than ten years ago, I followed the Lewis and Clark trail from St. Louis to the Pacific and back again. Since that time I have often thought about following rivers, following wherever they might lead, of learning tomorrow the source of the water flowing around me today. But I am a decade older than were either Lewis or Clark, and I know some of my limits. So I choose Cook's Run, a modest stream famous for its big trout, less than twenty miles long and, from its mouth to its source, close to home. And because in the past I have waded only two or three short sections of the Run, and those rarely, it will be an adventure, and I will write about it. Somewhere along the way I will find a subject, something that holds it all together, something to redeem my summer or some small part of it.

That was yesterday. Today as I sit at my desk in the loft not writing my book, the Cook's Run wade seems absurd. Then again, I decide, that makes the project all the more appropriate, a middle-aged foray, consciously ironic.

Elizabeth rushes into the cabin to tell me breathlessly that an eagle is flying over the lake, and outside Aaron is yelling, "Hurry up, it's coming closer."

August is the right month for the wade: an end of summer, a time of leave-taking. I will begin with August.

The children cry out again, and looking up, I see, through the skylight, the eagle swooping low overhead, banking against the morning sun, its wingspan breathtakingly wide, and I watch through the plastic bubble in our roof the long, low flight over the lake, watch the sudden dive and the backward thrust of legs and talons as it takes its prey.

A u g u s t 1

It rained hard this morning. When I awoke at 5:30 the storm had just begun, and by 6:30 the lightning strikes were close, barely across the lake, their flash diffused, a dull flickering across a curtain of white water. The sound came through unmuted, great house-shaking thunderclaps and the keening of trees as they beat against themselves, but I could not see the dock only fifty feet away, or the white canoe lying belly-up on the grass. Later, by the accumulation in a bucket on the shed steps, we estimated the rainfall at three to three and a half inches in less than two hours.

Apart from one or two brief sprinkles, there has been no more rain, but the day has continued gray and heavy, without any movement in the air. I have been putting off my start on the Run. The water will be high and too dark for fly-fishing. And, too, I am hesitant about wading the lower part of the stream. I've been on that stretch only once before, five years ago, and found it then, under better conditions, wild with boulders and white water, nearly unwadeable. I do not expect to catch fish in such turbulence, or even to keep a line in the stream, but I would like to avoid breaking a leg. This is not the day to begin. It is, however, the day I said I'd begin. At last, a little after three, I get under way.

The rain has cut channels into the edges of our lake road, made pools in the tire tracks, washed rocks down from the bank on either side, and where I am not expecting it, gouged a hole that grabs at the left front tire. Lifted off the seat by the jolt, I twist the steering wheel, but not quickly enough to avoid an encore with the left rear tire. I curse the rain, the township maintenance crew, myself, and wait for the roar that will testify to the second muffler I have dragged off in less than a month. The roar does not come.

The road to my grandparents' farm, though wider and better ditched, was a lot like this one, only with more clay, so that it became a river of mud with every hard rain, passable only by tractor. What was wanted, I came to understand, was something called a "kingbill road." I did not know exactly what this meant other than a path on which the going, regardless of weather, would be easy, but I thought the name, kingbill, must refer to some exotic bird, a bird I came to believe I had once glimpsed in an old National Geographic, *a colorful broad-winged, strong-beaked creature, free to fly wherever it chose, soaring over lesser traffic, its threatening aspect sufficient warning to all who would oppose it. Like my more practical elders whose primary concern was easy access to the mailbox, I longed for a road whose name promised so much. Only years later did I realize that what we hoped for was merely a blacktop highway, funded by the state of Missouri under a bill originally sponsored by a representative named King.*

Two miles from our cabin, I turn off the forest highway onto a gravel road that parallels what used to be a railroad track—this year the rails have been torn out, leaving only the narrow bed winding between the road and the river. Out of sight to the left, the Paint River runs through white pines and cedars. It is the Paint which I fish most often, preferring its wider water to the narrow Run, and I pass several places where countless times I have left the car and trekked in—familiar places. I make excuses, will fish here today and go to the Run when conditions are better. But I keep driving, four more miles along this glistening brown break in the timber, past the Wiegand farm, past Basswood—a nonexistent landing on a now nonexistent railroad—to the bridge where the road crosses Cook's Run. Here I pull into an abandoned gravel pit, or rather the cut-out section of a gravel hill, and park the car beside a horseshoe-shaped bluff of river-smoothed stones.

The only other time I fished below this bridge, exhausted by the rough wade, I sat on the tailgate when I had finished, pulling off my waders and stowing my fishing gear. Sometime in all of this, the car keys slipped from my pocket, and when I closed the car door, I locked myself out and the keys in. After trying every way I knew, short of smashing a window, to break in, and after several more minutes of swearing and car kicking, I walked the three miles to the Wiegands' through a drizzle and sheepishly asked for a round-trip ride to the cabin and Karen's keys. Today I check my pocket every few minutes, even unbuckling my waders for one last precautionary pat before starting toward the stream.

Just below the road a trestle made of great creosoted beams crosses the Run. Raspberries are full and red around its base, and I pick a handful before climbing the embankment to the old track bed. From that elevation I can look down at the water, fast and high. Large-flowered black-eyed Susans are clumped along the bank, long yellow petals drooping from the damp, blossoms bending heavily on their long stems until, nearest the stream, they nearly touch the water. Orange-and-brown butterflies, a nearly perfect match to the flowers, flit around the trestle and out over the big pool that has been impounded by debris wedged tightly between the bridge footings.

With rails and ties removed, the roadbed, now smoothed for a snowmobile track, allows easy walking, and though I appreciate the advantage to myself, I resent the encouragement it will give to others, the easy access for Jeeps and pickup trucks.

The main attraction of fishing these streams, for me, is not the plentitude of trout, but the scarcity of people. This is in part because I like to be alone and in part because I am not a very good fisherman—certainly not one who bears watching. The last is probably the result of impatience as much as anything else. Or more precisely, impatience coupled with a strange sort of perfectionism; I am always torn between a desire to fish every hole deliberately and the urge to move ahead and cover as much river as possible. I will, as a consequence, make hurried, almost compulsive, casts until I am convinced I have placed the fly everywhere a trout might be concealed (never mind that my first efforts have telegraphed ample warning to any lurking fish), will hurry into position rather than sidle around with the stealth appropriate to the serious sportsman. Also, I do not readily experiment with different flies, since I resist fumbling with knots and am reluctant, even in the slowest of times, to take the line off the water, no matter how briefly. Emphasis in my fishing falls on the physical, when the secret to any angling success lies with the mental. So I work a promising spot, using the same tired coachman, until, satisfied that I have covered all the water with at least one respectable cast, I move ahead.

But mostly it is the need to get away from people that brings me to the most isolated stretches of river, the need to be out of calling range. Because I am easily disconcerted by the presence of others, made claustrophobic even by the possibility that someone can phone or drop by, I need these streams as places to try in private to compose myself, to repair the damage of a year at school, the daily wear and tear caused by the proximity of other lives. Even when I was a child, my grandfather, noting my mounting anxiety as things grew increasingly hectic in the house, would say, "Go on outside. You look as though your bones itch." It is not an affliction that improves with age.

On the lake I fantasize that to the north there is only timber, that I am located on some outer edge of population, and, rowing to the other shore, could walk all the way to the end of north, to the point where south begins, without running into anyone. It is, of course, a notion best left untested, since, among other places, the not inconsequential town of Marquette lies in that direction.

About fifteen minutes up the track there is a break in the clouds. Abruptly the sun is bright and glaring, and I am sweating. I had planned to cut into the timber just below the trestle and push through to the Paint immediately below the mouth of Cook's Run, but I delay, afraid I will make my entrance too soon, and reluctant to leave the easy path I am on. The railbed crosses a drive, marked by a PRIVATE sign, a civilly produced print shop warning, then signs saying KEEP OUT, somehow more threatening because they are hand-lettered, appear on the largest birches and maples—an added incentive to stay on the straight and narrow. Too, ahead and about a mile below the Run is a large pool that reaches nearly to the track bed, and on a day in which I expect to spend most of my time merely keeping my balance, its quiet waters seem alive with promise.

For years our cabin was unreachable by phone. That changed before Elizabeth's surgery, during the time when her St. Louis doctor would allow trips to Michigan only if we could reach him at a moment's notice.

We knew there was phone service along Highway 16, but while we also knew it wasn't Bell, we didn't know what it was. Our first day in Michigan that summer, I drove down the road looking for a house connected to the lines paralleling the black-top. About a mile from the cabin I saw a pickup parked off to the side and a man leaning against a telephone pole.

"Do you know where I can find somebody that works for the phone company?" I asked.

"Pretty likely," he answered. He pushed his cap back and rubbed a finger along his nose, lifting his glasses with the movement. "I do. Or at least I did when I left the office this morning."

Two days later Bob Thompson, the man I'd met on the road, accompanied by the owner of Midway Telephone Company and the owner's teenage son (except for an operator, the company's complete work force), came to the cabin ready to hook us into the main line. They brought with them a tractor and a hollow point plow with which they ran the cable, the plow cutting through the rocky soil of our driveway, laying the line through the hole in the nose of the blade, then funneling the dirt back in place. It was all very neat in theory, but the plow continually hung up on boulders concealed beneath the road's surface, sometimes bulling them aside, but just as often grinding to a halt, until either the tractor tried a new route or the men levered the rock aside with pry bars.

Progress was slow and I grew increasingly anxious, knowing what lay ahead. The owner, looking down the drive to where it crossed the swamp behind the cabin, said with relief, "It will get easier when we reach that fill."

"Actually," I said, "that fill covers a corduroy road."

He looked at me carefully, making sure that I was not putting him on. "Oh, well," he sighed.

When they hit the filled area the plow snagged log after rotting log, raising each stiffly out of the gravel, the full width of the drive shivering and shifting as a ten-foot section of cedar or tamarack rose reluctantly from its damp grave. Bob, walking beside the plow, snaked telephone line around the butt end of the logs as the tractor crawled ahead. When the line at last reached the cabin, there remained a thirty-foot trail of stumps, irregularly set like antitank obstacles in a war zone, marking the underground path of all our messages.

Three hours already invested in our hookup, the men took another hour rebuilding the drive with the tractor blade. When that was done and a black phone hung conspicuously on the rear wall of our cabin, they sat and drank coffee, the owner carefully printing our name and number into his catalogue of customers. He gave Karen a list, printed just as precisely, as though it might be graded for penmanship, of the three or four other customers whom we could call "locally."

I fretted about the bill for all this, convinced we would be charged by the hour, convinced the meager savings we had set against the summer would be immediately depleted. But the men seemed in no hurry to leave, were already talking about the afternoon's work nostalgically, as though it had taken place in the distant past.

When they left, the owner almost shyly handed me the bill, the regular installation fee. Twelve dollars, as I remember it.

The pool lies just a few yards north of the track at a point where the river emerges briefly from the timber. The water here is about seventy-five feet wide and two hundred feet long, and the afternoon sun catches it at a slant, burnishing a surface still blackened by lingering thunderheads and setting it darkly agleam. Along the railbed a big garter snake flicks off the sand and into the grass ahead of me, roused slowly, then to a sudden darting as it reaches the high weeds. The muddy yellows and greenish browns of its back are for a moment separate creatures, writhing away of their own volition, and then all vanish in a thatch of storm-broken plants.

The water has risen into the grass, reaching five or six inches onto the stalks of the weeds and flowers, and I slide easily, from a sitting position, into the waist-deep stream. Above me and closer to the opposite bank is the deepest part of the pool, and beyond that, rapids where the river first rounds into sight. But I begin in the quieter, shaded water along the south bank. Here the pool bulges away from the main current, a backwater of logs and rocks cast aside by spring floods. Working the fly, an Adams dry, around and over this cover, I try for a regular casting rhythm that will drop the half inch of hook and feathers gently on an extended leader.

The Paint turns a dark, rusty color after rain, and except for the largest rocks and logs that loom shadowlike around me, there is little to be seen beneath the surface. Still I think I glimpse other shadows rising from the depths—not clear, brisk movements, but a slow drifting somewhere at the edge of my vision—that are evidence, if they are evidence at all, of nothing more than undefined possibilities. I turn away from the dark water, clearing my head of imagined fish, of the big browns that I know are here but also know I do not see.

The first time Karen and I came to the Upper Peninsula, we drove up with Kurt, a friend from graduate school whose parents own a place just outside Iron River. We came for Thanksgiving and drove back in a blizzard. The next summer we came again, returning from a long trip east during which I had begun the research for my dissertation.

On a drizzly morning Kurt and I went fishing, trolling in gray waters for anything that would come our way. As we worked the shoreline, the houses erased by fog and mist, we began catching northern pike, twenty-three and twenty-four inches, their long mouths filled with hundreds of back-tilting teeth, clear and sharp, like tiny slivers of crystal. After a time my lure snagged somewhere in the weed beds below. Kurt caught hold of the line and, while I reeled, began patiently, hand over hand, to pull it in. Weeds came up in great clots and then, at last, greener than

the vegetation, came a three-foot pike. Kurt cursed and dropped
the line as the fish, nearly in his hands, broke the water in one
heavy roll. I remember most clearly, after seventeen years, the
eyes, black, bulging with an old malevolence above that razor-
filled snout and glittering briefly in the light before plunging
down into the dark below.

I move to the other side where the current ripples beneath a
bank of grass and thistles, and where tall white pines lift fragile
needles against the sky. White pine needles come in clusters of
five, fine and delicate, a kind of lacework distinctive even at a
distance, and, like all pines, the limbs reach upward, thrusting
their slight burden high into the light. The water coils almost at
the roots of the closest tree, and at its margin a hummingbird,
bright throat iridescent in a show of gaudy color, hovers among
the thistles.

Snakes. Hummingbirds. But no trout. I had counted on this
pool to provide the day's bounty, or at least the excitement of
a near-miss, a little something to get the ball rolling, to set the
right tone. But there are only shadows, shadows that I catch with
the corner of my eye as they rise to meet me and then, as I turn,
fall from sight.

I enter the deeper water at the center of the pool and cast the
Adams into the rapids above. Nothing strikes, not even in those
few moments when the fly rides, a delicate brown fluff, on the
stream's rough surface.

I am taking notes as I go along, writing details in a small
blue-faced spiral notebook that I carry, together with two ball-
point pens, in my jacket pocket. This and that along the way,
disconnected points from which, I hope, a pattern will eventually
emerge. Jefferson sent instructions for all literate members of the
Lewis and Clark party to maintain a record of their journey,
convinced that when they made it home, he, at least, would see
the sense of it.

Above the pool, after clambering around the boulders at its entrance, I enter a long straight stretch of big rocks and fast water. Here cedars, some bending so low they stir the surface with their branches, parallel the water before turning sharply upward toward the light, shading the southern edge of the river. The entire fifty-foot width is a torrent, a series of rapids guarded by boulders, loud and unruly with high-thrown water that breaks against my lower body, turning me until I move against it sideways, wedging ahead, my hip and knee carving a path.

Something in the middle of the river reaches upward, falls clumsily, then reaches again and again. An arm, elbow crooked, lifts up stiffly, then drops as the body, buried in the overwhelming water, tumbles downstream. It reemerges, now clearly a big tree limb, and I watch as the river rolls it past me through rank on rank of rapids, watch as time after time the twisted arm reaches out in futile appeal only to fall once more beneath the surface.

When children disappeared from the small towns along the Mississippi, if they were not discovered in the first frantic search of nearby barns and woodlots, the fathers would go to the river with great pronged dragging hooks and, from the shore and small boats, cast into all the places where a child could hide beneath the surface. While mothers and children watched from the land, old men, river rats, toothless and unshaven, rousted from their shanties, pointed out the spots where in the past the water had stored its treasures, and we waited as hook after hook snagged submerged logs, castaway tires, the drift of a continent, waited as the men pulled against their catch, fearing that this would be the child, yet knowing that only if it were would the ordeal be finished.

In these rough waters I cannot keep the Adams afloat, and I finally replace it with a large muddler that I hope will be more visible in the dark stream, but am content merely with the fact that it can be allowed, guiltlessly, to slip beneath the surface.

The delicacy of the Adams is a consequence of the feathers that have gone into its making. Except for the gray floss body, it consists entirely of hackle—gray hackle for the tail, vertically tied gray hackle tippets for wings, and interwoven gray and brown hackle around the floss. By contrast the muddler comes from coarser stock: turkey tippet for the tail, mottled turkey feathers for the wings, a silver tinsel body, and everything topped off with bucktail behind the hook's eye, trimmed rough and round. A muddler is not supposed to look like some slight insect fallen to the current, but a minnow, a little bullhead swimming under its own power, its fat body moving in and out like gills and fins behind the thick and bristly head.

The sky is now completely overcast, a fact that usually improves my fishing, but fishing has become secondary to staying upright, especially when I push between the biggest boulders where the funneled current is most powerful. This is an endurance test, not a display of fishing virtuosity, not the artful sport shown in magazines and on Saturday television shows. I push ahead, guided only by the theory that if you keep a fly in the stream long enough, something will eventually come along, and by the conviction that even a blind hog finds an acorn once in a while. Too, there is an exhilaration that comes merely from plowing through, no matter how gracelessly, where the scoring is only for degree of difficulty, not for beauty of execution.

Still, this is more endurance and less artistry than I would like. Struggling to keep my legs from getting crossed as I edge around boulders, I let the muddler drift where it will, and, in the midst of white water, my note-taking has become a kind of crazy acrobatic as I try to keep the paper dry and yet not lose the fly rod pinched between my elbow and my side. But there is an absurd satisfaction even in this feat, and the writing provides much-needed breaks in my floundering struggle upriver.

This seems the nature of all writing: an awkward fumbling after grace, an interruption of everyday life in which we try to redeem something from that mostly graceless endeavor. Like fly-fishing, writing is an elaborate conspiracy to make lyrical an activity that is inherently a business of barbs and worms.

At the end of the straight passage I have been wading, boulders reach out from each bank in ten-foot barriers, forcing the river into a wide sluiceway. The Michigan Department of Natural Resources (DNR) has also constructed, in addition to these wing dams, a grid of logs—yet another breakwater—in the middle of the stream. All of this comes in a slight bend, and as I work my way around the grid I can see a bridge, half collapsed, about a hundred yards ahead and, to the left, a clearing for a camp. Here, casting backward into the jumble of rocks forming the spillway, I get my first fish. It takes the fly without breaking the surface, and, with the torrent's weight against it, does not fight, just drags water like an anchor, bending the rod as I try to play it properly. Only there is no play, merely the hauling in of seemingly dead weight. Finally, surfacing beside me, it is a six-and-a-half-inch brook trout, orange and red spots gleaming. The fish, too exhausted to resist, does not struggle as I unhook it but, upon release, revives and streaks toward the protection of the wing dam.

A shack stands just below the bridge, its windows boarded over, the grass tall around it. I wonder if this belongs to whoever put up the hand-lettered warnings by the railbed, but decide it must go instead with the PRIVATE sign.

The first summer after we bought the lake property, I came up to clear out the old cabin. It had been closed for eleven years, last used apparently during deer season in 1957 or 1958, the season before the previous owner's suicide.

Karen and I had seen the place the January before, the lot covered by two feet of snow—thus my confusion of a swamp as the perfect, level site for a future house—and the cabin concealed by curtains. I went up in July and joined Kurt, who had already moved into a place down the shore from ours.

The front of the lot was overgrown with brush from lake to cabin. Behind was the swamp, crossable only by means of a zigzag path across logs slippery with rot and standing water. The cabin, a green-shingled structure containing one 12-by-20 room, had two windows side by side on the lakefront, a small fixed pane of glass at either end, and a blank wall toward the swamp. It contained an ancient gas refrigerator and stove, a round table, four chairs (their dark varnish cracked and dull), a rocker, and jury-rigged double-sized bunk beds with mildew-blotched mattresses.

Decade-old newspapers and magazines were stacked neatly on the table, and antique cocoa tins together with milk bottles from a dairy in Green Bay lined the window ledge. There were dishes as well, yellowish-beige crockery plates and thick cups and saucers, dull and dingy in the green light filtering through the alder branches that rubbed against the front windows. Everything was unfinished, the walls just studs and exterior siding, the ceiling only the underside of the roof, supported by log joists. Still, the place was relatively clean. There were no mouse droppings on the rough flooring, no accumulated grime in the corners. There were only the neatly stacked leavings of the last occupant, long lost to despair, and, around the windows, hundreds of dead flies dried to brittle black flecks. But everywhere, scattered over headlines in which Eisenhower was President and Henry Aaron hit home runs in Milwaukee, and lifting in elegant fragments out of the desiccated fly remains, were the orange-and-black wings of ten summers' worth of butterflies.

Below the camp another rock funnel directs the river, and from behind the chain of rocks on the left I tempt my first keeper of the day—an eight-inch brookie. Not much, but I take it, gladly if not proudly, a sign of better things to come. And as I cast the fly close to the collapsed end of the bridge—the end away from the cabin—one of those better things swims up in a long brown line from under the broken beams to slap fiercely at the muddler, but is, at last, more irritated than hungry.

Climbing out of the water and over the bridge means a return to full gravity, and my earlier tendency to pitch sideways is replaced by an inclination, out of the current, to lurch forward.

On the other side, as the fly slides past a log, a brown trout sucks the muddler down in a sudden swirl. The fish is small, no more than nine inches, but, unlike the brookie, it fights, even tries to jump, though the turbulence sweeps its effort aside.

The alder grows in four- and five-foot thickets, lower limbs submerged and constantly writhing in the water at the river's edge, some great anguish continually reenacted. The river goes on like this for so long that I am surprised when I round yet another bend and see the Y where Cook's Run enters the Paint. To the right the Paint is wide and surprisingly calm, as though all the turbulence has been the slighter stream's bad influence. And on the left Cook's Run seems to flaunt that wild spirit. Narrow, it breaks in a frenzy of falls, tier upon tier of boulders, lined by banks that, between white birch and popple, are covered with long grass glistening from the wet.

Tree limbs sweep the water, reaching in some places halfway across the Run's twenty-five-foot width, extending out from both sides like lines of frantic launderers beating their wash against the rocks. The current is overpowering as it sweeps around the boulders, and I cling to branches, rising and falling with them as I feel my way along. On the higher ground above me, dead elms stand, skeletal watchmen against a gray sky.

On long drives, whenever they got bored, the kids would ask for a story or for questions. Since a story was the more demanding request, I usually went with questions: "Name six cities beginning with D" or "Identify three pairs of American Presidents with a shared name." As the oldest, Sarah usually answered first, leading to complaints from the other two, and so I would ask "favorite" questions. Once when I asked for favorite trees, Sarah said, "white pine," Elizabeth answered, "red maple," and Aaron, five years old and not to be outdone, declared, "Dutch elm." When the girls teased him, telling him he had picked a disease that killed trees, he insisted, "That's right, I like dead trees." For the rest of the summer, whenever we passed some large ruined maple or birch, Aaron would point it out and extol, to his sisters' dismay, its many beauties.

Seventy-five feet into the Run, there is a stream-wide fall of nearly two feet, the first step on what looks like an irregular stairway of white water. Trees are down, reaching far into the rapids and adding their bit to the turmoil, and in the middle of the stream a huge boulder splits the current, shouldering it to either side. There is, on the right bank, a path that bypasses the blown-down trees, the rocks, and the rapids, and along it, growing peacefully beside the twisted roots of a fallen birch, a clump of black-eyed Susans. The temptation to take the high road is considerable, but I remain in the water, holding on to limbs as I slide around the birch and force my way ahead.

The stream is waist-deep and rough—though not so bad as it had first appeared—the footing treacherous and the undercut bank a mass of grasping roots. I avoid looking down; the water's movement is too disorienting, dizzying in this confined space, the visual violence more threatening than the pounding my lower body is absorbing.

Above this series of breaks, the Run turns before being disrupted by another set of rapids and, to the left, leaves a pool that is miraculously serene. I accept the breather, fishing the pool carefully, and its surface, which rotates in slow, continuous circles, is twice broken by rising trout. Neither takes the fly, and so I move forward, ease back into the fray, and see, or imagine I see, a big fish rolling toward me like a chunk of wood. I watch for it and in a moment think I've glimpsed it again, but this time it does not look quite so fishlike. Fishermen are prone, in the midst of wild water, to such hallucinations.

The stream makes a sudden right turn and divides around a narrow island. Both banks are lower here, and the water, though still difficult, has calmed considerably. Between rapids there are pools, especially at the head of the island. I am nearly back to the trestle and the gravel pit. I fish sloppily, in part because I am tired—I've been in the river for nearly four hours now—and in part because I assume so accessible a spot is overfished. As if to confirm my suspicion the bank has become parklike; on the left, there is even a campfire site, and flowers—purple, yellow, orange—are everywhere.

Again I see what looks to be a fish tumbling toward me, showing dully as it rolls beneath the surface. This time I jump ahead of it, tugging at my net, and in my rush I break the elastic shoulder cord, nearly losing the whole thing downstream. I bat at the tumbling body, as though playing some absurd game of water tennis. I miss, bouncing whatever it is off the net's handle, delaying but not capturing. I try again and this time can see that it is a fish and that its fins are moving erratically as the current carries it away.

Netted at last, it is a fourteen-inch sucker, but I have no idea what it and the fish I saw earlier are doing in the main current or why they are behaving so strangely. When I lift the sucker from the water, its hue is dull and sickly, in contrast to the brightly colored brookies. Grayish-white scales, a half inch wide, cover its body, and its mouth twists downward in a thick-lipped pout. It is an ugly fish and stinks even now.

Halfway through the trestle, leg-weary and frustrated at a creel that contains only two small trout and a displaced sucker—kept as evidence of these strange happenings—I stop, suddenly depressed, not, I realize, by the day's trivial catch or my stiffening legs, but by something I cannot quite get a hold on, something that drifts almost into view, like the shadows in the big pool, and then evaporates when I try to face it.

Above me the thick timbers of the trestle brace their dark burden against the sky. On the bank flowers grow with a foolish abandon as though this were April and not August.

After my father came home from World War II, he tried for a while to sell life insurance in rural Missouri. He wore a double-breasted wool suit and drove an old Ford, a prewar model with everything rounded so that it looked like a series of metallic green hills. And some days, when I was about four, he would come home in mid-afternoon to gather up my baby brother Jack, my mother, and me and drive to a place where he had spotted a patch of wildflowers. My earliest memory of him is not in uniform but in that dark suit, jacket unbuttoned, wide tie loosened, crouched in a meadow of pansies or sweet williams or bluebells, repeating their names as he picked them and handed them to me for delivery to my mother. We could not live on what he made selling insurance to farmers, and so, after a year or two, he put the suit away and went to work on a paving crew. I do not remember our picking flowers after that.

My doubts seem ludicrous. There are better waters ahead, big trout, and easy wading. I leave the trestle and, crouching, enter the tunnel paved with water that runs beneath the road.

A u g u s t 2

More rain last night and this morning. A gentler rain that fell steadily and without yesterday's fireworks, but still, according to the bucket, more than an inch. By eleven it had stopped, and Karen and I, taking advantage of the dampness, have been burning more of the rotted wood from the cabin next door, piling the boards so high that the fire's heat shrivels popple leaves ten feet away, shakes the higher maple with its updraft, and forces us to keep our distance.

Karen loves this work, attacks it with the enthusiasm of a Scandinavian Guy Fawkes, and will not give it up. She is wearing jeans and an old flannel shirt, holes at both elbows, and when the heat lessens even slightly, approaches with another armload of siding, flicking her head to toss a strand of blond hair from her face. She throws the wood into the flames, then straightens with watery eyes and a pinched grin as the fresh fuel pops and crackles. Sarah has come from the house to watch. I neither see nor hear her approach, but when I look up she is there, standing on the perimeter of the fire's warmth, her eyes dark slits squinting against the heat. She stretches like a long dark cat, rubbing her back against the popple trunk, then wrinkles her nose in a tight little circular movement. As she watches her mother, a smile starts to curve her mouth, then is stopped, called back.

We had a kerosene cookstove in the little house in Wyaconda, Missouri. The house sat beside the railroad tracks and shook when the Santa Fe Chief roared by, passing less than twenty feet of weeded right of way from the bed I shared with my baby brother. One day when my mother, only twenty-three or twenty-four, and tall and thin with long, dark hair, was canning peaches, the fuel line caught fire. The stove stood beneath a window and

*beside the only door. Jack, no more than a year old, was sleeping
in the little bedroom at the far side of the house. I sat in the
middle of the main room—there were three rooms in all—
watching the blue and yellow flames shoot up toward the curtain.*

*"Take care of your brother," my mother said, pushing her hair
back with both her hands; then she picked up the stove like a
waiter delivering a flaming dish. Smoke clouding her face, and
bent by the awkward weight, she backed through the door,
feeling her way with her feet as she stepped down into the yard.
While I watched, her upper body rippled in the heat, and she
wavered spectrally in the doorway as though about to leave more
than the house.*

Now seems a good time to head for the Run and to take
advantage of the overcast sky. It is 2:45.

Again I park at the gravel pit and again the clouds break,
letting the sun through at the very moment I enter the water
above the bridge. Fed by the morning rain and wedged between
a clump of pine and a high bank of birch, the stream runs as fast
and deep as yesterday. Because of the swift current and the
overhanging branches, I can manage only an occasional cast, and
I spend most of my time edging around big rocks, struggling to
keep my balance in water that turns me sharply whenever it gains
the leverage. Hip-deep now, it is nearly unwadeable, worse even
than yesterday because, narrowed to ten feet, the current hits like
a body block, sometimes sweeping me a step or two downstream.
The footing, too, is difficult, not because the rocks are slippery
but because they sit so closely together, forcing me into the hard
Vs that separate them and pinching painfully at my feet, sometimes wedging me tightly, holding me off-balance as I try to
wriggle free in the swiftest current.

I spoke to Joe yesterday afternoon, showed him the sucker, and
asked for an explanation. He thought maybe the fish had washed
from some side pool and had been carried downstream by the

high water, but he seemed doubtful. When I told him I had seen another floating by, he shook his head, dismissing his original theory. "Crazy things are happening," he muttered, adding vaguely, "that's why I'm staying away from the river." The remark contained an implicit judgment on my project, from Joe's perspective a pointless wade through unpromising waters, a wade he believes I cannot finish. But in sixty years he has covered, piecemeal, all of the Run, and so, despite his doubts, he advised me—albeit reluctantly—as to what lies ahead, adding mournfully, "There was a time . . ."

After what seems like several hundred yards—more likely only a hundred or a hundred and fifty feet—the left bank rises abruptly into a ridge. A tall cedar, leaning over the Run, stands high above a fallen companion whose trunk, stripped of bark, lies half on the slope and half in the water, protecting a small pool from the onrush of the stream. Twice I try to sidecast into the eddy, and both times the fly—an Adams—falls short. I whip the line back and forth to dry the hackle, then sidecast again. It floats for a moment, a brown-and-white wisp at the outer edge of the pool, and once more the current grabs it, drowns it, sweeps it away. I try again, only this time I raise the backcast too directly overhead, and eight feet above me the living cedar takes the hook. I try to work it free with light flicks of the line, but the flat needles hold firm, and all that I shake loose is the sharp, sweet scent of the tree. I am still standing in the main current, and as I tug with increasing force against the unyielding limb, the water catches my right foot, forcing it in front of my left, nearly tripping me. At last, furious with the loss, I set my feet and pull. The leader breaks just below the fly.

I sort through the cigarette cellophane in which I carry a half dozen new flies Joe has given me. There is not another Adams—I've left without the two I put on my desk last night—and finally I choose a wet fly, a royal coachman. I watch to see the white wings and the red body band visible beneath the rusty water, catch the glitter of peacock herl on either side of the red floss.

The first discussion of artificial flies I ever encountered appears in The Compleat Angler, *a remarkable seventeenth-century book whose significance I completely missed in that initial reading. Izaak Walton's decision to pursue a fisherman's life rather than a political one—and in his day nearly everything was an expression of politics, and therefore potentially dangerous—resulted from careful consideration, was neither an act of frivolity nor of laziness. In the opening chapter he informs his reader that just as theologians dispute whether God finds greatest pleasure in His action or in His contemplation, so must man also ask in which of these pursuits should he seek satisfaction. Fishing, Walton declares, provides a third alternative, one that is both honest and harmless. To sit by a river is to enjoy the fittest place for contemplation even as one awaits a struggle with whatever monster might reside within those depths.*

If Walton's vocation promises both contemplation and action, it can be understood as a way of avoiding them as well, a means of contemplating safe subjects—things made of feathers and deer hair, of fins and scales—and an action whose only end is itself. Construed either way, fishing lacks the seriousness the theologians had in mind, is a form of play, an effort to avoid the risks of more dangerous thoughts and acts. In this, too, the angling of the fisherman resembles that of the writer; it is unlaboring work and contemplation with little likely consequence—a way of being active, both physically and intellectually, without really doing anything. Teaching offers much the same privilege. The problem with all three, however, is that, despite our best intentions, they become serious endeavors, and eventually as threatening to our security as any more worldly form of engagement.

The Run continues, narrow and canopied for the next two hundred yards, and as I cast short, flat casts, the velocity of the stream carries the fly past me almost as quickly as it hits the water.

Still, I work the breaks behind rocks and fallen limbs, fish the edge of the bank as closely as the underbrush will allow, and closer, since I frequently snag the coachman and have to ease toward the shore to set it free. Despite the lack of evidence that there is anything in these waters save one clumsy fisherman, I keep the ritual intact, casting into the bank regardless of snags, maintaining a steady, unhurried pace upstream. This is what fishing books say to do. While I am not a patient man, I believe in books and am trying to do this by the book, or at least as much of the book as I have had the patience to read. But mostly I am trying to establish a tempo for the passage that awaits me.

In one small way, my coming north has, like Walton's choice of angling, involved a rejection of politics. Throughout the seventies I, from the disadvantaged point of an electricless cabin, missed every Presidential nominating convention. This is remarkable, since from my first discovery in 1952 of television and politics I had not only watched every such gathering, but had watched nearly every minute of all of them. At fourteen I found the contest between Kefauver and Kennedy for the Democratic Vice Presidential nomination more gripping than Larson's perfect game in the World Series, and so what began in 1952 as a fascination for a still ghostly medium, became near obsession by 1956 with that which, every four years, took over the screen for two separated but full weeks.

Then I began teaching, left Chicago the day after the final gavel fell on the 1968 riot the Democrats called a convention, started coming to the lake, and missed every subsequent nominating caucus. But last month the Democrats were at it again, and I found the old interest stirring. It did not stir so much that I installed the TV set early, but enough so that I went to some length to hear the keynote address. The static, a gift of local iron deposits, was too great inside the cabin, so I took the radio into the boat and rowed out to mid-lake in the hope that oratory would carry more clearly over water. And it did; Cuomo's eloquence came through distinctly, movingly. For a while it was like old times here at the edge of Reagan's America.

I had thrown a spinning rod in the boat, thinking to catch perch while the politicians talked. The sun had already dropped behind the trees across the lake, and I thought the fish might be feeding. They were not, but the dusk was warm and comfortable, the sky a darkening blue, shot with purple to the west. As the broadcast continued, though, I found it difficult to attend to talk so far away, found the longing calls of the loons more compelling in the dying light, and let the old game slip away once more.

The land on my right has fallen to an alder swamp while the ridge on the left rises straight out of the water, lifting a stand of white pine so high over me that the roots, protruding from the gravelly soil, are well above my head. Then, around a slight curve the ridge slides back, gives way to a large pool, and the alder marsh becomes a meadow of long grass, thistles, and broad purple flowers. On the bank there is not only the blackened remains of a night fisherman's campfire—evidence that someone believes brown trout inhabit this pool—but even a fire pit lumpy with wet ashes, and, beside that, a coffee can.

I suddenly recognize this pool, remember it from seven or eight years ago when I fished through, moving downstream in calmer water. I caught nothing then, but, if I remember correctly, I fished in near darkness, fished neither carefully nor wisely. Now I cast to the outer edge of the bend, working a large submerged log. It is a mistake; too late I realize that I am wading into the deepest part of the pool, doing everything backwards, standing where I should be casting, casting to where I should be standing.

An inlet, concealed by the long grass, has carved a deep hole just in front of me in waters I have already disturbed. I remember now that I made the same mistake before.

Angry that I keep repeating the same errors, that I profit so little from experience, I clomp through the pool into another narrow stretch of rapids and shallower water. The low bank has been undercut, and, trying to wedge through the anger as though it were the swift water below, I force myself to make slow, deliberate casts, dropping the fly where it will be swept beneath the suspended sod.

These are cold waters, ideal for trout, and yet I have seen nothing, not even a minnow. I blame the swiftness of the current, the sun—only the sun has drifted behind clouds—and the forgotten dry flies. But there remains the gnawing suspicion that the fault lies with me, that I am doing something wrong. There are trout in Cook's Run, and yet I've seen nothing since leaving the Paint.

I wade on through an aisle of alders—the swamp extends on both sides now—until the brush gives way to more meadows, and the depth of the stream falls below my knees. The sun finds another rift in the clouds, its light striking the water at an angle, staining it with deep purplish tints as though responding to the purple blossoms that have returned to the banks, this time interspersed with the smaller yellow flowers called butter-and-eggs. Bumblebees crawl on every bloom, their thick yellow-and-black bodies flecked with purple pollen as they lumber about their business. The meadow would be noisy with their buzzing if it were not for the roar of the Run.

Aaron has for some time now been reluctant to go into the woods, either to cut wood or dig for worms, because he is afraid of bees. Four years ago he and Sarah and a group of kids visiting down the lake were hiking to the site of an old logging camp when Aaron stepped on a yellow-jacket nest. The wasps swarmed up his pants legs and he was badly stung, would have been more severely hurt except that Sarah pulled off his pants, scraped the wasps away with her hands, and then beat the discarded trousers with a rock—in the process getting nearly as many stings as her brother.

A year later, when I had convinced him that his encounter with the yellow jackets was only a fluke, not likely ever to happen again, he believed and went into the woods with me to dig worms. On our return I stepped onto a fallen limb, heard the whine almost immediately as the hornets lined out of the nest, not at me, but at Aaron several steps behind. He took more stings, the worst around his eyes and on his forehead, and developed a healthy disrespect for his father's opinions.

Above distant pines an eagle flies with slow deliberate strokes. As it crosses the river, the light glints off its white head and leg feathers. Yesterday a hummingbird; today an eagle. Now if only the size of the fish would increase at the same rate. But the fish improve neither in size nor number. Still I feel better for having seen the eagle, better for having the roughest rapids behind me. And, too, there is now room to cast, to fall into the regular rhythm that is the point of fly-fishing and less of the clumsy flailing about of the previous hours and day. There is more dignity to the whole business. With that in mind I stop to retie the net cord, broken yesterday when I beat at the tumbling sucker.

It was such shallow, swift flowing water that led to Thoreau's line "Time is but the stream I go a-fishing in," a line that trivializes rivers, not to mention runs, trivializes them for not being self-contained, oceanic, unfathomable, for being in time, even being time. Their transitory nature, I decide, is precisely what draws me to rivers as to some alter ego, some secret sharer. They seem less smug than oceans or even lakes, bodies of water which remain the same each time you step into them. And if the romantic hero is to be drawn to the masthead, to landlessness, surely there is something to be said for waders of rivers, for those of us who walk in shallow waters, who always remain within a few feet of shore.

Still, there must be some purpose to such endeavors, some small treasure to be pulled from these waters, a subject to validate the exercise. I intended an essay about fishing, something, per- haps, that Field and Stream might buy, but in fishing essays fish have to get caught. Perhaps this will be an essay about walking a river, an essay where what is sought remains unfound. I do not know what can be made of this. That is the nature of any essay, that it be—like those of Montaigne, who invented the genre—a little trial, a test of the author and his capacity to make something of his subject and himself.

The stream is now one I recognize. I am entering a long S curve which is the one section of Cook's Run that I have visited regularly, sometimes to fish but often just to look at from the high ridge to the north, a vantage point overlooking half a mile of the stream valley. I am pleased with the thought of familiar waters, with the awareness that a beaver dam lies ahead and a series of pools from which I have, in the past, caught trout. My confidence grows. I know how to fish the stretch I am entering, will not foul up these pools.

To prove the point I cast to the right bank, and though the water, deeper than I remember, hides the rock that lurks there, it does not conceal the sudden gleam of a trout as it flashes up and hits the fly. The fish breaks downstream and, aided by the current's weight, pulls heavily, steadily on the line, bending the

rod and causing me to misjudge its size. I haul too eagerly and
it skates along the surface until I net it, an eight-inch brookie,
which I then watch fall through a tear in the webbing. So much
for dignity. Still the trout clings to the hook, and I grab it and
put it in the creel.

*When, years later, I asked Sarah how she had the presence of
mind to attend so sensibly to Aaron when the yellow jackets
attacked, "Pa explained it all," she said, "in* Little House in the
Big Woods." *There are fathers, it seems, who know what they
are talking about.*

I have one fish, and the best water lies ahead. But when I reach
the bottom bend in the S, the place where, two years ago, the
beaver dam crossed the stream, only the outer ramparts survive,
broken fingers reaching out helplessly into the current the dam
once held in check. I realize in retrospect that no fresh cuttings
were visible in the meadow, no sign of recent beaver work along
the shore. He has either moved on or been trapped, and no new
occupant has taken his place. I have never known a time when
there was not a dam here; I am shocked at the change.

*Because the road is only a short hike through the woods to the
north, this is where I brought my children for their first look at
a beaver dam, where Sarah and Elizabeth once found a canoe
paddle—a paddle we still use—pressed against the latticework of
sticks and mud, where Elizabeth and Aaron, engulfed in my old
boots, waded for the first time, giggling as they crossed the
shallows below the dam, holding hands, these two natural opponents, for communal balance. Here, too, the spot where Karen
and I took friends who came to visit. One even wrote a poem
about it.*

But the dam is gone, broken by this latest onslaught or some previous one, and with it the familiar contours, the reliable holes. I move on, fishing, as much as possible, as though nothing were changed, casting to remembered waters, deeper than those swirling round my legs. Beyond the first bend, behind one of the three boulders I named the trolls, a trout rises, mouths the coachman lightly, then lets it go. Farther on, just before the second curl in the S, the abandoned beaver hut slumps in the shallows, its bleached ruins bearing raspberry vines and a few purple flowers. I cast into the sticks at its base where once, two years ago, a huge brown rose and tossed its tail contemptuously; today the fly sweeps downstream undisturbed. For some reason, looking at the hut, I remember, "Little pig, little pig, let me come in, or I'll huff and I'll puff and I'll blow your house down," and I think of the message D. F. Carlysle left for me all those years ago.

When we raised the first of the trusses for the new cabin, I straightened from my hammering and stood for the first time on what would eventually be the loft floor. I had never before seen the lake from that height and was deeply moved by this new version of the landscape. I stood there so long that those watching me on the ground began, themselves, to wonder.

The sound of the water has changed from the unbroken roar of the lower stream to an irregular chatter, and more than once I stop, thinking I've overheard voices.

Around the last bend in the S lies the most promising hole. One quiet, overcast morning, with Sarah—then eight or nine— wading beside me, I caught two good-sized browns, luring them from the brush piled in the deepest part of the curve. Both fish came out of the Run in great heart-stopping leaps, heads high, backs still curved from the effort that had carried them into the air. After netting the first, I looked to my daughter. Her face was serious, even grave, as she scanned the pool, then pointed to the next place she thought I should try, keeping silent, holding her pleasure for noisier waters. Now I work the same stretch carefully, through the pool and into the rapids at its head, but to no avail.

As a child Sarah watched "Captain Kangaroo" mornings while Karen and I held out for a few more minutes of sleep. It was her regular routine: Get a banana or a slice of bread from the kitchen and then sit in front of the television until breakfast.

One morning she awakened us with sorrow-filled screams: "Captain Kangaroo is dead! Captain Kangaroo is dead!" Weeping, she led me to the TV where, seven hours away, Charles de Gaulle was being buried before an audience of world dignitaries that did not include Sarah's baggy-coated captain.

It is time to stop, and the easiest exit is back at the old dam. Walking downstream and hoping for a last-minute reprieve, I work the S in reverse, past the hut and the trolls, then, just before the last bend, I notice that the current, unchecked by the beaver, has cut into the bank of the meadow, has cleared a channel in a spot once silted in by the dam. This is precisely the kind of realization that, in fishing magazines, is rewarded by a record catch. I stop and, in a perfect cast, drop the fly on a fully extended leader a hand's width from the bank. There is an immediate swirl, and a three-inch brookie takes the coachman, then hangs on until, with moistened fingers, I set it free.

The land climbs sharply above the river past a margin of scattered birch and into a plantation of jack pine. After stumbling up the hill through raspberry vines and popples felled by missing beaver, I lean against a broken birch, look out over the Run as it winds through flowering meadows and thick alders, and catch my breath. In this dull light everything has a slightly leaden hue, the tinge of a daguerreotype to which, in an afterthought, color has been imperfectly added. The restless water curls and eddies through bends and pools, and beyond, the distant edge of the valley rises, first with popples and spruce, then with birch and white pines. It is a stark beauty haunted by an arctic light that is already autumnal. A haze dulls and yet gives the metallic glint to the landscape, even to the air. I think of all the times I've seen this place—by the first vague light of dawn, by the brightness of midday, by the eerie illumination of a full moon. So much is changed, and yet it remains, somehow, the same.

Or does it? As an academic I've become so accomplished at both seeing similarity and noting difference that I no longer understand the significance of either. Yet that seems the whole point of analysis: of seeing the world as a place in which everything is unique and yet in which there is nothing new under the sun.

As I watch, the sun breaks through, gilding the scene in slow-moving bands of light, picking up the yellows in the butter-and-eggs and setting ablaze a branch of highbush cranberries. Along the shore the skeletons of trees killed by generations of beavers rot away, and in the marshy meadows the remains of drowned alder stick up in whitened clumps. Beside the stream, living bushes nod, like old men on park benches, as the water tugs at their branches.

I straighten for one last look at a scene I've photographed countless times, a scene that has hung above my office desk for seven years, aware that without the beaver the popple shoots around me will soon block this view.

A u g u s t 3

The alarm sounds at 5:30. I stayed up late last night, first watching Olympic gymnastics with the kids—the reception grainy, sometimes rippling from the newly purchased generator's interference, but a picture nevertheless, the first in sixteen years—and then, writing up my notes from yesterday's wade.

After the supple grace of the athletes soaring in elegant vaults, gliding along the slight width of the balance beam, swinging perfectly into the uneven parallel bars, then the awkward, hesitant work of my own hand fashioning sentences, angular and puny, all elbows and knees, the only point of similarity provided by the electronic failure, the television's frequent dissolution into flickering waves and ghostly images. Haunted by that analogy, I squinted over my notes and the pages previously drafted from them, seeking whatever lay, blurred and distorted, within. Though at moments, rising behind one or another image or phrase, I caught glimpses of something, it always eluded me. Perhaps tonight the reception will improve. Perhaps tonight things will begin to cohere.

The morning is so foggy that there is no horizon. Through the skylight the gray of the lake and the gray of the air form an unbroken wall, and I wonder what this means for the Run. Because its water is colder than the lake's, I suspect the fog will be less of a problem, perhaps will stay out of the river valley altogether. I hesitate between the warm bed and the cold stream, but finally choose the latter.

Stumbling down the stairs from the loft, I call the dog. For thirteen years, when I have gone fishing, he has gotten up with me, following first from the old cabin and then from the new. Even young, he was not an eager riser and would stumble into the predawn air as clumsily as I, shaking himself awake and then walking deliberately to lakeside for his first drink of the day. But when I carried the waders to the car, roused by their peculiar scent he would rush round me barking and growling, calming only when the boots had been stowed and the car door closed. It was a ritual, with slight variations, performed daily, ending when I scratched his ears, rubbed his back, and shut him once more in the cabin. This is the first morning that I have forgotten he is dead.

Fog hangs over the road, cutting visibility to less than fifty feet. On both sides, beyond mist-blotched ferns and goldenrod, shadow trees loom up, then disappear. The ferns have already begun to yellow, and a few reddened leaves show on a maple branch that reaches through the gray air. I think about Smeagol, missing him in this dull light.

It is odd how in death, when I am conscious of his death, he joins the other dogs I have known, memory of him merging with memories of his predecessors: of Major, who brought me through a childhood of constant moves, then, when I was eight, was poisoned and, after hours of lying trembling on a bed of gunnysacks in my grandfather's barn, died. I thought of his dying as I held Smeagol's convulsing body, surprised at how quickly that old grief rose to join the new one.

The second dog we owned, more my brother Jack's than mine, got distemper, and I, just turned sixteen and licensed to drive, took him to the vet. The doctor, recognizing the symptoms, sent me and the dog home, then called my father to bring the animal in again to be put down. When I discovered what had taken place, I was both relieved at being spared ultimate responsibility and aggravated at being thought too young to deal with death.

Without warning or movement a doe appears in the middle of the road, first her muzzle and ears showing through the fog, then her body and legs. She looks at the car incuriously, then

ambles into the shrouded woods to the left. I wait, but when no
fawn follows let the car roll slowly ahead before gradually
accelerating.

I plan on parking at the edge of the gravel and cutting through
the trees to the S curve, but I usually locate myself by the show
of light where the Run swings close to the road and the timber
thins. Today everything looks the same, and I park by guess. It
is not yet six o'clock, and the fog seems as thick here as at the
lake; I decide to wait awhile in the car, and I turn on the radio
hoping to catch a weather report. The first station I find is playing
a whiny country lament, the nasal voice sounding vaguely bored
with its own account of heartbreak, as though the deceit and
disappointment it details have become too commonplace to take
seriously. I move the dial and pick up John Prine singing "That's
the way that the world goes round/ be up one day and the next
you're down," but I can't hold it, and the voice falls back into
static and is gone. I fuss with the dial in a last effort to recover
the song and, when this fails, switch the radio off in irritation and
roll down my window. There is no sound. No wind. Nothing.
I roll the window back up, get out and start pulling on my
waders. A four-leaf clover curls against my foot.

*There are few talents more bizarre, more useless, than the ability
to see four-leaf clover. When you are walking with someone and
reach down to pluck one from the grass—there is never the
option of not picking them—or reach into your pocket for
change and pull out shards of clover, brittle and broken but
clearly clover, the explanation always sounds like an apology and
always evokes the same response, a bewildered look and a clumsy
effort to find some appropriate compliment for so childish a gift.*

*My grandfather would move through an alfalfa field, bending
every ten yards or so to pick a four-leaf clover. Even when he
walked to the hospital where they diagnosed his cancer, he*

stooped twice to pluck them from the neatly mowed lawn. At seven I could think of no more desirable skill, envied his mysterious knack, begged him to teach me the secret. "It can't be taught," he always insisted. "The trick is not to look for them." And of course I looked, looked futilely for three or four years, then gave it up and began finding them, just a few at first, then more and more, the telltale pattern declaring itself in the yards I mowed, in center field during a ball game, in the sidewalk cracks on the way to school. I pushed them into jeans pockets or, if anyone was around, gave them away. This present was always received with confusion, pinched between thumb and forefinger, carried awkwardly until I discreetly looked away and the small burden could be tossed aside.

After Karen and I were married I began carrying them home to be taped to the refrigerator, row after row of pressed green, drying to a yellowish brown against the enameled door, eventually giving way to the crayon drawings of our more properly educated children.

Sometimes when I've not seen one for a while, I am torn between relief at being freed from this trivial charge and sadness at losing yet another fragile link to my disappearing past. But eventually, both to my delight and my frustration, the familiar pattern declares itself once more.

I guessed well and have cut in only a hundred feet or so below the old dam site. I was also right about the fog. It hangs above the stream like a dome, but the valley, at least over the water, is relatively clear. Nothing moves in the marsh. Even the chatter of the rapids is muted. I work my way back to the bluff above the dam, pushing through jack pines whose interlacing branches hold shards of fog like a fence studded with lint.

The cold and noise of the water are welcome today. And, too, I like this part of the Run. Despite the closeness of the road, it seems pristine, and in the half dozen times I have fished it I have never encountered another fisherman. Today it feels more isolated than usual, the fog providing a thick ceiling that separates this valley from the rest of the world, casting it in a surreal half-light, and yet, for all its strangeness, it is a comforting, comfortable place, alive with flowers and moving waters. It is a storybook landscape, a child's fantasy world.

Just above the dam's debris, a brook trout hits in the rapids. It is not a large trout, but it hits hard, not the tentative strike I've known for most of the summer. The fish breaks past me in the current, and I guide it back slowly, the line telegraphing to my hand the sudden surges of life at the other end. Three casts later another trout hits, this from the undercut bank I noticed yesterday. Another, larger, rises in the upper part of the S, charging from the depths of the big pool, but then brakes at the last minute and bites short.

The water has dropped a couple of inches since yesterday and is clearer, shining in this odd light, more luminous than the air. I walk confidently, work the submerged rocks and logs aggressively.

Above the S there is a stretch of shallow rapids, and beyond these, in calmer waters, a large mound of foam clings to an alder root. Once I read an article where a fisherman cast into a pile of foam and hooked a huge rainbow. I follow his example, but the fly does not penetrate, merely lies on the yellowed top like a raisin on a meringue pie. I jiggle the line hoping to break through the foam, but on top it stays. Finally I yank the rod back, pulling the fly free and throwing a string of bubbles thirty feet downstream. Magazines should watch what they publish. There are people out here who will believe anything.

Around another bend and into another pool, and a trout leaps for the fly just as I retrieve the line. Both of us look foolish. Checking the backcast, as though I could somehow withdraw my motion, I let the line fall clumsily, well away from the willing fish. And the trout, trying to change the direction of its jump

while twisting after an elusive prey, flops awkwardly on its side.
Graceful work, this.

*When I first started fly-fishing it was largely because of the idea
of casting, that incredible suspension of the line overhead, the
sweeping curve following, in a delayed reaction, the motion of
the rod. The point of all other fishing was to bring home meat,
but with a fly line the process is itself the purpose. The elegance
of casting justified the endeavor, regardless of the catch. So I
believed. And so I still believe, but more during the winter than
in trout season, and more when I keep the fish in the water than
when I fling them around like potatoes.*

The Run widens into an alder marsh, and for the first time in
my three-day wade I am forced to put on insect repellent. The
mosquitoes swarm above the surface, cover my hands, invade my
ears. This, in my eagerness, I take to be a good sign, evidence of
life in a place where one show of life provokes another.

And I do begin picking up trout, catching one on every second
or third cast, but all of the three-, four-, and five-inch variety.
An eager lot, they leap from the stream as they attack the fly,
accepting the ride as I tow them to me. I seem to be running an
amusement park for baby trout. With each minuscule catch I
dampen my hand in the cold water—diluting, of course, the
insect repellent—then hold the fish lightly as I slide the hook free.
I should paste little pieces of parchment to their sides, the kind
sometimes found on the first pages of library books: "This fish
contributed by Wayne Fields."

A ten-inch trout breaks from the rapids and takes the fly hard.
No sooner have I unhooked that fish and cast again, when another
brookie, only slightly smaller than the last, hits from under the
alder. Things are finally picking up, and I hope for a big fish
today, a brown, the kind you only catch when the weather, the

light, or something else is just right. Actually the kind someone else catches the morning you sleep in.

Karen needs to go to town, and I promised to get the car back early, but the only way I know to get out is to retrace my steps and exit the way I came in. I can, maybe, cut cross-country and hit the road somewhere to the north, but that could just as well take me through swamps and even longer delays. I decide to double back, but there is one last pool I want to reach first, one I fished with Sarah the time we caught the browns above the beaver lodge. Blocked by a fallen popple that piled up water halfway across the stream, it seemed a perfect spot for trout. But that time, as we approached, we discovered—concealed by the still leafy branches of the fallen tree—other intruders, two otters swimming and diving like uninhibited children. When at last they realized they were being observed, they took turns rising high in the water, bracing on each other's backs, and chattering shrilly at us. I told Sarah we would come again and, in the absence of otter, catch the trout which this secluded hole must house. This will be my first return.

No longer slowed by the hunger of little fish, and eager to get to the otter pool, I move quickly now but still don't know how far I have to go. And it is nearly 8:00, the hour I had said I would be home, and guilt begins to nag at me. But before I make up my mind to quit, the stream opens behind another washed-out dam, one that was not here when Sarah and I came this way, and yet is already abandoned. When I cast, hurriedly, to the beaver's debris, a ten-inch brown sucks the fly down and runs hard up-stream. Against the pressure of the line, he slows, drifts back on the current, then turns and runs again. When he slides back this time, it is into my mangled net.

The pool is wide, but the current remains swift. Dead alders show where the beaver's high water had reached before once again receding, and sharp-pointed branches reveal his work. But all has grayed with age, no new growth shows through in green promise, and the reexposed ground is dark with silt and decay.

Spiderwebs sequined with dew hang between the alder spears, some broken and torn, their dazzling geometry distorted. Others, complete, shiver lightly in the air, the precision of their making, the delicacy of their composition dazzling. Where did these patterns originate? Are they somehow programmed into the spider? Do they precede the weaver, making him their servant? Or does the maker improvise, adjusting his art to the whimsy of the imperfect world in which he finds himself? It seems a noble work, this finding a design with which to bind up so much fragmentation, holding all together with thread finer, nearly, than sight, this rendering the world whole with so slight a line.

Thus Whitman's "noiseless, patient spider" throws out its thin filaments in hope of being joined to something, anything. So old Walt, fishing with his wordy lines, struggled for attachment. Deep in middle age when he described spiders, was he casting for some safe anchorage, or for something alive and fierce that would pull him beyond himself, pull him into more demanding depths?

I hurry on, hoping along the way to spot an alternative route back to the car.

The fallen popple that I have been seeking as a landmark has broken up, leaving only a five-foot length of trunk, and that entirely submerged. A little beyond, however, lies a newly fallen spruce, uprooted by high water, and beyond the spruce, oblivious to my presence, is an old man reeling in a little brookie.

I am doubly frustrated, first that someone is here, and second, that he is *here* in this hole that I thought only Sarah and I knew. He sees me and waves, friendly. Because he is fishing with bait on a spinning outfit, he has to be heading downstream, but where in hell did he come from?

I am not sure of the etiquette of this situation. I can't walk downstream ahead of him, and I don't really want to go around him. Where did he get in?

I approach cautiously as he, smiling, continues to fish, casting out his bait, letting it drift briefly, then slowly reeling it back. He is at least seventy, maybe seventy-five. He has a little white mustache and a nice face, the sort that kindly old grandfathers have in children's books and in 1940s movies—the kind of grandfather that would take a kid fishing. He is thin and straight, and I feel guilty for being so upset at his presence. I push back my hat, trying to look civil, even good-natured, remembering the comment of a lumberjack friend who once, surprised as I came out of the river one evening, said I looked like an ax murderer.

I need not have worried; this old man would be hard to intimidate. He greets me, his words lifting and falling with a Scandinavian lilt, and shows me his catch of four eight- and nine-inch brook trout. "Ya," he says, he is going downstream. He wishes he could fish with flies, he adds, but has never developed the skill. He is almost apologetic in a dignified way, and I half expect him to bow. I feel as though I've wandered into a diplomatic reception. "Not really skill," I mutter, trying to look something other than disreputable in my torn jacket, my stain-blotched hat, my untrimmed beard.

"Just where did you come from?" I blurt out.

"Sweden, of course," he says, a small smile working below his neatly clipped mustache.

"I mean, where did you get into the river?" unsure if he is joking. He points behind him and says there is a trail about four hundred yards away, and up the trail a dirt road on which his car is parked. I can get out there.

It is after nine. I tell him good-by and hurry past, calling back that I hope I've not disturbed the water too much. He says there will be no problem; he has plenty of time and will fish here until things have had a chance to settle. I look at him, suspecting that he might be talking about more than fishing, that there is another conversation taking place and that I am missing it, but he has already turned and is contentedly reeling his bait once more.

Immediately beyond the old man the Run narrows, and alders

cover much of its width. I fish hurriedly, finally leaving the coachman and three feet of leader somewhere in the branches of a spruce. I would not replace the fly except that the loose line will take more time and trouble than will the tying, and so I quickly knot a muddler into position and hurry along. A king-fisher, crying wildly, hurries downstream, darting close by my head.

Where is the trail? I know I've gone more than four hundred yards, and yet I've seen no evidence of a path. The kingfisher returns, passing as close as before and in full voice, like an ambulance with a fancy siren. Why do I believe old men when it comes to estimating measurement?

It is now 9:30. Here and there gypsy moths have mittened the alder branches with large egg sacs.

My grandfather on my mother's side, the four-leaf-clover grand-father, was uncanny at judging distances and weights and heights—any measurement. Once I won a "How many jelly beans in this jar" contest by turning in his estimate. He was off by only seven.

But now, old man or no, I've covered at least six hundred yards and there has been no trail.

My grandfather—the old Swede physically resembles him, or my memory of him—was a peculiar mix of piety and impatience. Once he decided at the last minute to drive from northern Missouri to Texas for the Southern Baptist convention, all be-cause he had a sudden desire to see Billy Graham address the faithful. My mother went along, taking my baby brother and me, in order to visit her sister in Houston. We were joined by her Aunt Ethel.

As we headed south, Grandpa became increasingly convinced that we were going to get there late, would miss the very sermon that had motivated the eight-hundred-mile jaunt in the first place. He drove faster and faster and grew increasingly reluctant to make food and rest room breaks. Someplace in Arkansas the fullness of bladders and the emptiness of fuel tank coincided so that even he had to admit the need for a stop. He snatched the hose from the filling station attendant's hand so that the windows could be more quickly washed and the oil checked without unnecessary delay. He shooed the others of us to the rest rooms, urged us to a swift completion of our errands, then shoved the exact payment at the attendant and jumped into the front seat like an Indianapolis 500 driver. As he hit the accelerator there was a shout from behind the car followed by a clatter of metal and a great snapping sound.

"Loyd," Aunt Ethel said calmly and not unhappily, "I believe the man hoped you'd leave the nozzle for the other customers."

The bank climbs higher on the right and is covered by tall trees, and threading up it, running between two maples, is a path. Fifty feet from the river it strikes a dirt road. But there is no car. Another two hundred feet and this road joins a better one, but still no car. I begin to think the old Swede an apparition.

The road winds through ridges of thick timber, and after three quarters of a mile, pulled to the side, is a rusting brown Chevrolet with a Reagan sticker on the bumper. I am vaguely disappointed—not that he would vote for Reagan, but that it was the sort of thing he would care to advertise. But farther along, where the dirt track meets the gravel road on which, a mile away, I am parked, is a second, smaller car bearing a bumper sticker that proclaims in proud letters, blue against a yellow background,

CARL AND MARIE

MARRIED 50 YEARS

A u g u s t 6

I get up slowly this morning, perhaps because the muggy weather, along with intermittent rain, has continued through the weekend, and I have not slept well. That and the prospect of running into Saturday and Sunday fishermen have kept me away from the stream since Friday, and the heavy air does not make today seem much more promising. And of course there is the writing, both the writing I should be doing but am not and the writing I am doing that is going, as far as I can tell, nowhere. "So then I cast to this pool and nothing bites and then I cast to that one and nothing keeps right on biting." Not just exciting, but elegant stuff this. And the Run! One bend after another, alder to spruce to popple and back to alder again. There is more variation in the Peoria phone book. Still, I said I would do it, told more people than I care to remember that I was doing it. Not the noblest of incentives but sufficient. And time, as always, is running out, if I am to complete the Run before we leave for St. Louis.

The risk of essay writing according to Montaigne—and he ought to know—is that, once a subject has been opened, we may find nothing in it, or more to the point, nothing in us that the subject can evoke. Few things are less reassuring than a dead Frenchman.

As I stumble toward the door, a puppy meets me at the foot of the stairs. Saturday we went to Eagle River to see a movie and buy groceries, and on the bulletin board at the grocery store Sarah saw an ad for Labrador/Chesapeake Bay/Golden (all the same litter) retrievers. On those few occasions when we've discussed getting another dog, each of these breeds has been mentioned, and so we went to see the last remaining puppy.

A woman, stooped to block her toddler's rush for the screen, came to the door, then took us around to a pen in the backyard. The mother dog was off with the woman's husband, but the puppy, looking like a light-coated lab, almost white and all ears and feet, came to the gate in a rush, missed the opening and bounced off the chicken-wire fencing, rolled twice, recovered, and plowed out to us, hitting the toddler broadside and knocking him to the ground.

Elizabeth and Aaron decided immediately that we had to have her, Aaron most insistent, perhaps because there is something puppyish in his own awkward bearing, his own shyness, or, perhaps, because his blond hair, further lightened by sun and water, is the same color as the dog's. But Karen—and, to some extent, I—felt reluctant, as though we were betraying Smeagol. Sarah attempted to remain aloof. The puppy managed, as we deliberated, to knock the crying toddler down three more times. We got the dog. Two fors, no againsts, and three abstentions. Her name is Brandywine, she is nine weeks old, and she cost five dollars. And this morning, as she attempts a gallop across the vinyl floor to meet me, her rear end goes into a slide, and she tumbles into a half-roll at my feet, no doubt disappointed to find me more substantial than her ex-owner's child.

We bought Smeagol from a doctor living in the most affluent of St. Louis's affluent suburbs. The doctor had hoped, since a grand champion lurked somewhere in the background, to sell the pups at a premium, but so had twelve other lab owners who advertised in the same day's paper. Desperate to be rid of the extra mouths and digestive tracts, the doctor settled for twenty dollars a head.

Sarah was three; Elizabeth was a baby, a baby with heart disease, a baby whose future was at best uncertain, and we were afraid of what lay ahead. Karen, worn down by the recent death of her mother and by the even more recent discovery of Eliza-

beth's illness, was wary. *We did not, she argued, need any more complications. Katrina, our cat, was pet enough for this time in our lives. I argued for the dog, argued that cats qualify as residents but not as pets, and that the fenced-in yard behind our newly purchased house would be wasted without a dog. Poor steward-ship, I piously declared. When we went, just to look, the other puppies ignored us as they tumbled over one another, but Smea-gol came quietly from behind a privet bush, stumbled slowly to Karen, and licked her ankle.*

I always thought of Smeagol as a puppy. Even when I held him, convulsing, in the back seat of the car or, later, in the vet's office when he was being given the final injection, I said to him again and again, "It's O.K., pup. It's O.K." Despite the gray muzzle, the dull veneer of cataracts, and the deafness of his last year, I could always see the puppy he had not been for more than a decade. Now I look at Brandywine and see only her decline and death. Does the clumsiness suggest a joint disorder? How long till we have to contend with her aging, her dying? She bounds in front of me, refusing to be ignored, and I let her trail along as I walk to the outhouse.

When my mother-in-law, after a long struggle—not really a struggle, there was too much grace in her resistance, but more a dispute, a disagreement—with cancer, decided to die, she com-pressed the process into a single day, saying good-by to children and husband in the morning, then lapsing into a coma. I stayed with her through much of the afternoon, responded as best I could to muttered phrases, unintelligible but spoken with convic-tion, and when she began to thrash her wasted body against the bed, I held her shoulders with my hands, held her awkwardly, and tried to talk her into immobility. She did not convulse with

the violence of Smeagol's dying, but perhaps it was the memory
of her that gave so much urgency to my efforts to quiet him, the
accumulated weight of old failures and of those that lie, inevita-
bly, ahead.

After I've loaded the car, I take the dog back inside. Karen calls
down from the loft, and I climb the stairs to show her, on the
topographical map I got from the U.S. Forestry office, where I
plan to go. And because I've never been in this stretch, I draw
a crude copy in my notebook, marking all possible exits. As I start
off once more, Karen reminds me to take my poncho.

Today I turn off the main road onto rough gravel and drive
the trail I walked Friday, parking behind some bushes just yards
from where I last got out of the river. The entry point, the one
the old Swede told me about, is a place where the bank has been
faced with three cedar logs, one on top of the other, allowing
a clean access—no alders to fight, no muck to wade.

Though the weekend rains have totaled at least another two
inches, the stream does not seem higher, only darker. There is a
haze above the water, almost a mist, and the sky is dark. The
threat of rain pervades the morning. I've forgotten the poncho.
The air, oppressive and heavy, weighs on my first casts, and the
fly plops rather than floats to the surface. With the dark water
and the leaden casts, I give in and switch almost immediately
from the dry fly to a muddler.

A crow calls from the hillside, then is answered by another.

Last summer, when Smeagol would lie in the sun, warming
himself and dozing in the front yard, a raven would come to pick
through the fire pit, prospecting for garbage left from last night's
burn. In previous years Smeagol would have kept such an in-
truder away, but deaf and arthritic, he no longer awoke to the
rustle of ashes just inches from his head. And the raven, always

the same raven, distinguished by a crooked feather in its tail, full of strutting arrogance as he made his rounds, would step casually around the sleeping dog.

At the next bend there is an island thick with the purple-topped plants which, thanks to the *Golden Guide to Flowers,* I can now identify as joe-pye weed. The bumblebees clinging to the fuzzy, flat clumps of blossoms seem dead or frozen.

Ahead, beyond a fallen white birch, the stream opens again, a slight rise of water backed up by the tree with its fluttering strings of bark and, to one side, an old bridge timber. The timber is about thirty feet long, with a heavy bolt sticking through it, and I cast for the still water just beyond the bolt. I forget the fallen birch's still upright twin and snag the muddler ten feet overhead. After a five-minute struggle in which I tighten that which I seek to loosen, the leader breaks.

I hate tying on leader tippet anywhere, but I especially dislike doing it in the river. My fingers are clumsy under the best of circumstances, but here, cold from the Run's water, they could be carved from wood. I start the barrel knot a dozen times, getting the first three loops in place, then losing them as I try to feed the line back through. My hands are small, fingers short and stubby, my excuse for not being the great basketball player I once longed—still long—to be, my justification for being unable to type or play a musical instrument and for innumerable other shortcomings; the ironic conclusion of my unusually long arms. Even out of the water I fumble with knots as though I were wearing gloves. Hands wet and chilled, it is as though I am wearing mittens.

Finally I get the loops on the one end tightened, then take the parallel piece of line to complete the connection. The idea is to keep the new line straight with the old, instead of elbowed as it would be with a conventional knot, the storyteller's "and" or "so," a rolling conjunction that minimizes any break and confirms continuity; not the lawyer's "therefore" or the scientist's "because," the assertion of change, of a new direction proudly taken. The barrel knot conceals disjunction, neither judges nor repudiates what went before, as it presents a line that flows, smooth, seductive, graceful. A wonderful knot if you are a proper fly fisherman or a heart surgeon. I am a wrecker of defunct cabins and have hands like Ping-Pong paddles.

Perhaps because of the pawlike shape of my hands, they lack the three distinct lines basic to palmistry. The lifeline is there, reassuring both in length and clarity, though troubled on my left hand by a flurry of last-minute disruptions; but the width of each palm is dominated by a single thick seam that runs from one edge to the other, a great fault, double-sided, cutting through the pale topography and yielding nothing to the surrounding hummocks in its undeviating straightness. Here the lines of heart and head have fused to form some mysterious new wrinkle, a simian crease—one of the characteristics of Down's syndrome. What would a palm reader make of this text? What can be made of all these entanglements?

At last, the barrel knot completed, I put on a wet coachman and begin again. It is misting now, but a fish rises, flutters up like a yellow leaf from the edge of the rapids, gently tugs the fly and, releasing it, flutters back down so that for a moment I think it is a leaf.

The Run narrows, breaks over the rapids that have created the pool, and again enters a thicket of alder. An eight-inch trout takes the fly, but before I realize it, I've lifted him from the water on my retrieve, and he flops free with a heavy splash just a few feet from me. Instead of fishing with flies, I am flying fish.

What looks like someone's snagged leader attached to a big, poorly tied fly dangles above the water ahead of me. As I approach, the fly becomes a spider, the leader his only thread as he faces me in the middle of Cook's Run, and we watch, bewildered, at the ends of our respective lines. He more resembles the Puritan's spider than Whitman's, the one dangling over the fiery pit of an angry God. Granted, water would be the better destiny, offering—perhaps—a damp deliverance rather than old Edwards's eternal sizzle.

When I was in second grade and my father was between road-construction jobs, I served for the first time as a pallbearer. We were living with my mother's parents and it was winter, two or three months before my seventh birthday. The corpse was that of an infant, and thus the casket was carried by children, boys from neighboring farms. The baby was a stranger to me, never seen except for that day in the coffin, but, since my grandfather and Major were still alive, it was my first death. Within four or five years I would know other children who died, would carry into a city cemetery the boy who had—on the morning of his dying—delivered newspapers with me, would, during the polio epidemics of the fifties, look down at several children, hair carefully groomed, cheeks rouged, whom I had originally known in life and not in a mortician's still arrangement. But this first one was a stranger, a little girl whom I had never seen move, never heard cry out.

I realized at the time that this was a special privilege, that while I could not share the sorrow of the family members seated around me, I could watch, note all the details of the occasion, and keep them in mind. There is much about the funeral that I have forgotten—especially the colors! What survives does so in black and white—but I remember that commission to observe, that commitment to detail. Even at seven I was troubled by the detachment, sensed the Peeping Tom element in it all, but also found a pleasure in the work. It became a kind of hobby, collecting experiences the way another child might have saved bubble gum cards. Eager to add new entries, I welcomed the memorable, whether an albino squirrel or a blue bullfrog or a tornado or my first car wreck. I tried imprinting each event exactly in memory, but without any sense of purpose or value.

Now I wish that in her last moments I had held my mother-in-law, lifted her like a fretful child and rocked her in my arms. Probably I was too afraid of hurting her and so did nothing to ease her passage. Or maybe I was afraid to draw death so closely to me, saw it, in the end, as more real than the woman it was claiming.

The stream begins to open once more, and the sun comes out for the first time. Surprised, I look up and see blue tears in the gray cloud. And farther west, even more blue is visible. I look behind me into the light. The Run shines, black with blinding streaks of silver. As the break in the clouds lengthens, the light moves forward and catches me just as the brush along the bank retreats and thins. White pines rise a short distance from the Run, and here and there elms, a few bearing one or two limbs still in sickly leaf. Although the stream has not greatly widened, and hints at narrowing once more, its mood is changing.

Butterflies—brown-and-orange fritillaries—dance above the water, the fly line snaking among them on each cast and again on the return.

Last month, whenever I made my four-mile run to the mailbox and back, black butterflies with white markings surrounded the small puddles along the road. They rose up in fluttering clouds as I jogged by, lifting three or four feet into the air before settling back to their damp claim. Then one day they were no longer

*black, but brown-and-orange, as though overnight word had
been given and the costumes changed.*

*Across the road from the mailbox, the phone company main-
tains a small cement-block building with a light over the doorway that burns round the clock. On Friday I discovered, clinging
to the wall amidst sphinxes and cecropias like a delicate lime-
green leaf amidst the dull debris of a forest floor, a luna moth.
Its long tails curved down to small white circles outlined in
brown, the punctuation mark at the end of that startling pale
green. It was the first living luna I had ever encountered, and as
soon as I finished my run I drove Karen and the kids back to see
it, stopped again on Saturday morning, then found it by carlight
on our way home from Eagle River with the puppy.*

*On Sunday the telephone building was bare of wings—green,
brown, or otherwise—and the children, who had not gone so
long as I without finding such a marvel, seemed relieved to be
spared one more dutiful show of enthusiasm for an insect on a
block wall.*

Along the stream, bent by the morning damp and tended by
fritillaries, black-eyed Susans lean from the bank. And from
behind a broken alder limb, a merganser comes out squawking,
beating the water with frantic wingbeats, the rust-colored tuft on
its head adding to a slightly hysterical look.

Beyond the alder branch I see an opening, a clearing to the
right, and, up a way, the back of a Jeep. I've known, though I'd
forgotten until now, that there is a camp somewhere in here and
have heard strange stories about the owner—that he blocks the
Forestry trail and threatens fishermen when they wade by his
property. Supposedly he is in a constant state of war with the
DNR and the Forestry Service as well as with the rest of us. Still,
though more elaborate than most such accounts, this is standard

fare for fishermen discussing waters they do not fish or those they fish often and want to keep to themselves. I struggle to see the cabin, but it must be hidden by the trees. Something, I suspect, like the deer shack I saw by the broken bridge on the Paint.

The merganser is still ahead of me but at last takes wing, churning his way like an eggbeater until he manages to get into the air. He leaves two feathers floating in his wake.

The sun shines without interference now, and I've no fish in the creel. It is 8:35, time to find a trail leading out of here. I am going to get skunked for the first time on the Run.

Actually this will be the second time I've failed to catch anything in Cook's Run. The first time I fished this stream was on Joe and Vi's thirty-ninth or fortieth wedding anniversary. We ate and, after several martinis, toasted the event with brandy, and then Joe decided that the two of us should go fishing. Karen protested, Vi shrugged, and we went to the Run. Joe waded upstream and I went in the opposite direction, walking stiffly, painstakingly, among boulders that refused to stay in focus. Joe, normally the quietest of fishermen, was singing a sixty-year-old schoolboy's ditty to a constant accompaniment of splashes. I caught nothing on that occasion either, while Joe, unsobered and still hymning the benefits of proper living, brought in seven trout.

Ahead, although there are still no signs of fresh cuttings, I hear a roar and the sudden promise of a beaver pond. But when I round the bend, I enter what looks to be a park. There is a rock dam, every stone carefully placed by hand, the kind found in the middle of resort towns, and a footbridge with steel supports mounted on concrete pilings. And on the left, in the middle of a two-acre lawn, is a house—not a cabin—a house made of brick supplemented by board and batten cedar siding, and bearing a cedar-shake roof. It is a low California house encircled by a deck, a golf-course clubhouse for young businessmen on their way to greater things.

"*Little pig, little pig, let me come in.*"

The dam diverts water before releasing it through a center spillway to a trout pond on the left, water that then circulates back to the stream through an underground drainage system. All this is too new to be legal, not some old construction that predates stream-protection laws. How did they ever get away with it? And regardless of the law, none of this belongs here. It is as though I've somehow gotten into the wrong stream and am gazing at an alien landscape.

I look to see if anyone is around. The place seems deserted, although the lawn has been freshly cut, presumably by the tractor mower that is visible behind the house. The trout pond presents a major temptation; I know it is an illegal pond and suspect it has been stocked, but I resist entering, motivated by virtue, I tell myself, and not by fear. This, I realize, and not the regulation deer shack I'd expected, must be where the wild man lives, and he is clearly a rich wild man—an irritating combination—able to buy his way around nature and the law.

The pool below the dam yields only little trout, and I trade the coachman for an Adams dry.

The knot I use for flies—a turle—is easier to tie than a barrel knot, is in fact little more than a slipknot, tied after the line has been fed through the hook's eye and then looped back over the fly. Somewhere—I think in Buckminster Fuller—I read a discussion of knots that explained them merely as intersecting planes. From this view, in knotting the line I've added nothing to it, only turned it against itself, thus it alone brings the pressure and holds itself in thrall. With knots so with words and most other things.

I remember, not long after my discovery of this passage, being asked by Sarah to tie a broken jump rope, and, while I complied, I gave her the simplified version of Fuller's explanation, showed her how the knot was nothing but the rope refigured. She looked at me with daughterly indulgence and asked, "Does that mean you don't think it will hold?"

Larger fish occasionally break the surface but without enthusiasm, as though in this indulgent setting even they have grown arrogant. I work the dam futilely, then the bridge pilings and the shoreline in between.

For some reason, during my sophomore year in high school, I taught myself to flip rope one-handed, into knots—though actually not rope which was too thick or string which was too limp. What was just right was the cord on my classroom window blinds. In three of my classes and in study hall I sat next to the window, and whenever the teacher's attention was diverted, or when the cord was long enough to pull under my desk, I practiced. Eventually I could toss an overhand knot into the line four out of every five attempts, but somehow, once I had mastered this skill, it lacked the power to amaze that I had expected it to have.

Above the pool the stream narrows and turns, and immediately it is as though nothing I have just seen could have been. Then in confirmation, threading through the trees and barely visible, a cyclone fence marks the border of the private land.

I check on my roughly sketched map but see no trails, no evidence of the place I've just passed. I could return and cut through the drive to the road that runs back to my car, but I'd rather be finished with the too perfect lawn, the cultivated stream. Surely I'll find some other exit soon.

I've succeeded in dredging up the words to Joe's nursery song:

> *"The best six doctors anywhere,*
> *And no one can deny it,*
> *Are sunshine, water, rest, and air,*
> *Exercise and diet.*
> *These six will gladly you attend,*
> *If only you are willing.*
> *Your mind they'll ease,*
> *Your will they'll mend,*
> *And charge you not one shilling."*

He tried to teach the lines to the kids when they were little, but to no avail. I, however, have kept them stored—not filed, just dumped randomly in my mental attic—to be periodically retrieved in the middle of a trout stream.

Seventy-five yards upstream I strike, first, a little island, and beyond that, an enormous pool. The sky is a brilliant blue, and the quiet waters provide a giant mirror, reflecting not only sky and fluffy clouds but the duplicate of a big three-trunked white pine that soars above the left bank. To the right is a meadow of joe-pye weed and Queen Anne's lace and, joining a multitude of fritillaries, white butterflies, dazzling in the bright light. The water is colder as well as deeper here. The cold must come from springs, but neither the topography of the land nor any evidence of recent beaver work explains the depth.

I cast to the meadow side, reluctant to leave without trying some small part of the pool, but as I edge into the deep water, I feel the first wet evidence of a leak in the right leg of my boots. These waders are only three months old and, on sale, cost thirty-five dollars. A friend once told me that Korean manufacturers, who seem to have a monopoly on the business, have perfected a water-soluble wader. I can believe it. But there is nothing to do. Not only is the sporting-goods store where I bought them six hundred miles away, but it has gone bankrupt as well.

I climb out of the stream before taking in any more water and then start up a track that runs to the east and, I hope, toward the car. But after one hundred feet the road is blocked by a steel gate bearing a No Trespassing sign. I backtrack and swing north. I am not certain from my map which of several possible trails I am on, but I seem to be heading away from where I parked. After about four hundred yards, fifty of which are under water and inhabited by a congregation of frogs, I find an overgrown path that cuts back toward the Run, and, convinced that the road I want lies in that direction, I take the turn.

The trail winds for another quarter of a mile, then narrows and is blocked by frequent blowdowns. But for the first time there is evidence of other travelers: the ferns are broken, weeds are mashed over. Encouraged, I trudge on and, after another hundred feet, nearly step in a pile of bear droppings, still steaming and filled with blueberries. More bear sign lies ahead, including smaller paw prints.

I do not worry about bears, only about bears with cubs, and what we have here, or somewhere close to here, seems to be a bear with a cub—this in a week when the *Milwaukee Journal* has been specializing in bear-attack stories, one on a farmer in Wisconsin and another on a camper in Yellowstone. A third account might seem too much of a good thing.

In our first years at the lake, a time when we were filling in the swamp for the new cabin site, something kept knocking over the garbage can outside our northeast window. I inspected the daily damage and declared the culprit to be a raccoon.

One morning about six—I was already in the river—Karen awoke to a racket outside the cabin. She got up to see my raccoon and found instead a bear inches away on the other side of the windowpane. *Shaken but eager for proof of her encounter, she got the camera and photographed her bear rummaging through our garbage, the bear working among corncobs and fruit cans, the bear looking at the window. Finally, alerted by the clicking, the beast saw her and ambled away.*

By now Smeagol was going wild, barking the deep, fierce bark he reserved for bears, and Karen, worried about Sarah and Sarah's Uncle Jimmy, who were asleep in a tent behind the cabin, let the dog out. Trembling but determined, Smeagol drove the bear away, endearing himself to Karen for the rest of his life.

I come to another cutoff, this one heading more directly east, and, for no reason I can explain, I take it. Gradually it occurs to me that the road I left after walking through the frog holes had to have been the correct one, that I have simply been wandering in a large loop and, at some point, will come back to that earlier trail. I have just finished depressing myself with this discovery when I hit gravel once more and am only thirty yards below the car.

A   u   g   u   s   t   7

I awaken at 5:15 to the cries of loons and to the sound of Karen letting the dog out. The loons, one at each end of the lake, are keening long, mournful refrains, as though they never expect to find one another again. Karen, on the other hand, is trying to sound cheerful as she encourages Brandywine to climb, unassisted, down the front steps. The loons seem more sincere. Finally Karen gives in and, grumbling about the wet, carries the puppy across the porch and into the grass.

I attempt to sleep, but I am covered with a thin film of sweat. The muggy air lies on me like an extra blanket. I feel as though

I have been awake all night—but I have slept through another rainstorm. Still, despite the dripping maple leaves outside the window and the moisture beading the skylight, all is blue and cloudless overhead. The sun will be on the water almost as soon as I reach the stream, the big pool unfishable in bright light.

I walk onto the dock to wash, and, as I kneel to the water, a loon surfaces less than twelve feet away. In this stooped position I am on nearly the same eye level as he, my head craned to one side, his upright above a long, pinstriped neck, black feathers shiny from his recent dive, eyes an unfathomable deep reddish hue, chips of ruby-colored obsidian. We remain like this, unmoving, for a long moment; then he wriggles his head, as though working a stiffness from his neck, and hunches his body slightly, calmly. After another hesitation he stretches his wings in an unhurried gesture and sounds a cry like hysterical laughter, a crescendo of sharp wavering blasts somewhere between a cackle and the staccato of a machine gun, his lunatic call.

Elizabeth, for several years, was afraid to go onto the dock. The half inch of water visible between the decking seemed the pro-founder reality, and she would not trust the wood except on hands and knees, eyes downward, watchful of the lake below.

Aaron, on the other hand, little more than a toddler and freshly shod in expensive corrective shoes, would head for the dock every chance he got and, once there, would walk quickly to the very end and unhesitatingly into the water. He did this repeatedly, then would climb to his feet and stand quietly, knee-deep in the lake, until someone pulled him out. In time he found other ways to inform us of his dislike for the heavy-soled shoes which, of course, were always removed when they got wet.

Last summer, while I was casting from the dock in the twilight, checking a reel Aaron and I had just repaired, a long shadow, its shape distorted by the rippling lake, followed the lure

toward me. When only six feet of line remained in the water,
I dragged the lure into the shallows toward shore. At the very
last, its belly furrowing the sand, a pike somewhere between three
and four feet in length made a lunge for the red spoon, its teeth
sparkling in the dark water. With a flick of its head it threw the
lure before I could set the hook and turning, slowly, arrogantly,
swam under the dock, the dock on which my children play, and
into the darker pool in which, in better light, they dive.

Basswood is one of my favorite places, though it is in fact
hardly a place at all. To the north of the main road, across the
abandoned railroad right-of-way, a turnoff leads to a National
Forest gravel pit, the pit where we got the fill on which our new
cabin is built, a pit no longer in use. The last stretch of water I
fish each year, a ritual of leave-taking, lies a mile walk above
Basswood along a high ridge that parallels the Paint, and then a
short downhill hike through a swampy stand of cedars. Here a
big spring hole—and a quarter mile to the west another—contain
trout even in dry seasons. I landed my first good-sized brookie
and my first brown in these pools. Here, too, is the hole where
I hooked my largest trout—a brown more than two feet in
length and with orange spots the size of dimes—played it out
from behind a log until it quit fighting and came side up to the
surface as I drew it to me. Less than a foot in front of the net,
even as I was deciding whether or not to break principle and have
it mounted, it suddenly righted, sent the hook flying, and flashed
by, bumping heavily against my leg as it passed. I stood in the
middle of the Basswood hole shouting obscenities and beating at
the water with the net until I lost my balance and filled my
waders with chilling spring water. Sometimes, in the middle of
a class, I find myself thinking about that trout, see it perfectly as
it rides up on the water, defeated. And I dream about it, usually
in the dead of winter, two states removed from Basswood. I have

spent more hours not catching that trout than I have, in forty-two years, spent in rivers.

When Sarah was fourteen, I brought her to this same spot, left her to fish alone for the first time while I went upstream to a smaller spring hole. We got a late start, and by the time I started fishing, the river was already deep in shadow, a full moon just breaking through the trees along the ridge. The water began to steam in the evening air, and I gave up and, rather than wading back as planned, climbed the hill, and crossed over land to Sarah's pool.

The swamp was dark beneath the cedars, the moonlight only rarely filtering through the needles, and I could not hold to the path, stepped time and again into the grasping slime of the bog. When I reached the water, the moon had cleared the ridge and lay, a perfect circle, on the surface of the river. But Sarah was nowhere in sight. I called out, then, guessing that she had grown bored in this confinement, rushed downstream, yelling her name and stumbling over the rocks. She did not answer. I hurried back to the pool, then through the swamp and up the ridge. One of the Wiegand girls, on horseback, saw me as I broke free of the timber, and rode over to warn me of a sow bear and cub she had seen crossing the railroad tracks to the west. She promised to keep a lookout for Sarah on her way back to the farm and rode off through the moonlight.

I ran along the ridge, tripping over the waders, then halting to call my daughter's name, until, nearly back to the small hole, I got an answer, rising from the river and weaving through the trees with remarkable clarity and strength, unmarred by the anxiety that hoarsened my voice.

Sarah had snagged her line, lost the fly, and, frustrated, had come upstream to meet me. Two years earlier she had walked this route with me to see the hornets' nest that hung for a season over the upper pool. When tonight she had made her way back and recognized the spot even without the paper hive, she guessed how we'd missed each other and was retracing her steps. We talked, her voice, calm and reassuring, climbing to me, deepened by the valley and the trees and carrying just the hint of an echo as though it had traveled a great distance. Then, continuing to call to one another, though less frequently now, we walked our separate paths to the Basswood pool.

Basswood also is the site of an old homestead, that of a Civil War nurse, foundations still visible, and remnants of her apple orchard still producing tough, gnarled fruit.

Just to the east of Basswood is the Wiegand farm. Relocated Detroiters, the Wiegands are a large family—there are fourteen children—and nearly all of the boys are employed in one phase or another of construction. The father, Charlie, and half a dozen of his kids helped us pour the slab for our cabin, and in the years since, they have, with advice or assistance, befriended us repeatedly.

But all I know of the land to the east of the farm, the land directly across from Basswood, is a red pine plantation that fronts against the road. Last night I called Lawrence, one of the Wiegand sons, to ask about a way into Cook's Run someplace near where it cuts behind his parents' place and turns alongside the forty acres on which he is building a house of his own. He has an excavating business and works compulsively, with no concession to or even thought for leisure. He told me the rutted path that turns from the main road into the pine continues down nearly to the Run and, if I am careful, can be driven. Upstream, he said, an old logging trail leads back to a turnoff where the car can be parked. But he was less encouraging about the wade, thought the big pool from yesterday too deep and silted to be gotten through, and warned against other holes farther upstream. When he realized that I intended to go anyway, he said, "Well, at least I know where to look for you." Lawrence, who is a serious young man, said it as lightly as he ever says anything, and yet he seemed worried. Lawrence, I remembered, cannot swim.

When I asked Joe about the big hole, he said it was dug in the seventies by the DNR in the hope that it would collect silt and keep the lower waters clean. He has not been in to see it since the excavation but thinks it all expensive nonsense. I also asked about the fancy cabin with the dam and trout pond. He told me the name of the owner, a local businessman, and of how he had been taken to court by an outraged DNR, but that the judge simply imposed a fine and told him not to do it again. "Even a rich man probably doesn't need more than one dam and pond," Joe concluded.

Past the Wiegand farm the sun breaks free of the distant trees, a garish orange-and-red bubble burning through the mist that hangs over the hayfield below the barn. At the edge of the gravel a raven, balanced arrogantly on long thin legs, straddles a dead rabbit and darts its beak where an eye used to be. It is six o'clock.

I turn into the pine, into heavy ruts—truck ruts—and the trail disappears under a pool of muddy water, then reappears thirty feet away only to disappear once more. I ease the car along, holding to the high ground between the deep tire tracks, and the weeds, like choiring crickets, scrape against the undercarriage with a constant high-pitched chirping. The tracks lead downhill into a valley of maples, and after a half mile of straddling ruts and fording pools, I turn onto a side trail and park.

Before pulling on my waders I check the patch I put in place yesterday. Because rubber cement wouldn't bind to the layer of fabric on the outside of the boots, I tried "super glue," smearing it to the piece I'd cut from an inner tube and then clamping everything firmly in place. The claims on the package were extravagant, but the patch does appear to be holding; still, I expect to get wet again today.

Last night, writing up yesterday's wade, I grew even more frustrated with the whole endeavor. While there is a certain quaint appeal to the descriptions of flowers and trees, how long can that appeal be sustained? I still cannot see what is to be made of this and suspect it would take more than a big fish, more even than a record-breaking brown, to salvage things. Clearly then, this cannot be about fishing; fishing is a way of keeping your balance as you wade upstream. But what is it about?

About midnight came the discomforting thought that I am writing about nothing happening, about middle age, an in-between time, when the things that, in youth, I hoped would happen have lost either their appeal or their possibility, and when the things I fear will happen, know will happen eventually, are still being held at bay. This is a time when the prospect of change has not lost all of its attraction, but, simultaneously, when I realize that what is likely to come is not at all the thing longed for.

When Nick, in Hemingway's "Big Two Hearted River," fishes another Upper Peninsula stream, he does so in order not to think, in order to unclutter his mind. Recently returned from war, he wants to give himself over to the ritual of line and knots and technique, to be absorbed in the external. That is, in part, what I had in mind when all of this began, wanted the "happening" to lie outside of me, wanted it to be at once more and less than me.

What is the longed-for thing? Would I dare name it even if I knew?

Ahead and to the south the triple-trunked white pine rises above shorter growth, and then the path I came out on yesterday appears. The far side of the pool is all that remains in shade, and there only because the downstream curve has provided trees that will shadow the water for a short while longer. Everywhere else the sun glints as though reflected off chrome.

Within moments the tippet I added yesterday has worked itself into the most intricate maze imaginable, and I have no idea why. There were some small kinks in the leader, though no more than might be expected for something you carry for weeks in your pocket, and perhaps I tied on more than necessary, but here are knots that would bewilder a sailor.

After ten minutes of picking and cursing—during which time the sun takes complete control of the pool—I have unraveled the mess and have straightened the leader by pulling it through a piece of inner tube I keep in my jacket pocket for just this purpose.

Once something did "happen" to me while fishing the Paint. A few weeks after Jimmy Hoffa—who owned land not far from Basswood—disappeared, I was wading about half a mile above the hornets' nest pool, a stretch new to me, heading for a wooden bridge and a dirt trail that would take me back to the railroad tracks.

Except for its undergirdings, the bridge was hidden from my view by fog, the result of a warm, humid evening, but gradually, as I pulled in eight- and nine-inch brookies, I became aware of something being rolled over planking, and then of voices, angry and cursing. Finally, no longer casting, only crouching as though fearful of inadvertently poking through the cloud overhead, I heard a great splash above the bridge.

Quietly I worked my way downstream, taking the long way back to the car. For the next forty-eight hours I was the only semi-honest man in America who knew the location of Jimmy Hoffa's body. After the second day I decided to go back and

*confirm this knowledge. I returned on a cooler August evening
and, without benefit of cloud cover, crawled under the bridge
and found a fifty-gallon oil drum sitting upright in shallow
water. Bloodstains shone red against the lighter red of the barrel
and a rank smell hung in the air. I listened for footsteps, then,
with a sharp-edged rock, began pounding upward on the outer
rim of the lid. When the top at last popped free, and I peered
inside, I found the bloody garbage left by unusually fastidious
deer poachers.*

The pool is cold and deep, the great mound of dirt on the
north bank witness to the extent of the excavation. The only
available passage is wide to the left, a route that makes the most
promising spots along the south bank virtually unreachable. It
also is chest-deep in weeds, apparently some hybrid of algae and
moss, concealing a silt that sucks at my feet and, often as not,
gives way abruptly. And even holding to this course, I manage
to keep the water below my wader tops only by standing on
tiptoe and feeling my way along with the greatest of care. This
does not make for good fishing. Every step sends out ripples
across the quiet pool and, worse, releases bubbles and a stink like
that of rotting cabbage, telegraphing my presence in every direction and mucking up all the water within casting distance. What
this is good for, I discover, are foot and leg cramps, constrictions
that work their way from arch to calf with wondrous efficiency,
laying down a path of pain as neatly defined as the river on a
map.

It is now after seven, and I've covered about a hundred and
fifty feet without seeing any sign of fish. I find as secure a footing
as I can, let the water settle, and begin casting to the far bank.
The Adams constantly drowns, and I must dip it in silicone
solution—from an hourglass-shaped bottle I carry in another
pocket—every few minutes, because with the amount of line I'm

now using I can't dry it in the air. Exasperated, I tie on a wet royal coachman and immediately hook an eight-inch brookie.

When I reach for my net, the webbing is bound up in the algae/moss that surrounds me like putrefied lime Jell-O. Instead, I grab the fish with my hand, pleased not to be skunked today. It slips the hook and my hand in the same movement. I tell myself how much worse I'd feel if it were a nice trout, one like the brown I lost at Basswood. I think this and yell "Shit!" the memory renewing an old aggravation rather than providing consolation. An eagle, which must have been all the while observing from the white pine, lifts suddenly, indignantly, hugely above the pool, circles once, and then heads upstream on strong, deliberate wings.

I try to move on, but I have become rooted. Neither foot will break free of the silt's suction; I am caught in a sea of green hair, like stuff pulled from clogged bathroom drains. After what seems minutes of struggling, I wriggle the right foot until I can ease it backward a half step, then start twisting the left. Eventually I get free, but in the process I've allowed the fly to sink into the weeds and when it at last breaks free, it comes complete with a foot-long streamer of slime. I move closer still to the south bank, searching for a safer path. At first the silt seems shallower, then without warning it gives way and I begin to sink. My left foot scrapes against a limb hidden in the muck and I backpedal until I find a precarious balance. It is like quicksand here. I inch back to the path I had taken before, a path nearer center pool, where the silt, still treacherous, nonetheless seems firmer.

The leg cramps continue, threatening to bind up the muscle once and for all. I cannot remember whether to point my toes up or down to ease the pain, and thus try to avoid either movement for fear it will be the wrong one. The strain of fighting the cramps has tightened my back and shoulders until they, too, ache.

Six years ago, while we were living in Connecticut, my brother Jerry—third in the family order—came to visit. He had been going through a difficult time, and neither of us was very good at intimacy or, for that matter, even small talk. So we played basketball, long, exhausting games of one-on-one, hard games in which we banged into each other and forced our way to the hoop. Jerry has a shoulder that dislocates easily, and sometimes in the midst of play it would slip out of place. He would roll on the gym floor, screaming curses at the pain, yet directing me until I caught hold of the offending arm and worked the joint back into proper position. Then he would get up, thank me, rotate the shoulder a couple of times, and we would resume the game.

Lurching clumsily along, more intent on staying free of the silt than on catching fish, I manage four more trout, all less than seven inches in length. Three crows land stiffly in a dead birch to the west. They watch, all three heads turned in the same direction, all cocked at the same exaggerated angle, like spectators at a dull sporting event waiting for the action to begin. I do my best to satisfy them.

The pool ends by a stand of fireweed, their tall pink spikes surrounded by the flutter of fritillaries. My right sock, as a result of all the foot wiggling, has crawled down on my foot. The lump it forms under my instep bothers me, but less than the feeling that the sock is creeping farther down with every step. I flex my toes daringly, worrying my foot inside the boot. Finally, exasperated, I lean against the bank, loosen my suspenders and work my hand down until, hunched up like a folding chair, I catch the sock top between finger and thumb, and tug it back to its proper position. For the first time in my life, garters seem a marvelous invention. So, too, in the absence of leaks, does "super glue." I am prepared, with a single tube and sufficient patching, to bring the Korean wader industry to its knees. Though tired from fighting the muck and weeds—and still fishless—I feel oddly elated, and I gaze out over the big pool with pleasure, though try as I might, I cannot identify what in it pleases me. Looking back into the sun, I see only a glaring sheet of water beneath a glaring sky. Even the white pine is indistinct, and the entire view seems bleached of color like an overexposed photograph.

I must have been six or seven, and it was some kind of family function because several of my uncles were there when the two men, not family but known to the family, appeared and talked about a creek hole filled with big catfish. They had a seine in their truck, and my father and uncles—David and Ralph, still teenagers, Lee, and Merle and Merle's brother, Buck—all bored with polite conversation and fried chicken, together with my cousin Bob and me, followed in cars. I see, as though still standing on that bank, the males—some boys, the others, including my father, men for less than a decade—stripped to their shorts and dragging the wide net through the pool, taunting one another and laughing whenever someone slipped. The few fish they caught were either carp or bullheads, and the family members, as they pulled on their clothes, mocked the two outsiders who had promised something better.

They were still joking and deviling when the game warden arrived. Seining on Sunday, even with a license, even in Missouri, was illegal, and the holes in this seine were too small, even if the other regulations had been satisfied.

When we got back to the picnic, the men, chastened in the presence of wives and older relatives, tried a false bravado but were unconvincing, and my grandfather, who took a stern view of such frivolity on the Sabbath, shook his head in disgust and went home.

The sandy bottom continues, providing soft but stable footing, and the alders and spruce on the shore cool the air even as they

shade the edges of the Run. Here, as downstream, though fueled
by a slower current, small riffles and submerged timbers provide
fish cover. I approach a spring hole where logs jut out from both
banks. A big brookie jumps by the log on my left. The fly drops
exactly where I want it, my best cast of the day, but returns to
me undisturbed, and I head on into a big curve, deep enough on
its shallow edge nearly to swamp my waders. Another ten- or
eleven-inch trout hits at the top of the bend, jumps once and is
gone.

A blue heron, surprised in a runoff pool, lifts awkwardly into
flight, folding and unfolding its great body as it gains the air, legs
stuck out apologetically behind, as though they should be doing
something useful, carrying something, perhaps.

*Last year the kids and I regularly went fishing on the lake.
Whenever the bigger perch weren't biting, the girls would grow
bored and want to go back to shore, but Aaron, ten years old and
inspired by their irritation, would dangle his hook and worm just
a few inches below the surface, teasing up little fish, minnows so
small that they couldn't take the hook but could only clamp onto
the end of the worm. He would then lift them into the air and
talk to them as they clung with an overwhelming possessiveness
to their slight hold on his bait, inquire after their families, explain
the importance of brushing after meals, declare the dangers of
gluttony. Soon Elizabeth would be giggling uncontrollably and
Sarah would watch, bemused, over the top of a Mary Stewart
novel. When at last the minnow lost its grip, Aaron would
chastise it for its failure to say good-by, then dip the worm back
into the water and tempt another baby perch into the same
conversation. He sustained this effort for the better part of a
summer, a summer during which we caught very little but in
which I had no difficulty getting others to go fishing as long as
Aaron was in the boat.*

The water is louder ahead, and as I come out of a sharp bend I see the dam, relatively new and narrow but ingenious. Shaped like a big spear point with spillways on both sides, it is anchored to an island in center stream, an island spiked with ironweed and one huge thistle. The beaver has backed up four and a half feet of water in a relatively narrow spring hole, but I can only fish it by standing on the dam and dangling a few feet of line straight down from the rod. I feel like a kid fishing in a mud puddle, and the results are about the same. Maybe I should tie a bent pin to the leader. Aaron could make something of this.

Above the dam the stream narrows and once more there are alders overarching the deepest pools. I snag the fly on a branch behind me and retreat to free it.

Back turned, I hear a splash like a log falling into the water, and my first thought is that I've surprised the beaver, builder of the fancy dam. Since I am deaf in one ear, it is nearly impossible for me to locate sounds, to pin down their source. I look carefully but see no beaver. The circles, however, seem to be coming from under thick brush where the bank is cut by a spring. In confirmation, a trout, an enormous brown, rises once more, this time just curling its broad back above the surface as though scratching itself on the low-hanging limbs. I can do nothing but watch—and wish for a stick of dynamite.

Suddenly the Run is very deep, even next to the alders, and it sloshes over the top of my waders. I take my notebook from the waders pocket and clutch it between my teeth while I struggle along by clinging to the grasping limbs. Where the hole ends, so do the alders, and the stream enters a broad grassland that extends outward more than a quarter of a mile to either side of the Run. Is this Cook's Meadows? Overhead an osprey circles, dipping low in a flash of white, then circling upward higher and higher till it is only a spiraling black speck against the blue.

Watching the stream, I jump at the sound of a blow followed by a long series of yelps like the cries of a stricken dog. There is a thrashing among the low bushes and high grass on the north

bank and then a sound like that of a hog rooting around in mud.
Another whack, more yelping, and the scurrying of a cub followed by the more deliberate, heavy movement of an adult. A
ridge of brown fur rises above the vegetation, plunges and rises
again as mother and child crash on their way no more than five
yards to my right.

*I have never believed, really believed, that our children would
one day become independent from us, not until this summer
anyway. The annual return to the lake has been a persistent claim
on my part—one tolerated though not accepted by Karen and the
kids—that things need not change. In spite of the effect of six
summers of wheeling yard after yard of gravel until the very
shape of our land had been transformed, despite the years of cabin
construction that has disrupted the skyline of the lake, despite the
previously unthinkable television antenna that juts up from our
roof, I have maintained by the glow of evening gaslight the
illusion of control, the dream of constancy. Change has always
been the enemy. I mourn the loss of every tree, resent the mod-
ernizing efforts of other lake residents. Perhaps I have hoped, by
relinquishing electricity and running water, to escape time and
deny its power for at least these brief summer months. I know
that, beyond all else, I hoped to hold on to the children, hoard
them up for myself. Karen, of course, has always known better.
And so, I am discovering, have the children.*

The river continues, unchanging, through a series of sharp
bends. On the bank, tall thistles with purple blossoms, big and
bristly, entertain a host of butterflies. (If a bunch of larks is an
ecstasy, what is the collective term for butterflies? A squadron?
A churn? A delight?) On the bottom of the Run everything is
visible, and, aware that I must be visible from any point visible

to me, I nevertheless cast to submerged logs and even to the occasional trout I spot in the water ahead. One surprises me, and I avoid a shutout by the narrowest of margins.

We had an aged movie camera, old when we inherited it from an aunt and uncle, and with it an equally old projector. The camera got little use, only one or two reels of 8 mm film, but the kids play that brief footage over and over again. Aaron, who does not appear on screen, since the events predate his earthly debut, even recorded a sound track to accompany the show.

In the movie, made only weeks before Elizabeth's surgery, Elizabeth plays on the ground while her older sister climbs on the monkey bars. The camera follows the confident ascent. Periodically Sarah looks determinedly toward the lens. Then she is at the summit, gripping the bar beneath her with one hand while she laughs triumphantly. There is still a plumpness to her face and limbs, still the baby she so recently had been as well as the leaner child she is growing into. She lifts her hands to wave and plummets downward. The camera follows only a blink behind. On the ground she cries, less in pain than in anger, humiliated by the fall. She refuses to be comforted by her mother, who rushes to her side, and berates the father who continues to film her defeat.

Sarah finds the movie amusing in a small way. Aaron and Elizabeth find it uproarious. They like to tell her how little she has changed, how little all of us have changed.

And then the road, actually more a trail, and that only on the south bank. On the north side the undergrowth is as wild as ever, until, around the next bend, a more proper road appears, and I realize that what I have just passed is a turnaround with a footpath to the stream. On my right the bank, though still overgrown, is broken by a cross section of old bridge timbers that reach out into the water from beneath a burden of dirt and alder.

I climb carefully around the timbers, trying to preserve my waders, then take the path that cuts through the thicket to the north.

A u g u s t   8

Raining at 5 A.M., and I go back to sleep.

Six o'clock and the rain has stopped. The sky is overcast and the air remains heavy. Karen, already up to let Brandywine out, will drive me to Cook's Run, and Sarah, awake because the puppy keeps jumping up and licking her face, will ride along. I eat a doughnut and stick a banana into my jacket pocket. Today's will be a long wade, all the way from where I got out yesterday to Forest Highway 16, where, later in the morning, Karen will leave the car by the bridge and pedal home on her bicycle.

I called the Forestry office yesterday to find out the best places to get in and out of the Run once I cross U.S. Highway 2—probably the day after tomorrow. The ranger was reluctant to offer advice but told me happily that they are doing a fish survey at various points along the stream, shocking the water and counting the stunned trout. They have been moving just ahead of me, leaving the Run full of groggy brookies and browns. "They'd be off feed at least four days after we hit them. Bad luck to be fishing then." I swore softly and sincerely. He added that they had worked just above the gravel pit on Thursday, August 1, then again on Friday, and on the second day had clocked the Run at four feet per second, the fastest anyone remembers. "It would have been even faster on Thursday after all that rain," he added, "but we forgot to time it." When I told him that I had waded upstream from the Paint on Thursday and up from the bridge on Friday, he seemed skeptical. The story of the sucker convinced him. "That would have been some pounding," he said, then, either as a reward for my effort or an apology for his initial doubt, offered to sketch in some hunting trails if I would bring a map by the office.

Once, driving back from town, I saw a DNR pickup pulled over by the bridge on Highway 16. Four men in waders were unload- ing a short flat-bottomed boat and a small generator. I stopped and asked what they were doing. The oldest of the four, a man in mid-forties, wearing a cowboy hat, and speaking with a coun- try twang, told me they were doing a fish count. He introduced the others: a DNR fish specialist with a neatly trimmed mustache, and two helpers, college kids, one squarely built and wearing a University of Michigan T-shirt, the other tall and thin and noticeably shy. The one in the cowboy hat, a teacher at the University forestry camp, invited me to join them, an offer that the DNR man did not greet with enthusiasm. I rushed to the cabin for my waders.

When everything was ready, they started the generator, now aboard the skiff, and the chunky kid, harnessed in a kind of rope halter, dragged the whole thing upstream. The two older men probed the water with metal-tipped rods that were linked to the generator by thickly insulated electric cables. They shocked along the undercut bank and behind logs, flourishing their peculiar weapons like misplaced harpooners. Stunned trout, mostly small but a surprising number measuring eleven, twelve, on up to sixteen inches, rose like manna all around them. Each of the four carried a long-handled net, and they swept up the bobbing fish that in their helplessness were being carried downstream. Periodi- cally there was a break in the action and the nets were emptied into holding tanks aboard the boat, the trout kept inactive by an anaesthetic powder the fish specialist sprinkled in the water. In the more densely populated holes, the men darted around, scoop-

ing up the larger fish, catching the small ones that drifted into
the backup nets, and calling out whenever the leads started to
tangle or when they had resurrected more fish than they could
gather in. Everyone except me had on long-sleeved rubber
gloves, and I had to keep my arms folded in order to be sure I
didn't, in the excitement, join the chase and get jolted myself.

After the four had cleared an area, they would shut down the
generator, strip off their gloves, and measure, one at a time, the
trout, record length and species, take scale samples in order to
establish age, then release the fish. The man in the cowboy hat
and the squarely built kid would often get excited with the catch
and grandly describe the beauties of a particular trout, sometimes
praising color, other times shape. The DNR officer, impatient
with their enthusiasm and the delays it caused, regularly called
them back to their work. The tall kid spoke only when giving
data, reporting kind and measurements as he held each fish, in its
turn, against a wooden ruler. He had long, delicate fingers and
handled the slippery trout, even the smallest of them, gently,
skillfully.

The man in the cowboy hat could not resist his teaching
instincts, kept on professing in his easy drawl; the squarely built
kid listened, occasionally breaking in with a question; the DNR
officer, a look of boredom on his face, recorded; and all the while
the tall student's long fingers moved with a potter's grace through
schools of trout.

This morning we approach the Run from Highway 2 rather
than from the Basswood road, turning off the pavement onto the
trail I spotted yesterday. While the road is better than its counterpart on the opposite side of the stream, it is deeply rutted with
long puddles and jutting rocks. Here, too, I try to ride the ridges
in order to keep from dragging off the muffler, even stop at one
point with the intention of walking the rest of the way, but

Karen wants to see the Run and we drive on. There are tracks, recent tire prints leading out of the puddles, and I begin fretting that someone has gotten here first. Karen and Sarah think I am paranoid, absurdly possessive. "Who else would drive in on this?" Karen asks. "At this hour?" Sarah adds. She is in the back seat, holding the puppy. But when we reach the stream, we find a new sports van with a Wisconsin plate, and across the clearing to the right I see a fisherman. He looks like a vacationing executive complete with new L. L. Bean vest and hat and a Orvis graphite fly rod.

"Which way you headed?" I call. The words come out hard, accusing, and he looks up, startled, but relaxes when he sees Karen and Sarah. He points downstream.

"Good," I say. "I'm going up," and I point to the left.

"Good," he says and continues casting but hurries now as though eager to get around the bend.

I pull on my waders while Karen and Sarah inspect the Run, then I say good-by and head for the opening to the left of the turnaround. When I get to the water I find another executive, identical to the first, walking upstream. I feel as though I've fallen into a mirror.

I yell at Karen to wait. Furious, and without taking off my waders, I get into the car and drive, much too fast, up the rutted road, all the way swearing at the "goddamned flatlanders"—imperiously exempting myself from that category—who muck around where they don't belong. I am genuinely enraged, and I make the whole business an issue of class—the issue to which I always resort when my rage is greatest, an issue now fueled by the expensive outfits and the van—ranting and raving, half aware of the absurdity and self-consciously playing the buffoon but serious at the same time. I am shaking with anger, burning with a nonsensical righteousness. Karen and Sarah laugh. The dog throws up in the back seat.

After we have stopped the car and cleaned out the dog vomit with roadside weeds, I deliver Karen, Sarah, and the puppy to the cabin and head for the Paint, to the spot near Elmwood where, two weeks ago, I lost a big trout.

Only long stacks of pulpwood, a couple of equipment sheds, the shell of an ancient bus, and an abandoned one-room house now declare Elmwood's existence. When we first came to the U.P. the house was inhabited by an aged ex-logging cook and his dog, an arthritic Saint Bernard named Bruno. The old man used to let me get drinking water from an outside spigot in return for sitting and listening to him talk. He was well into his eighties, and, when Bruno died, they moved the old man into a nursing home, and he, too, died.

This morning I have Elmwood to myself, and I walk up the track bed a third of a mile before cutting through a thick stand of spruce and birch to the river.

On the first cast, the fly riding the turbulence along the far bank, I catch a ten-inch brook trout and begin to calm for the first time since I spotted the second department-store fisherman in the Run. Ready now for the big spring hole and the trout that got away, I've come to reclaim that which has been lost, to be vindicated, to recover my dignity.

Twice I have tried this pool at night, hoping to catch a brown feeding in the dark. The first time, a year ago, the whole family came, but I had not gone beforehand to cut a trail through the alder, and by the time we got from the railroad tracks—there were still tracks here a year ago—to the river, everyone except me was tired and mosquito-bitten, and when they realized they would be fishing through body-wide holes in the thicket, the others immediately lost interest. Karen and Elizabeth, unhappy with the cold, the dark, and the bugs, soon retreated to the car. Aaron and Sarah tried to fish, but their lines kept drifting into the tangle of roots and weeds along the bank. Finally, in desperation, I waded to the middle of the river and held their lines in center stream until they hooked one trout each, both brookies and both somewhat smaller than the monster I had been hoping for.

Last month I talked Aaron into trying again, only this time we cut in above the pool and crossed the stream—Aaron riding piggyback and embarrassed even this far removed from any onlookers—in order to fish from a cedar-sheltered ledge on the south bank. We had a lantern, but the lamplight only added to the intensity of the darkness. Aaron asked almost upon arrival if we couldn't go home. We got the lines in the water just as a coyote began to wail somewhere behind us. I told Aaron what a good experience it was, being here away from people, where we could listen to a coyote and fish a pool no one else had stirred up ahead of us. He said he was cold and sleepy, that he didn't like coyotes, and that he thought it was a good time to go home. We went home.

Today I work the pool carefully even though nothing breaks its surface. So it was, I remind myself, the day the big trout hit, and I move into position to cast towards the spot where that fish had appeared, a place where the current curls into the upper edge of the spring hole. The fly floats back unmolested. I repeat the cast, and the fly returns again. My left foot is cold and, I suddenly realize, wet. An icy trickle is running the length of my leg. So much for "super glue." So much for defeating planned obsolescence and Korean free enterprise. Nevertheless I cast once more, proud not to give in to the numbing cold that is filling my boot. The fly snags on a branch, and I have to ease along at the edge of the deepest water until I can release the line.

My anger at the fishermen, I realize, was directed at the conspicu-
ous costliness of their gear, the excessiveness of the new van,
because otherwise I would have to acknowledge them as other
versions of myself. Frustrated because they were where I wanted
to be and were doing what I wanted to do, I tried to divert the
issue to how they were going about it all. I tried to make it an
argument about character rather than envy. So, too, I fear is my
hostility to the ranch house and trout pond downstream. How
different is my swamp filling and cabin construction from that
effort at revisionist geography? Still, I did not presume to divert
a stream. True, I displaced stagnant water with sand and gravel,
but I did not interfere with the ongoing life of a river. The
distinction, however, seems fragile, even desperate.

By the time I climb out of the river, the water inside my
waders is up to my knee.

A u g u s t   9

The weather seems to be changing. At 5:30 as I collect my gear
and load it into the car, the sky is cloudless, and while the
temperature must already be in the sixties, the air is less heavy
than it has been.

Yesterday afternoon I went over to talk to Joe. He was sitting,
shirtless, in the screenhouse, exhausted from trimming the forest
of trees he has, over the past thirty years, planted behind his cabin.
He shapes them, cedar, spruce, pine, all the same way—like
Christmas trees—so that they will not be mistaken for the wild
timber he cleared away to make room for his own handiwork.
He labored for breath, complaining about the heat and humidity.
The temperature was only in the high seventies, but that can be
regarded as hot in the Upper Peninsula.

After fly-fishing, history is Joe's greatest love, and he was eager to tell me what he knew about the Cook brothers, whose logging company cut over the land along the Run, took out the "cork wood"—timber that would float—on a flood of water they created with a series of dams. He said there were a couple of lake-sized impoundments, including one in Cook's Meadows, the area he says I am about to enter, and he thinks the brothers had a big logging camp someplace near Basswood. But there is an uncharacteristic vagueness in his report, dam sites imprecisely located, the fate of the brothers unrecalled.

When I repeated this to the ranger at the Forestry office, he was doubtful, and even suggested that the Meadows were farther upstream, the beaver ponds below Highway 2. This was a possibility I had never heard before. When I asked Lawrence Wiegand, he said he didn't know about the Cooks but thought maybe the Meadows were a myth. Joe, however, is my reliable witness, and he says today's stretch is the place. And I remember that Millie, then the Beechwood postmistress, told me years ago that her husband, dead for thirty years, used to hitch a ride on a logging train to get to the Meadows. That would mean he must have fished the Run somewhere before it makes its swing to the south and away from the railroad tracks.

"Big holes in there," Joe warned. "Way over your head. And lots of quicksand. Watch your step." Joe is about five feet five and worries about water depth.

He reminisced, naming fishermen he knew who had favorite spots in the Meadows. All are dead. "Good men," he said, nodding sadly, then, catching himself, "Not all good," and he described some of the worst. Vi sat on the couch shaking her head. She tolerates all this fishing talk, but her look made it clear she thinks the subject childish. Joe ignored her and went on. "If I were only forty," he began.

"And a good man," Vi added.

He stopped and looked at me. "Watch your step."

He took me to the shed for contact cement and a rubber patch for the waders, then pulled four royal coachmen from a cigar

box. "There are deep holes," he said. "Fish wet. Let it sink." He
returned the cigar box to its shelf. "And fix those waders before
you drown."

*During our first years in the U.P. the Beechwood Post Office was
our only mailing address. The actual "Post Office" was only a
small room at the back of the general store—one wall composed
of boxes, the kind with glass doors and numbers on the front—
where Millie went about the Government's business. All of this
seemed somehow out of my childhood, the store/Post Office at
Neeper, Missouri, a "town" consisting of that, its most important
building, one house, an abandoned church, and the Methodist
cemetery. At night, hunting rabbits by carlight, I rode the gravel
roads with one of my uncles or my father until, tired or bored,
we somehow found our way to the Neeper store with its bubble-
topped gas pump like the one in front of Millie's, its oiled
wooden floors, glass display cases and Hadacol sign, all repeated
twenty years later in Beechwood, long after Neeper had been
abandoned.*

*Before Elizabeth's surgery we didn't have a phone, and when
my mother felt neglected she called the Post Office, and Millie,
whose own children were grown and not always the best of letter
writers, would report on how we looked the last time we'd been
in, tell what we had been wearing and repeat any conversation
that had taken place. She would describe Sarah, insisting that she
had visibly grown since our previous visit, and generally reassure
an anxious grandparent. Later, when my mother related these
exchanges, I was always amazed that so much had been said by
a woman who rarely spoke in my presence, only stood, arms
folded against her print dress, smiling benignly as I glanced
through our mail or examined the yellowing postcards that had
been for sale in the store for more than forty years.*

After Millie lost the Post Office to the gas station on U.S. 2,
she continued receiving our mail—now addressed "c/o Beech-
wood Store"—and then, the year rural delivery began bringing
our mail to a mailbox on the corner of Highway 16 and the
Basswood turnoff, Millie died. There was an estate sale and
people came to comb through old furniture and kitchenware and
to browse among stacks of once popular religious books, tracts
on prayer, spiritual healing, and celebrations of positive thinking.

The house and store also went on the market, but now, ten
years later, remain unsold.

My sister, Marilyn, and her husband, Rick, came last night.
Marilyn is awake and comes out of the cabin with Karen to take
me to the Run.

This time there are no vans, no executives in fancy outfits, and
while I pull on my waders Karen and Marilyn go look at the
stream, calling out when they see a mink darting along the
shoreline.

I start slowly, carefully, fishing along the bridge timbers and
around the first curve into what immediately, instinctively I
know are the Meadows.

Cedar waxwings, their feathers like crushed velvet in the
morning light, stir the branches of a bush high on the stream
bank, but there are few bushes and fewer trees on these margins
to the Run. Instead, on both sides, there are tall grasses and
long-stemmed flowers. The early sun gives the distant spruce a
pale greenish tint and, off in the Meadows, the alders glow
golden-hued.

The best hunting, whether in the woods or just shooting rabbits
along the roadside, was with my father's father, Grandpa Guy.
Guy—he is alive and well and living on his farm—has remark-
able vision, and with the possible exception of his second son,

who resembles him in many ways, is the best shot I've ever
known.

Grandpa, when I was a boy, was a quiet presence, rarely
speaking, and then with a strict economy of words, leaving
conversation to my grandmother, who always had something to
say. At hunting he was patient and easygoing; mostly he watched.
His favorite game was quail, largely because he enjoyed training
bird dogs, but when I was first learning to shoot he'd take me
after rabbits. Sometimes in the evening as we drove in one of the
endless procession of Chrysler products that made their way from
active service to a cowless pasture behind the house (Guy doesn't
trade cars but keeps all his old ones either for parts or sentiment
or the pleasure of watching them rust), Grandpa would slow to
a stop, then direct me to take the rifle and shoot a rabbit somewhere in the darkness ahead. I'd get out of the car and look and
look and finally announce there was no rabbit out there. Guy
would come around, take the rifle, aim, and fire, and then we'd
drive what would seem an incredible distance to pick up the dead
animal. It became a joke with us—my failure to see, his making
a distant kill—but it was a serious one. Guy had lived a subsist-
ence life too long not to regard hunting as food gathering, and
he had too high a regard for what had over the years come to
him this way to allow killing to become excessive.

Above a small island and at the head of a curve, I hook an
exposed root and walk into one of the deep holes Joe warned me
against. But this hole has been diminished from what he remembers, has filled with fresh sand so that the water doesn't even
threaten the top of my waders. Still, it would have been a likely
fishing spot if I could have gotten the fly in before my feet.

I met Joe at the lumberyard. Our first summer at the lake, living
in an old deer shack with a swamp for a backyard and—for most

of the summer—no neighbors, we decided to put up drywall on the unfinished walls and to cover the rough plank floor. It was Joe from whom we ordered the building materials.

When Karen asked about delivery, he said he guessed he could drop the stuff off some evening. And he did—but without mention of the fact that he owned land less than a hundred yards from ours.

He continued to keep his distance until, after cancer surgery three years later, he retired and began spending his days either at the lake or in a trout stream. Elizabeth had surgery that same winter, and Joe decided their fates were intertwined, that if one got well the other would get well, too.

He and I started going to the river together that year.

The pattern of Cook's Meadows quickly becomes evident. In these low-lying marshlands the Run follows a series of sharp turns like a switchback path on a mountainside, a big pool in each bend gives way to a sandbar, then another bend and another pool, and so on. And at nearly every bend, old timbers are visible, sometimes just a single beam, sometimes a pair, sometimes whole cribs. That there should be so many is bewildering.

The banks of the Meadows continue to be grassy, themselves two and three feet above water level, and the grass another three feet above that. When the wind picks up it is like walking through a prairie. The grasses, head-high around me, shift and moan, a sound like the breathing of some restless sleeper, and I think of descriptions of Kansas and Nebraska written by eighteenth- and nineteenth-century travelers, and earlier, of Coronado's frustration with grass that could conceal a man on horseback. I have not since I was a child walked through weeds that rippled above me, and today I find the sensation oddly familiar and comforting.

In the absence of cover, the sun illuminates the entire river bottom, reveals the smooth, fan-shaped bars as well as the sharply banked channel and the rounded holes that are often divided by a ridge of fernlike water grass. The sand is fine-grained and pale with a look and feel that suggest it has only recently arrived at its new resting place and waits to be moved, in time, farther downstream.

During my freshman year in college we directed a flow of water through a bed of sand in the science-building basement and watched over several days as a newborn river found its shape and formed its valley. Looking down through the clear waters of Cook's Meadows, I remember that creation process, the water's molding of the sand, the day-to-day changes in its oxbows and deltas, and twenty-four years later I recognize here the same configurations. Around me the Meadows, alive and swaying, provide sharp contrast to the basement walls containing that other stream.

And, too, I recall spring in Walden, *when the snow melt flows across the wound the railroad has made in Thoreau's wilderness, the new water carving primal forms, organic shapes in the exposed sand. On such evidence did Henry declare life unbeatable.*

I am unable to read this topography. If, as Joe has suggested, logging dams impounded water throughout the Meadows, where were they placed, and what have they to do with the recurring timbers? Joe became excited describing the old business, the spring drives when the dams would be broken and the water released in a torrent, freighting logs to the Paint and beyond, to the sawmills in Wisconsin. I thought of the rain-swollen stream I fought the first two days and imagined that multiplied a hundred times and carrying whole forests rather than an occasional limb.

But though the Meadows have the look of a new land where the diluvian age has just ended, a place recently emerged from the water and still fresh and clean like the world being shaped on the Run's sandy bottom, they hint at neither the violence of logging nor of torrents greater than those created by a spring runoff. They look, instead, peaceful, pastoral in the early morning light, a broad and lovely margin between the thick stands of second-growth timber that rise in the distance to either side.

Rural Baptist churches, churches with names like Woodville, Ballard, Liberty, Providence, churches where my grandparents and their parents worshiped and are buried, did not have the indoor plumbing that allows baptistries to be neatly concealed at the front of a sanctuary, and of necessity they did their baptizing in livestock ponds or rivers. The congregation gathered on the bank among newly sickled weeds and, with Sister Brookheart in the lead, sang in steady but subdued voices "Softly and tenderly Jesus is calling." Latecomers stepped carefully through the new-cut vegetation—"calling to you and to me"—and old Aunt Minnie (not "sister" but aunt to an entire church, an entire community, in which not one person had lived so long as to have ever seen a young version of the woman), watched with a warn-ing eye as the procrastinators found their proper places—"Come home, come home, ye who are weary come home." And, as the end of the refrain drew close, Brother Alex, who twenty years ago sang once on a radio station in Quincy, lifted his nasal tenor above the others—"Softly and tenderly Jesus is calling, calling O sinner come home."

The preacher, Uncle Ivan—my great-uncle, but Brother Cull to most of the congregation—a tall, leathery man wearing a white shirt under bib overalls and standing waist-deep in the river, spoke in a rough yet melodious baritone, beginning so softly the congregation had to strain to hear, then slowly grow-ing in volume: "Hear my prayer, and let my cry come unto thee."

Except for a sparrow singing on the opposite bank and the soft murmur of the water as it purled round Uncle Ivan's body, all was hushed. "Hide not thy face from me, for my days are like smoke, my heart is smitten and withered like grass. I am like an owl of the desert." A breeze sprang up, rippling the river and moving from the west as though in answer to Uncle Ivan's call. And then, that sun-beaten face, etched by time and disappointment but softened by self-knowledge, looked up from the water and gazed out over the small cluster of believers on the shore. "As for man, his days are like grass: as a flower of the field so he flourisheth. For the wind passeth over it and it is gone. But the mercy of the Lord is from everlasting to everlasting. Bless ye the Lord."

Then he waded into the shallows, away from the current and into the quiet inner waters of the bend, took the hand of a gangling farm boy—a Justice or perhaps a Grinsted—a boy clumsy and uncertain until, in the preacher's grasp, he grew confident, almost graceful as he followed into the deeper water. And the congregation began again, softly, little more than a whisper, "Come home, come home, ye who are weary come home," and the boy leaned backward on Uncle Ivan's arms until completely buried in the river. Then in a strong lifting motion he was brought again to the surface, returned to his feet, and Uncle Ivan, with his calloused fingers, brushed the water from the boy's eyes.

And I, who had already lived in many houses, thought I could understand something of the weariness of which the hymn spoke, was moved by the promise of home, envied the boy who had emerged from the river, and listened intently for that voice that could end all loneliness, could somehow make me whole. I heard Sister Brookheart's voice and Brother Alex's and one or two of the others. Never "the" voice. When, years later and in a church with an interior baptistry, I, too, was immersed, it was, I suppose, an expression of hope, hope that there could be a place, a refuge, even for one who had not heard the call but had listened diligently.

Of course, all those little Missouri streams merely pointed to that river central to the imagery of faith, the stream that had displaced Styx as the soul's point of entry. "When I tread the verge of Jordan, bidding anxious fears subside; death of death and hell's destruction; land me safe on Canaan's side." But Jordan is to be crossed, and the faithful delivered to a home on the other shore. I wonder what it means to be a wader, always moving the long way. I wonder what Uncle Ivan would say about that.

Clumps of flowers fleck the bank, mixed in with the tall grasses: the fancy little blossoms of lobelia rising in long spikes at the water's edge, and asters, daisylike, some with purple and others with white petals, and, sometimes under the taller plants, the delicate orange blossoms of jewelweed. The Meadows have a garden look to them, and at the next bend, when the stream cuts to the south, the sun catches the white trunks of the paper birch seventy-five yards to the west as though reflecting on the columns of a distant manor.

There are the names. So many I had not thought of in all these years, names somehow washed up by this thin current, blown in from these meadows; Grinstead, Justice, Brookheart, Alex, Aunt Minnie, Uncle Ivan. Names somehow struggling up from these stones, released from these drifts of sand. Has time undone so many?

Despite the sudden drop-offs and the softness of the sand, it is hard to understand the awe, that runs like a refrain through talk of the Meadows. Joe's fretfulness seems unjustified. It is puzzling. Stretches of the Paint, bottomed with boulders that give way to sudden drowningly deep pools, have been much more intimidating, and he has never questioned my wading there. Perhaps I have misunderstood.

Not so puzzling is why I am not catching fish. Even though I work the south bank, the one least brightly lit, even though I cast around the redundant and mysterious timbers and into the runoff inlets that enter from the north, I expect little return. The sun reveals every nook and cranny of the bottom and, I presume, exposes as much from that perspective as it does from mine. Even the fly line leaves the slightest hint of shadow as it snakes across the water. And there was a full moon last night. When I awoke at 3 A.M., the glow was coming through the skylight, revealing every object in the loft. In such light trout could feed at their leisure on the abundance washed into the stream by last week's rain. They can be choosy now and, in the absence of any hatch, are exactly that. Or I could, of course, be incompetent.

Three hundred yards into the Meadows, the wind, now blowing directly into my face, picks up, covering the noise of distant traffic with its own rustling journey through the grass. It sounds as though it has traveled a long way and carries the whisper of that distance beneath the murmur of vegetation. It also whips my line into the shore so that the fly catches the heads of wild rye as firmly as if they were alder branches, forcing me into the bank time and again to free the line by beheading stalks of grass.

Other names come unbidden, names from my earliest memory, and that seem so alien in the world I have grown into: Emmett Craig, Roscoe Colvin, Justin Moncrief, Pleasant St. Clair, Otho Webber. And later names, these accompanied by faces less blurred by time; Steve with whom I spent so many high school Friday nights, usually in the back of a bowling alley, playing euchre and pretending that we did not want to be with our more popular classmates, exulting in our superiority and keeping a careful lookout for girls; Phil with the owlish eyes who always looked, behind his round glasses and Harvard ways, as though he had just been awakened but would not allow that rudeness to spoil his good manners; Andy who could endure the worst insults in the name of passive resistance and then play four-square or touch football unforgivingly, and now frozen in my memory as he stands on a balcony and points toward a distant assassin; Tahti speaking softly in the darkness about some personal betrayal, and then, virtually without transition, her lean body swaying, about the excitment of our time and the painful pleasure of being alive in 1961; Bill, skinny, freckled, and crewcut—the look of a Mormon missionary—gyrating through some uninhibited California dance to the amazement and consternation of native diners in a New Delhi restaurant, a place where we had gathered for a makeshift Thanksgiving celebration; the girl who, one rainy day while on break from her clerical job, led me to her favorite paintings in the Chicago Art Institute, explaining without pretension or embarrassment how much they meant to her at a time when I feared all sentiment and most emotion—her name, I think, was Rosemary; another Bill—this one older, but still young in those days before his cancer found him, more intense than the other—a lawyer who, his small frame magnified to prophetic dimensions by righteous indignation, had addressed an audience of more than a thousand church and civic leaders, chastising them for their hypocrisy, their failure to serve justice, and then, that evening in casual conversation, had backed into a closet, its sliding doors pulled on either side nearly to his nose, and had spoken through that crack to his cocktail-drinking friends; Will in his semi-Amish clothes painfully plucking a guitar and singing, badly, every song Jim Reeves had written and, when he finished at 3 A.M., repeating the entire performance; Jitsuo, head thrust forward as though its weight were pulling his small body toward the speaker, listening intently to the naive anguish of an eighteen-year-old boy, listening as though the words, blurted out so clumsily, had not been heard countless times before.

Once started the names keep flowing, a surge of nostalgia that can only be stopped by intense effort, the current so strong it is nearly overwhelming.

I give up people reluctantly, feel their absence long after they have gone, and have become, as I grow older, hesitant to take on cause for further grieving. I think sometimes that I have known and relinquished enough, that I prefer to be left alone, to cut my losses.

The sun is directly behind me when I wade the short straightaways between bends and it casts my shadow far ahead, projecting a larger man on the narrow waters before me. I slow down, work more deliberately, trying to reduce the rippling circles sent out with every step. I feast on Fig Newtons picked up from the table on my way out of the house.

The sharp turns continue, and, as the lazy crow flies, I am covering very little distance. As though to prove how tortuous is this path, the Run bends sharply to the left, and I am momentarily doubled back, headed due east into a blinding sun. But the stream curves again, abruptly and to the right, turning me once more to the southwest.

More old timbers, this time jutting out from both banks.

The pool here has been almost completely filled with sand, and in the shallow water hundreds of trout minnows hang in the current, head upstream, bodies wriggling to keep the most aerodynamically—or hydrodynamically—efficient position. They break sharply as I pass, slivers of life rushing to both sides three feet ahead of me, then rejoining ranks a yard behind. The wind calms and a "chic, chic, chicaree" song comes from an alder bush a few yards from the bank. I see a movement among the branches but not the singer.

My own name, now cut to two-thirds of its original length, somehow placed me midway between the Emmetts and Justins of my father's and grandfather's generations and the names of my contemporaries. In classrooms filled with Bobs and Terrys, I was always the only Wayne. Most of the time I liked that arrangement, even liked my name though it sometimes sounded odd to the other kids, and mostly I resisted the substitutes I was regularly offered. I always preferred it to Otho or even Pleasant.

In recent years it tends to appear most often in print as the name of escaped convicts fleeing Indiana or of Idaho serial murderers. A perennial favorite on death row, the name remains agreeable to me despite the company it keeps, and has, I suspect, done more to define me than I it. Wayne Fields is a distinctive name though not a distinguished one—the name not of a President but of a secretary of agriculture, perhaps.

It is 7:30 now, and the height of the banks has lessened; the stream has widened and shallowed to knee-deep. Alders are advancing on the right toward the water's edge, and behind them clumps of willow appear. The delicate water grass that grows on the stream bottom forms troughs of curved green over the channels where the main current flows, and from one of these, near the right bank, a foot-long trout emerges, makes three quick circles around my legs, then slides back under the weeds. As I watch the green furrows, other, lesser trout dart out and back to note my passing.

My father's mother called her first three sons by their middle names. Thus my father, William Wayne, was called Wayne, forcing on me a double name, Wayne Dale, to make clear which Wayne I was. But the two boys who were drafted were retitled by a government firmly committed to the principle of first name/middle initial, regardless of a mother's intentions. So James Richard became Jim and my father ceased to be Wayne and became Bill. Except in Grandma's house. She did not yield regardless of the opposition. The last time I saw her alive, she did not recognize me but spoke of me to this stranger I had become, all the while referring to me by a name no one else has used for more than thirty years.

My mother was renamed by the state of Missouri, a misprint unchallenged by a family more respectful of authority than my grandmother, converting her name from Dorothy to Dortha.

Karen and I took our children's names very seriously, drew for each of them on biblical precedent. And they have fit each in its own way, each child appropriate to his or her name, each name remade by its new bearer.

River debris has heaped up against another old timber and from its tattered shelter twenty or thirty six-inch trout come darting downstream toward me, dark arrows that shoot forward in a wide barrage, then, glittering, catch the light with their speckled sides. Only at the last do they swerve around my legs, then flash through a dark grid that shimmers deep in the water as the light catches and is held by the ripples on the surface. This cross-hatching moves like an electrical field along the streambed and turns the trout from brown to gold as they flash through bands of sunshine and on into darkness again.

Crows call in the distance, waxwings flutter in the bushes along the shore. Ahead, hundreds of fingerling fish blanket the sand.

Even as I take in this place, delight in its patterns and colors, I despair of ever being able to recompose it, think anxiously of this evening's frustration when words will fail me once more. I am not so arrogant that I write to tell some great truth, that I think the world has much to gain from my undersized hands; I write in the hope of crafting a page, a paragraph, even a line that is filled with the grace I lack, that sings with a voice beyond mine. I write in the hope of forgiveness, in the hope of making something better than myself. Tonight, as on other nights, the old tangle will prevail. What I have seen can never make it from my mind to the page with the lyric power of this landscape, rather it will be defeated by the disjoining disease that is our human inheritance. Inevitably I will only compound the very debt I try so desperately to repay.

Sparrows sing in the bushes, and the switchback path of the Run continues uninterrupted, sometimes swinging nearly due east in the enthusiasm of its turning, then breaking back toward the southwest and its headwaters, and always with the recurrent timbers, reminders of an old but indecipherable intention. The spruce to the northwest have drawn closer and are now only a hundred yards distant.

I've been so absorbed in the Meadows and in watching the streambed that I've paid little attention to fishing. The movement of rod and line merely provides the meter for my morning, a rhythm for my wade, and, too, it helps me keep my balance, since I find it more difficult to walk upstream empty-handed than to use the leaning movements of casting to stabilize my body. The fly rod is the wader's equivalent of the high-wire artist's pole, a steadying aid against the temptation downward. Balance is equally difficult to maintain on the straight notebook lines on which I compose, and there I work with neither pole nor net.

Though I've caught nothing in these fabled fishing waters, I am content with the place itself. My great hunting expedition has turned into a pleasant walk in the country, a satisfying descent into tourism despite an occasional nudge from my conscience as it insists that this expenditure of time and effort should produce more tangible results.

I remember, as a child, walking to school during one of the springs when my family stayed with my grandparents on the farm. I crossed a half mile of pasture before reaching the main road, and though it was in unbroken snow a rough crossing, in spring it was a constant delight, was in fact very much like this walk has been. I think for a moment of taking my children to that place, then remember that the land has a different owner now, and that the pasture has been reshaped and cultivated in the years since I walked it.

It is now eight o'clock, and I eat the last two Fig Newtons at the site where yesterday's fisherman must have stopped for lunch. Piously I retrieve the fancy French yogurt container he has left behind and drop it into my no longer empty creel.

Deep holes continue to appear at every turn, each with its alloted timbers, and I fish them deliberately, if ineffectually. An osprey, more competent than I, flies overhead with something in its talons.

Between curves I find a dead seventeen-inch brown trout lying side up on the bottom, and judging both by its color and its location, death has been recent. I've never come upon a dead trout of any size before and have not encountered a trout this large, living or dead, in more than two years. I lift him from the water and find on his underside two punctures an inch apart. The deep gouges look like the work of talons, perhaps the osprey. Blood still oozes from the wounds, and I return the fish to the water, saddened, not because he is dead, but because I did not have the opportunity to catch and, inevitably, kill him myself.

This last thought bothers me. I do not like killing, dislike fishing for lake fish—perch and bass and pike—because they are still alive when it is time to clean them, still resisting the inevitable until I crack them across their heads with the filleting knife.

There was a time, when I was about Elizabeth's age, when killing pleased me, when I shot the sparrows that flocked to my grandfather's barn, shot bullfrogs, rabbits, and squirrels, and longed for larger game. Some of this could be called hunting—we ate the frog legs, the rabbits, the squirrels—but much of it was merely indulging the power that enabled a boy to make something dead. That is the only explanation for the inebriating binges when I would shoot dozens of roosting sparrows at night among the hayloft rafters, or when the prey was even smaller, bumblebees picked off as they worked the hollyhocks around the farmhouse. I stopped not because of the windows that had to be replaced when neither insect nor blossom broke the flight of BBs, and not because of the chilling scream a dying rabbit can muster, but because one morning I fired my uncle's rifle into a squirrel's nest, hoping to stir up some kind of life, and a bird, a robin, fell to the ground, dead not from the bullet but from a single twig driven through its body. The fact of one dead robin didn't stop me so much as the realization that the death was not directly my doing, was not, after all, a thing in my control.

Trout die silently, unobtrusively and out of sight, their colors dulling in the darkness of the creel.

With incontrovertible evidence that big trout are in these waters, I try to take the work of catching them more seriously.

A small green caterpillar hangs from a thread nearly into the water below the bank. The thread gives way, and the caterpillar floats downstream—one more for the Reverend Mr. Edwards—

and, at the next bend, out of sight. As was the case with the bee, nothing rises to take him. I tie on a small yellow-and-brown fly, but without much hope, and continue on. A sparrow suddenly darts from an alder and drops a little white blob in the water. Instantly a small trout leaps and lunges for it. How can I imitate that?

Fish, some large enough to keep, glide along the channels in the water grass, but they seem like occupants of an ornamental pond rather than wild trout. Nonetheless at the head of this pool one jumps from a line of unimposing riffles—the first such disturbance of the day—and takes the fly. I release him even though he is of legal size, a token of appreciation, an act of generosity. And, too, he is not that large, no more than eight inches.

Sarah loved the Laura Ingalls Wilder books, as did her mother. They read them separately and together again and again until both knew the entire series virtually by heart. Whenever Karen would be reading aloud and would come to a sad part—as when Jack the dog dies in On the Banks of Plum Creek—*Sarah, aware of how easily her mother could be moved to tears and already at six or seven alert to the approaching grief, would call for the book and, while her mother wept, read in her steady and unflinching child's voice of loss and separation and death.*

The Meadows begin to narrow before an advancing line of spruce, the trees soon separated from the stream by only fifteen feet of alder and backed in turn by tamarack and birch. In breaks among the alders black-eyed Susans and coneflowers appear once more, together with thistles and lobelias. At the next dark tumble of timbers, these slumped in decay, fritillaries and an occasional sulpher flit over joe-pye weed.

The high whine of two phantom jets, a training flight out of Marquette, passes overhead as the last evidence of the Meadows slides away.

The Run flows between alders and trees now, the branches of dead elms clawing the sky at nearly every bend. I check my watch. The crystal has fogged, it is losing twenty minutes a day, and yesterday the winding stem broke so that I cannot adjust it. But if I add today's twenty-minute error, the time must be about 9:15.

With shallower water has come a faster current. There is, as well, a return to heavy alder growth on both banks. When the branches from opposite sides nearly touch midway over the stream, I try to split them with my cast and, amazingly, manage to do so, threading the yard-wide gap perfectly both on the backcast and the forward carry, but as the line descends it stops in mid-flight, the fly suspended four feet above the water. Incredibly it just hangs there, leader invisible in the light, as though it has become a real insect hovering in the morning air. I wait for it to fall, but the suspension continues, and I approach slowly, reverently. The leader has caught on a spider thread, a single line crossing between alders, a cunning trap to snare unsuspecting fishermen. Perhaps an army of spiders waits on the bank to bundle me up in their webbing and cart me to the banquet hall. Then again, they may be looking for something, if not larger, at least more appetizing. I tug on the line, breaking the thread, and the fly drifts back to the stream.

The first dock I built was mounted by U-bolts to six-foot lengths of pipe that every summer had to be driven into the sand. It was a stupid design that I clung to for years, long after I recognized the absurdity of all the labor involved. When everything was in place, the lengths of pipe rose above the dock floor, a sort of metal honor guard standing attentively at eight-foot intervals, and every dawn a crisscross of spiderwebbing stretched the three feet between the upright pipe. The first person each morning who went to wash up had to break through these gossamer lines.

Penelope, as she awaits Odysseus's return and keeps the suitors at bay, weaves a shroud for her father-in-law, and because she must choose a new husband when the work is done, she picks the threads apart by night, delaying the inevitable. So with the dock put together in June, only to be dismantled in August, or the cabin built to be torn down half a lifetime later, always with the material saved for other, future constructions. So too with the words that I write, then rearrange, then change again. This is nighttime labor as well, work done quietly and against the dark that can only be delayed—but delayed nonetheless.

The trees fall back from the Run and both banks grow thick with alder. A musty smell, the heavy, dank aroma of swamp and decay, sharp contrast to the smell of meadow flowers that has drifted over much of the morning, hangs in the alder branches and rises up from the silt in the shadowed margins. It comes and goes like the memory of my grandparents' basement, a memory at once pleasant and wearying. It is the smell of resignation, I think, and then wish the thought could be undone.

I snag an overhanging alder, and, rather than trying to tug the line free, I reverse the rod, hold it three-quarters of the way along its length and hook the offending limb with the reel, then, using its weight, bend the branch toward me. I do this often among the pliable alder branches—when I am sure no witness is around—in order to save flies. This time the reel, somehow loosened, drops off the swaying rod and falls into the water, draping the line over the branch in the course of its descent. Line and leader, together with the snagged fly, are now entangled in alder. When I pull the whole mess to me, retrieving the line as though I have taken to fishing above the Run, I break off limbs and leaves until I have freed everything. Behind me the stream is littered with green debris. It is now ten o'clock.

The Run has entered a series of broad curves with a high bank on the right that carries mature trees—first a stand of apparently undiseased elms, then hemlock, followed by cedar. A cave-in has tumbled ferns down to the water's edge, leaving a deep, reddish scar beneath the trees, and just where the current swirls past the slumped bank, a fat brookie attacks the fly, hitting hard and running upstream until I retrieve him. The day's first keeper.

I enter another stand of cedar, stepping into the cool air and rich smell of their shadow, and it is as though I have passed from one room into another. Branches covered with small, pale green cones bend heavily over the current.

The reverberating noise of a car crossing the bridge cuts through the subdued chatter of the Run, and then, on the left, I can see a clearing, and in it an Upper Peninsula special—a forty-foot aqua-and-silver trailer house complete with woodpile. The owner has cleared his land to the water's edge, making it seem naked as it had never been in the Meadows.

Forest Highway 16 is carried over Cook's Run by a narrow concrete bridge with solid, waist-high sides, a bridge scheduled for demolition as soon as federal funds are allocated. It carries a metal plaque, raised lettering badly worn, that reads "Trunk Line Bridge 1915 Built by State Highway Dep't. Frank F. Rogers Com'r. Connihan & Barnum Contractors, Iron River, Mich."

It is eleven o'clock, and the car is parked above the bridge. The patch on my waders has begun to curl around the edges.

A u g u s t   1 0

The heat has broken, at least momentarily, and the sky is clear. But there is something unsteady about it all as though no firm commitment has yet been made. The weather can still go either way.

Last night I took Marilyn and Rick, together with Aaron and Sarah, to the big DNR pool where, two days ago, I worked my way through the muck by the far bank. We carried in wood for a fire, together with our fishing gear and a thermos of coffee. After the lines had been baited and a fire was burning, I slipped away to try for another look at the Meadows, moving back along the trails behind Wiegand's farm, picking out the paths I had trampled over the past days. The full moon cast an eerie light over the tall grass. Nothing moved, and the ribbon of water, gleaming under the light, threw back the moon's reflection and remained, itself, impenetrable, even threatening. The far bank loomed up in silhouette, the holes before it deepened by its shadow.

I knew that the heavy runoff of last spring and the more recent rains had, at least temporarily, overwhelmed with sand the Meadows of Joe's memory, but I recognized his Run before me, a different terrain from the one I walked yesterday by sunlight. The high banks and grasses, the spectral alders, the vacancy, gave a haunting power to a place at once familiar and unrecognizable. I struggled through weeds to a low hill and from its height could see the glistening stream as it wound through the first of its endless curves and knew that ahead, in the dark, it swirled past ancient timbers that repeat themselves with every turn. To be in the Meadows, I suspect, is to be both someplace in particular and no place at all. There are no discrete plots of land here; I was never in any "meadow" in the singular but always in the "meadows" plural, never anywhere more precise than that.

For a moment in all of this I glimpsed one aspect of my identification with this slight stream, a recognition more clearly illuminated last night than now, but one having to do with the fact of multiplicity and the simultaneous aspiration for singularity, wholeness; something to do with several selves yearning for reconciliation.

Flying from Washington to St. Louis one November night, I grew bored with the novel I was reading and turned to the window. The sky was clear, a half-moon gleaming above the plane's wing. Nothing below was recognizable, but I watched the ground, waiting for some familiar city to show itself against the dark. Suddenly an explosion of light blossomed, mushrooming like a Fourth of July rocket. Another burst, and I grew fearful, convinced I was witness to some terrible chain of catastrophes. Then more light, this a careening line, a brightly lit roller coaster, a mountain train out of control, appearing, then disappearing, without any discernible rhyme or reason. I continued watching, bewildered, as the eruptions kept pace with the plane over hundreds of miles, intermittent bursts and sudden swirls, breathtaking in their implication but still inexplicable. I considered asking the stewardess if the pilot had an explanation. Instead, I kept silence and maintained my post, forehead to the Plexiglass, watching the awesome display below.

When, eventually, the plane paralleled the course of the Ohio River, I realized at last what I had been witnessing. The light spread on that broad current like a luminous curtain, unhurried now, moonshine expanded by the water and moving with the angle of our flight. The squiggles, ribbons, racing off in sudden escape, were smaller streams, illuminated as they twisted through bends and oxbows until they disappeared beneath branches and foliage. Along the Ohio, tributary after tributary picked up the performance as the moon mapped each new waterway in a quick, deft stroke before moving on to the next creek or pool. On the river, between turns, barge lights reached in long, straight beams, unwavering for miles, while on either side the light was alive, leaping up, twisting away, slowed only on the broad, pale curtain flowing along the great stream's breadth.

When I returned to the big pool, I could see, from the clearing's edge, Marilyn tending the fire, and as she bent over the flames I realized how much she resembles her mother. At the edge of the dark, Sarah was baiting a hook and, looking up, she called to me in Karen's voice. Rick stood silhouetted on the bank, casting toward the weed bed across the pool, and Aaron, hunkered over his fishing rod, collar up and wearing the earphones to Marilyn's radio under the pulled-down earflaps of his cap, swayed to music only he could hear. He had caught a big muddler, nearly all ugly head, and was using it as bait. Before the night was over he caught three more, but no trout.

The triple-forked pine stood darkly, holding the moon in its upper branches, first on the shore and again in the water. People talked. Aaron, deafened by the radio, yelled whenever he spoke, then looked bewildered when we laughed. We drank coffee and watched the darkness of the pool from the high bank.

Sarah caught an eight-inch brown, and I caught an eleven-inch brookie. Except for Aaron's muddlers, that was our entire catch, though something large hit Rick's line, doubling the rod before escaping into the night.

At the bottom of the stair the dog has left a pile just in front of the last step. I am not so much angry—my predictable response—as depressed. Am I really ready for a puppy? This last year, before Smeagol died, whenever I was the first one up I checked to make sure he had survived the night, relaxing only when he awakened to a nudge from my foot. Now I must watch my step for the messes left by a puppy that cannot get by till morning.

I clean the floor and push the dog outside in the vain hope that she will see some connection between the two activities.

Karen drives me to the bridge on Highway 16. She got up to let the dog out at 3 A.M. and is not overwhelmed with sympathy for my complaints. "She's a puppy," she says. "What do you expect?"

"Smeagol never did this," I insist.

"It was thirteen years ago. You've forgotten." I'm sure I have not, but she has that look of absolute Scandinavian certainty, a look I have seen on her mother's face and on the faces of her aunts. I swallow the rest of my protest.

"Did you eat anything?" she asks. Whenever I am upset she assumes I am hungry.

"No," I answer. "I cleaned up dogshit instead."

"Builds character," she says under her breath, then adds, smiling a not completely convincing smile, "When do you want me to pick you up?"

"Rick said he will come get me. I'll meet him around nine at the hatchery."

"Are you sure he knows the way?"

"I showed him on the map."

"He's never been there."

I laugh. "Neither have you. Neither have I," I add sardonically. The hatchery is less than five miles from the cabin, yet in sixteen years we have never gone there. "Hell, maybe we'll all get lost." Karen is swerving the car to avoid the hummocks where old tree stumps are working their way through the blacktop. She looks like a slalom skier, crouched forward over the wheel and swinging her weight with each sudden turn.

"Why are you in such a foul mood?" she asks.

"I'm not," I object, but I realize that I am and that I don't know why. "Just tired, I guess."

Karen is silent for a moment, then, "You need to spend some time with Elizabeth," she says. She says it softly, trying to prevent my taking offense, her eyes still fixed on the road ahead, watching for the next obstacle.

I start to bridle at the remark but check myself. "I tried to get her to go last night, but she wanted to stay home with you." There is an edge of accusation in my voice.

"I know," she says, "but it is rough being in the middle." She pulls the car to the side of the road. "Be careful." She seems worried, though I have no idea why.

"No danger in this stretch," I tell her, "except the risk of getting trampled by tourists."

The parking area beside the bridge is surrounded by yellow coneflowers, their long, full petals curled back slightly, the dark cone at the center thrust outward, a badminton shuttlecock turned to blossom. A squirrel chatters at me as I straighten my creel strap beneath its tree. It, like the other squirrels here, is smaller than the ones I've known elsewhere, smaller and a brighter red, and much chattier. City squirrels are, for the most part, a silent presence, something seen running along a telephone line or lying dead in the street, but these squirrels in the middle of the woods or in the trees beside our cabin scold tirelessly, sometimes nattering away from perches barely head-high.

My first time north I thought these were flying squirrels, but, though fast on the ground and agile climbers, they do not take flight, cannot soar from tree to tree. That miracle I have never seen, but on more than a few occasions I've heard at night—or so I thought—a faint, high chatter, a rustle of leaves, and then a kind of sighing sound as something above me rode the air without benefit of feathers or wings.

I enter above the bridge at a point where the Run cuts under a white pine, the stream carpeted by the delicate water grass and littered with the small white five-pointed blossoms that look like stars against a green sky.

Though I have crossed this bridge hundreds of times, I have never fished these waters, in part because here, where it completes a triangle with the Forest Highway and U.S. 2, Cook's Run yields its mystery as well as its solitude. Here it is just a stream that flows under the highway, an occasion for a bridge over which everyone passes. Here it brushes public campgrounds and serves those with newly purchased spinning outfits and one-day fishing permits, people who want to fish but not to get away. The trailer camp on Golden Lake sends its clients—those who arrive early in the afternoon—to the bridge, where they dangle salmon eggs or pieces of corn in the current. They turn in the narrowness of that span toward every passing car, smiling their confidence in these shallow, overfished waters. I wonder what it is the trailer camp operator tells them and why he isn't governor of the state.

Or perhaps this is all snobbish nonsense. Perhaps I am afraid I cannot catch fish that have grown wary from experience. In any event, unlike the Meadows, this is not a part of the Run which I am anxious to wade. Still, the cedars that reach out horizontally over the water before turning upward to the light encourage me. I cannot fish beneath them, but I enjoy wading under cedars, and this morning find them calming as I bend to pass under their curved trunks, reassuring in their toughness and grace. Somewhere at the edge of my mind is a memory of other cedars, but I cannot bring it into focus. I reach back for it, then let it go.

The cedars give way to a power line that crosses the stream, its poles, like the measuring lines on a ruler, marking the distance to Golden Lake in one direction and to the highway in the other. A logging truck thunders over the bridge on 16, and I can hear a car on 2.

Electricity was so recent a rural convenience that in my childhood it was still not taken for granted. Rows of glass battery jars, remnants of my grandfather's efforts to be illuminated without federal assistance, lined one basement wall, and the poles along Missouri gravel roads had a new look.

One pole in particular I always noted in passing, usually on the way to the Woodville Baptist church and the burial ground where half my grandparents now reside, a pole I regarded with reverence. Recognizable by a black creosote mark in the shape of a four-fingered hand that pointed downward just below the wires, it was, someone told me, where Joe Columbus had been electrocuted while working on the lines. I had never known Joe Columbus or any of his family, but I admired the name and imagined that black stain the scorched print of his dying hand.

*We attended few services at Woodville, those mostly funerals,
and I remember little of what I ever heard there, but at every
passing I was moved by the sight of Joe Columbus's cross.*

I snag the fly in an alder, adding to a barely submerged anger
at work in me; my irritation at the sounds of traffic, the sight of
power lines, and whatever it is that Karen noted, threatens the
morning. To calm myself, I attempt a taxonomy of snags while
undoing the one before me, my version of the kids' "questions."

1) There are snags on grass, the kind I repeated countless times
in the Meadows, where the slender stem of a weed crowned by
a small cattail of seeds holds captive a line which is supposed to
catch twenty-inch brown trout. Such a snag usually occurs on the
backcast and announces itself when you snap the rod forward,
pointing to the place you want the fly to drop; but the line you
expected to obey that command falls limply to one side, reaching
behind you rather than ahead. The same effect can be created by
a bush or tree, but such occasions are less humiliating than the
weed snag which forces you, exasperated, to walk backward and
break off the seed cone or, something more irritating, the daisy
blossom that holds you in thrall.

2) The forward snag, the kind that comes from trying to cast
too close to the bank in front of you, is more tolerable, because
you see it happen, and because it represents an overreaching, and
because, sometimes, if the leader wraps cleanly around the branch,
the entire process can be reversed with a careful tug that sets the
fly spinning in the opposite direction. If the line and the snag do
not cooperate, if the leader ties itself in a knot on the first
go-round or slices into a leaf or catches on a little alder cone,
nothing will do but that you wade forward to free the line,
sloshing your way through the very hole you were trying so
deliberately to fish.

3) The most common snag, in streams like Cook's Run, comes
overhead, when you've forgotten how the curve just behind you

has positioned the grasping limbs, or when you've tried to split the narrow space between canopying branches, or when the wind takes your line. Or when you just screw up. Whatever the cause, the overhead snag is often the harder dilemma to resolve. You can try tugging the fly free, nearly always unsuccessfully, or, if it is a limber alder, find some way to bend the branch to you without overstraining the line.

4) The easiest snag to recover from physically, however, is the hardest to deal with psychologically. It is the one in which *you* are the thing snagged: your hat or jacket, or, in really extreme instances, your ear. Here you hunt, tracing the leader with your fingers, until you just manage to reach the hook in the back of your jacket or to knock the victimized hat askew with your efforts.

The smooth routine of casting, the taut line snapping back and then forward until it unrolls the fly across the water's surface, once interrupted, becomes a clumsy mockery, the line falling dumbly—as though stricken in mid-flight with some enervating disease—onto the fisherman, who points the rod impatiently ahead while his enterprise falls in tangles around him.

There are marked similarities between fly-fishing and writing; both enterprises represent efforts at some elaborate choreography in which energy, carefully controlled, and tensions, elaborately maintained, sustain a harmony that is itself as much the object as is catching a fish or relaying a message. Both lines are troublesome awkward contrivances that can as easily entangle their composer as reach out to his longed-for audience. Both are metaphors and, like all metaphors, are never completely under anyone's control but have lives of their own and act in ways we did not anticipate, lead to ends we did not choose as destinations.

When I first began thinking about such things—even before I realized they were things about which I was thinking—I as-

sumed fishing and writing to be metaphors for life. As I grow older, I've come to suspect that I have got it backwards, and that life, at its best, is a metaphor for fishing and writing. Or perhaps neither side of any metaphor is finally dominant, the one inextricably tied to its contrasting likeness, no longer merely a point of comparison but yoked in a new existence to its other self.

This snag is behind me on a reachable alder branch.

I enter an S curve where, despite the DNR's wing dams, the water shallows back to ankle-depth. The brush thickens here and then opens slightly. A low cedar has caught debris against its horizontal trunk, backing up water thigh-deep, and beyond this living tree a dead companion has become a peninsula carrying on its back a hump of dirt and weeds, even a wild rose, as it juts into the stream. A spring trickles thinly beside this finger of vegetation. I wade around both obstacles with as little commotion as possible, then cast back three times. Each time the Adams settles next to the branches, but to no effect. These are good casts, I think, but they go unrewarded.

I suddenly recall the elusive memory of cedar I stirred up a little while ago. It is of a single tree, not an impressive white cedar like these along the Run, but a scrawny Missouri red cedar, a volunteer that my grandfather let grow in the front yard and that I crawled under as a child. It stood in a fence corner only a few yards from the gravel road that ran by the farm, and on hot days I would crouch beneath it, waiting for a breeze to stir the cedar smell and watching through the wire mesh for something to come into view.

Somehow I do not expect to catch trout, even though the weather and the cloud cover seem right—or close to right. The waters through here are not, in fact, promising, but there is something else: a vague feeling that I should be elsewhere fishing big holes on the Paint or at my desk writing the book my colleagues expect me to produce. A sense of futility prevails. Even though I didn't catch fish yesterday, I found the stream a sufficient pleasure, but today in the shadows of alder, I am listless, unexpectant, distracted by old business that refuses to recognize its time and place.

Ten days into Elizabeth's coma the neurologist told me that she would never awaken, told me that too much time had passed without any sign of improvement and that I would have to break the news to Karen, who had begun to imagine evidence of consciousness. It was nearly midnight when he told me, the two of us standing in the half-dark of the pediatric intensive care unit and me holding a rigid and unresponsive daughter. Through the windows across the room I could see oaks beside the streetlights, their leaves still in place but dead and brittle in the December night.

When Karen came at 1:00 A.M. for her shift, I said nothing, only handed over the child like an exhausted runner yielding the baton in some never-ending relay, said nothing because I was tired and knew that Karen, unbelieving, would be angry, and because for us to say it would be somehow to make it true.

Sarah, three then, asked at breakfast if Elizabeth could play yet, asked if she had called for her older sister, asked if she wanted any toys. One of Sarah's toys was a jack-in-the-box that never failed, in the days before surgery, to frighten Elizabeth, and since the neurologist was constantly clapping his hands close to the child's head, trying to provoke some reaction, I took the toy along that morning in the hope that it had not lost its startling power and could, at long last, rouse the sleeping infant.

Standing in front of Karen, who held our child propped like

*a board in her lap, I cranked the handle in one last desperate effort
before accepting the inevitable. The box clanked out a frantic
version of "Pop Goes the Weasel" until, at the climactic moment,
the clown leaped up, startling even me, and Elizabeth began to
shake, shook until Karen, who could not see her daughter's face,
believed she was convulsing as she had in the days after surgery.
Then Karen, too, recognized the laughter, a deep body-shaking
laughter of a child no longer afraid of clowns on springs, a child
still rigid but alive, awake.*

The sun breaks through and plays on wet bark, drawing out
patterns of moisture like the lines in a woodcut or an engraving.
As though in response to the change in light, birds begin to sing,
but their songs are repeatedly overwhelmed by the noise of traffic
as I get closer to the highway, and the clouds return. The air is
still, undisturbed even by insects. It is, as I realized when I first
got up, as though something is about to happen but has not yet
begun. Two crows land in a dead elm and caw at me harshly,
their ragged feathers sticking up here and there in unruly tufts.

I fish more deliberately, try to establish a rhythm, a tempo that
will lend some harmony to my actions and my emotions. But the
throttle keeps slipping forward and my efforts at deliberation
prove fruitless; I rush the pace, moving ahead almost as soon as
I start my backcast, and my individual movements seem at odds
with one another. The line creaks in complaint above me.

*In 1977 we endured five cases of strep throat in the house. The
last case was mine. Shortly after my recovery the two girls went
into the hospital for tonsillectomies, but on the appointed morning the doctors became troubled by an abnormality in Elizabeth's
blood chemistry, some missing ingredient necessary for proper
clotting. Sarah went into surgery alone and Elizabeth was sent
home until more blood studies could be done.*

When at last Elizabeth was rescheduled, I stayed in her hospital room as Karen had with Sarah. We watched television for a while, and then I must have fallen asleep in the chair beside her bed. When I awoke and checked on my seven-year-old daughter, her eyes were wide open—not just open but truly wide—and her mouth stretched, severely stretched, in a rigid smile. She stared at the ceiling, unaware that I had awakened, the unflinching smile tight across her face.

"Are you all right?" I asked.

She nodded yes, eyes still locked on the ceiling, smile unlessened.

The look troubled me. I had never before seen such an expression on a child's face. I waited, but she did not speak.

"Can't you sleep?" I asked, and she shook her head stiffly. "No."

"Are you frightened?" I finally whispered.

"Yes." She nodded. I moved over beside her and took her hand, and we kept vigil, unsleeping, me watching Elizabeth and replaying all the awful hospital nights we had shared, and Elizabeth watching the ceiling, her strange smile unyielding.

I ease past a brush pile and cast back to the pool it shelters. The nooks and crannies within the debris are filled with the flowering grasses, their fragile stems reaching two or three inches above the surface. I hook a stalk and pull back a small bouquet.

The clouds have passed and light careens off the water, but muted, unglaring, more like a painting of light than actual light. Wider now, the Run is bordered by grassy margins and stands of spruce and cedar. In the shallows the flowering water grass forms little islands, and the banks, accepting this challenge, show back purple asters and joe-pye weed. Ahead, beyond a clearing for power lines, I can see the bridge and Highway 2. It is 7:15 or perhaps 7:35, depending on whether my watch is now off forty minutes or an hour. Its failings have lost any discernible pattern.

They operated on a little boy, a mongoloid baby named Mark, while Elizabeth was in intensive care, and though the long-range prognosis was not hopeful, the surgeon was exhilarated at having done so much with such a malformed heart. One afternoon just before Christmas, when the sun had already dropped behind the trees across the street, I held my daughter, had been holding her for better than an hour, staring out over the monitors and leads, out over Elizabeth's bed and Mark's, past where Mark's grandfather sagged against a metal chair as he kept vigil beside the unmoving child.

I do not know how long I had been looking at Mark's monitor, uncomprehending, watching the flattened lines of a departing life. When at last I realized just what I had witnessed, roused myself as though I were the sleeper, I cried out. A nurse rushed the disoriented old man from the room, sent the coded emergency call—Dr. Cart—over the PA system. Help came almost at once, banging through the swinging doors like the heroes in a western, pushing a shiny steel machine that brought to the child all the power the hospital could provide. The doctors administered injections, thumped the baby's chest, did all they knew to do, did it efficiently, quickly, and futilely.

In the hall, his voice penetrating the closed doors and swelling over the noise in the room, the grandfather asked repeatedly and with growing anxiety what was happening. I sat, holding my own child, and wondered how long I had kept my silence. When the doctors discovered that the heart had not failed, that Mark had choked to death on his own vomit, I wondered, too, at the guilt, unseeing, I had accumulated.

A monarch flutters down in front of me, its wings slightly tattered and its movements labored. "Juliet," I think, surprised by the strange swiftness with which the name comes to mind.

Two summers ago, before our cat died—a cat that Elizabeth always knew favored her older sister, and at a time when she was frustrated by her own lack of friends—Elizabeth found a monarch on one of the big blocks of milky quartz that sit below our patch of flowers and blueberries. It seemed unable to fly, would only move its wings slowly from full span to closure with a movement that consumed whole minutes. She named it Juliet and for three days carried it on her right hand, lifted before her by a palm curled in toward her chest, index finger straightened for a perch. The butterfly, its wings untorn but worn so thin in spots as to lack any color, would stay in place, occasionally rustling its antennae ever so slightly or unfurling its wings with almost unbearable slowness as Elizabeth introduced it to all her favorite places and told it the story of her life. At night she placed the monarch on a pillow beside her bunk, where it remained until she awoke the following morning.

On the fourth day it died. We buried Juliet, and for the next several days Elizabeth grieved. From its first appearance in the yard we knew—Elizabeth included—that the butterfly was nearly gone, and we treated it as a curiosity, like the mottled salamanders that we find under rocks or chunks of wood and keep in a bucket for an hour and then release, a curiosity that would soon lose its power to fascinate. We were unprepared for Elizabeth's eagerness to mourn so slight a show of life, so subtle a loss.

Today's monarch, though battered and obviously in decline, lifts high overhead and, fluttering in an erratic upward flight of ascents and falls, moves like a heartbeat out of sight.

It is peculiar to walk under a bridge, casting a line thirty feet beneath passing cars. But more peculiar is my sense that I am strolling through an eighteenth-century park or into a painting by some turn-of-the-century Frenchman. The clearing around the bridge is thick with flowers, gardenlike with daisies and asters backed by the bridge abutment's high wall. The bridge itself creates a grotto, open at both ends but sufficiently contained to encourage—at least in the absence of overhead traffic—a cloistered feeling. Beneath the concrete span, big stones have been placed—Seurat's dots writ large—in a rough mosaic that holds the banks against erosion. Where they have broken loose and rolled to the river below, their places have been filled by ferns.

But once I leave the shelter of the bridge, the banks again grow wild in a tumble of alder. Somewhere behind me loons cry hysterically. The eagle must be stalking Golden Lake. They fall silent, and a single loon appears overhead, beating its wings in the swift, short strokes that can, miraculously, bear up a loon.

When the last cries have stilled, a general quiet prevails. I am still in easy earshot of Highway 2, but there is no noise of traffic, only the water's low clucking as it burrows under a cedar that, uprooted, has fallen across the Run and created a wide pool.

Deep cracks, two and three inches apart, run the length of the bleached trunk, like lines on a topographical map, some indecipherable message printed in an exquisite calligraphy.

The water is cold and relatively deep; cover is abundant, and on the bank behind me the remains of an old campfire indicate that someone else thought to find trout here. I fish the pool, painstakingly but to no avail. I fish it again, doubt and frustration growing with each succeeding cast. There is a hatchery nearby, surely an unfailing source of trout, most likely stupid trout that escape or are released into the Run, but I could be fishing in a washbasin for all the life that breaks the watery flowers on the pool's surface. The dark boulders that line the shore, rounded and tight-grained, stand mute before my provocations.

The rocks came into our front yard by a variety of routes. Those lining the waterfront and breaking the waves that claw at the peat and grass that make up our lawn were hauled in over several years, but the greater part one summer when my youngest brother came to visit. Eric, seventeen years my junior but already at sixteen nearly four inches over my six feet and eager to prove himself his eldest brother's equal, lugged in stone after stone, then consumed all the food in the cabin.

The large gray boulders that curve around the stand of spruce came by wheelbarrow from somewhere in the forest behind our property, wheeled by my father and my Uncle Merle in a week when my mother and aunt found entertainment in antique shops, berry picking, and sisterhood. The men, after a day or two of sitting silently in lawn chairs and gazing aimlessly over the lake, eventually wandered off in different directions. Merle, a retired dragline operator, returned first and asked, casually, if we could use a few large rocks. Karen gave me an uncertain but doubtful look, and I shrugged what I hoped was a noncommittal shrug. Then my father returned and the two men left together, pushing a wheelbarrow and arguing about the best way to haul a two-hundred-pound stone. In the course of the afternoon they brought back eight boulders, wheeling them happily into the front yard with the explanation that anybody can find a use for a good-sized rock.

A year later, when we had already rolled the gray stones into a curving border on the south edge of the yard, Sarah spotted a large chunk of quartz—the rock on which Juliet was discovered—across the lake and half a mile away, exposed by a summer without rain. Karen, shopping in town, had Aaron—still a baby—with her. I had kept the two girls at the lake, supposedly so they could have naps, but both were wide-awake and both were grouchy. Sarah wanted the rock. I said, if it was a rock, which I doubted, we had no way of retrieving it, and took Elizabeth into the cabin in the hope of talking her to sleep. Sarah followed us, her face thoughtful. She must have been about six. "I think that rock will fit in our boat," she argued. "Perhaps," I conceded, "but we could never get it into the boat, and even if we could, it would probably sink us." She pursed her lips and looked out the window, then said, "We could get the rock into the boat the same way Grandpa and Uncle Merle got the gray ones into the wheelbarrow, and after we did that we could see if the boat sank." She was determined, had made up her mind just as she had at four when she enlarged her name to Sarah Willie Mays Dick Butkus Joe Frazier Fields, a name she kept intact for two years, earning in the process the largest name tag in preschool history. And Elizabeth had no intention of going to sleep.

With the two girls—Elizabeth's head just barely visible above an orange life jacket—and a labrador retriever who refused either to be left behind or to lie down, I cast off in a homemade rowboat that was incapable of holding a straight line and which was equipped with a pair of oars too long for the craft they propelled, causing me to smash together both sets of knuckles whenever I looked away from my hands.

We found the block of quartz, about two feet cubed, sitting high and dry among a field of lesser stones, and by tilting the boat on its side, and bracing it in position with the oars, I managed to roll the rock aboard. And we did not sink. Halfway back Elizabeth began to cry, and Smeagol nearly overturned us when a loon surfaced close at hand, but I rowed a zigzag course in a vessel freighted with a weeping three-year-old, a barking dog, and a justified Sarah wearing a baseball cap and seated on her milky-white perch, facing forward like the figurehead on a ship's prow.

I head upstream and promptly arrive at another pool, this one framed on both banks by the wide cut of a pipeline, running like a highway east and west. Cleared of trees, the right-of-way is a ribbon of flowers and ferns, a stream of plants: coneflowers, goldenrod, daisies, joe-pye weed, fireweed, tansy—a wide runner of flowers as far as I can see.

The water immediately drops from waist-deep to below my knees, picks up speed and decibels, though the latter are not so loud as to defeat the sudden pounding that erupts on the western bank where a woodpecker is trying to drive a tunnel through a dead birch. He hesitates, cocks his head at me, and after a slight twist at the point where black feathers give way to red—a movement that suggests he is trying to ease a not surprising crick from his abused neck—throws himself back into his strange, relentless work.

The first summer we stayed in the old cabin we were awakened one morning by an incredible pounding on the outside of the wall. More than a pounding, the reverberating series of blows sounded like a jackhammer on the cedar siding. A woodpecker was chipping away shingles for the insect larvae underneath. Before we managed to re-stain the building the following year, he had knocked three holes through to the tar paper separating the shingles from the sheeting beneath.

Again the river is blocked, this time by a fallen spruce on the left and alders on the right. I back through, shielding the rod and line with my body. It is, the best I can figure, 8:25, and I am to meet Rick at 9:00. According to the map the Run forks just above the pipeline right-of-way, the left branch leading to the hatchery and closed to fishing, the right bypassing the breeding ponds and open. But no fork appears. While my hand-drawn copy is crude and only vaguely reliable for distances, I distinctly remember from the Forestry map that the stream divides almost immediately after the pipeline cut.

Since a fork is not something easily missed, I press on. So thick are the bushes and so narrow the stream, I walk for the next fifty feet crouched beneath the branches, upper body parallel to the water. This I take to be a sign of things to come: a dwindling in depth and width, a burrowing under brush as the Run shrinks to the nothing of its beginning.

The left bank remains a low thicket, but the one to the right rises, providing the backdrop for another pool, deeper and colder than the last. But I cannot figure where the fork has gone, and it is already after 9:00. Denied any exit here, I double back through the alders, though this time my passage is eased by the fact that I am moving with the grain, all the while cursing cartographers. I get out at the pipeline and start up the gravel road that bends almost to the stream bank and that will take me to the hatchery.

A short distance later I come to a second pipeline cut. Somehow I failed to notice that a gas line parallels the petroleum line and that the stream fork lies just beyond the second of these. Even granting the twisting difference between stream distance and that of a road, I must have been close to the second cut when I began my retreat.

Leaving my fly rod and net beside the gravel, I walk the two or three hundred feet to the Run, walk through raspberries red with fruit and clumps of butter-and-eggs. A tiger swallowtail flutters up reluctantly from the blossom of a joe-pye weed, then settles on another twenty feet away. With his perfect wings and elegant tails, he bears no resemblance to the frayed and faded Juliet.

From the stream bank I can see the elusive fork, right where the map says it should be. I return to the road, gather my gear, and continue toward the hatchery.

When I approach the bridge that crosses the breeding pools, a Doberman rushes from behind a large log building, the caretaker's house, I presume, and charges toward me, snarling as he accelerates. I back against a popple so that he can't get behind me and, braced against the tree, grab up my net in the absurd hope of thrusting it over his head. I reach for my knife but realize I will never get it free of my waders in time, and so I wait, armed only with a landing net that even alders have managed to savage.

He comes in great bounds, lips pulled back, teeth gleaming, and, though it all is happening very quickly, it also seems slowed, and I am watching, detached, both the dog and myself. I am not so much afraid as angry and oddly exhilarated. For the first time this morning I have a quarry, something for my net, if not my creel, and, too, a legitimate target for all the unnameable irritations that are gnawing at me. I am thinking this and at the same time I can see the muscles flex and contract as the Doberman approaches.

When the dog has closed the distance to five yards, a woman calls from the distant cabin, and he checks his attack, continuing forward another ten feet before coming to a complete halt. He stands for a moment, glaring at me. His chest is barely moving, showing how little exertion I've required of him. My own breathing has quickened considerably. At last he gives a final snarl, more formal than vicious, and trots off easily toward the house. I let the net fall to my side and wonder how long the woman has been watching.

Beneath the plank bridge, thousands of five- and six-inch trout crowd the hatchery pool, the densest layers hovering under large plastic feeders that drip an endless stream to the fish below.

Somehow the fish remind me of the unfinished manuscript, of my several unfinished manuscripts. And, too, I think of Sarah on her alabaster throne, crowned with a New York Mets hat, serenaded by Elizabeth and Smeagol, her clumsy craft powered by a foulmouthed father who barks his knuckles with every return of the oars.

A u g u s t 14

I did not go to the Run Saturday or Sunday, claiming weekend fishermen and family visitors as an excuse, and, since Rick and Marilyn did not leave until Monday morning, I skipped that day as well. In fact I don't much want to go back to Cook's Run. While I was wasting Friday morning sorting out pipelines and confronting a Doberman—all for a single keeper trout—Joe was in the Paint catching his limit. This whole endeavor seems more and more foolish, a waste of time that could be more profitably spent on my academic book, a waste of effort since the familiar sections of the Paint seem the places to be fishing.

When I came home from the hatchery, Joe was sitting on the front step, his creel casually open, positioned so that the sunlight rekindled the pink-and-yellow speckles.

"Any luck?" Joe asked with apparent disinterest.

"Lots," I answered, opening my creel like a poker player calling a bluff. "None of it good," I added as he looked in, a troubled expression on his face. The look eased as he saw the single trout.

"Too bad," he said. "Used to be good trout in there."

"Still are, for all the damage I did," I said, trying to appear unconcerned. "I nearly had something big," I added.

"How big?" Joe asked, as though merely being polite.

"Probably more than I could have handled with my net," I said.

"A brown? There have always been big browns in the Run."

"Partly brown," I told him and then explained about the Doberman.

"I heard they had a big dog to keep poachers out of the hatchery." He said all of this as though it were common knowledge. Joe fluctuates, one day extravagant in his talk, the next cryptic, volunteering little. Last time he was expansive.

"It would have been nice if I had heard that," I said, irritated that the episode should be so easily dismissed. "It came as something of a surprise to me."

Aaron, who had seen Joe's catch, asked if he could clean my one trout, and as he worked he commented appreciatively on its thickness and its color, trying to cheer me up. He gutted the fish quickly, cleaning it without any need for my assistance.

And on Saturday I accepted the fact that we would return to St. Louis a week from Friday, committed myself on the phone. I had hoped to squeeze in an extra weekend, or at least to avoid tying us to any specific date. But it is set now, an official declaration of the end of summer. And, I feel sure, the end of something more than summer, though of what, exactly, I am unable to say. The suspicion has grown that the next equinoctial crossing will be irrevocable and not merely another redundancy in a life built on repetition, a suspicion that the circle has been broken, stretched out as a line, and the promise of recurrence dispelled.

The business of losing the children continues to haunt me, the matter of their growing up and away from us, and, though I knew all along that such was the nature of the contract, I had thought the ultimate settlement too far off for fretting. But like contracts entered in fairy tales, eventually the debt comes due, and the enchanter appears on the doorstep demanding what we, too young to know the price he was exacting, agreed to all those years ago. So I see Rumpelstiltskin's inevitable approach and watch helplessly as he comes to lay claim on our young. Pronouncing his name will be to no avail this time. And so it is I who howl the oaths of rage and stomp my foot into the floor while my children prepare for their departures.

I am aware of the self-indulgence in this melodrama and of the absurdity of the role I seem determined to play. Sarah at sixteen will return to the lake next year, and Elizabeth and Aaron at fourteen and eleven are hardly preparing to move out of the house. Still, they all seem changed, aloof, disinterested in the fishing and canoeing of previous years, reluctant to join the work when we are tearing down the old cabin. They prefer to be alone, reading, listening to their radios, playing by themselves. I feel left out, dismissed. As we work together stacking the salvageable lumber from next door, Karen and I talk about the changes. She takes them in stride, insists on being mature, and tries to ease me through the transition. She points out that I have always become depressed this time of year. But I object, telling her that while there is ever a kind of dying in leaving the lake and woods, this seems a more thorough sort of death, the loss of much more than a summer or even a year. She replies that I deal with change, any change, this way, brood on it, make it a wound to constantly pick at, willfully increasing the pain. As always she wants to get on with things, while I hang back, sullen and afraid.

And so, though I know she is right, I resist, and a part of my resistance is a reluctance to return to the Run. Now that it has entered the heavy timber below Highway 2, it seems far away from the family. It is now a stream I've never entered with any of them; its waters lack any personal history, have become the future I do not want to face. I long instead to return to familiar streams.

In a way, a way not altogether clear to me, I am troubled by the Run's headwaters. They are far from the beaten path, hard to get to, hard to get out of, and, from the hatchery on, the stream is surrounded by dense timber. Only the Run and a few half-forgotten logging trails cut through this wilderness. But normally these are conditions that I seek out, that attract rather than repel me, promising a privacy that, for a few hours at least, I have always coveted. If I worry about getting lost, and I suppose to some extent I do, it is not because of any danger, but only about the humiliation of being the object of a search, of being officially looked for like the forestry-camp students who, last spring, had to be brought out by a rescue team.

That of course is the bottom line, the fear stronger than any other: the fear of humiliation. And the direction in which this narrative has begun to move is hardly reassuring. I am not such a naive reader that I don't see the observations giving way before the observer, the present being shouldered aside by the past, not so blind to the implications of even my own work that I can't guess which headwaters I truly dread. This Run is threatening to become a river of sentiment, of uncontrolled reminiscences, undisciplined emotions, the turbulence that I have worked so hard to submerge, currents I've kept out of sight and at a safer depth. The danger here is that I will allow that stream to blend too readily with Cook's Run and to carry into this wade my own debris. Though I recognize the justice of such a punishment, I would like to be more than a reader of my own rubbish, to do something more than sit hunched over my own entrails looking for a prophetic pattern, a sign. While I don't believe that we ever rid ourselves of psychic trash, give it over to some impersonal agent to haul away, believe rather that we only box it up as best we can and trundle it from closet to closet, trying in the shuttling not to disturb the lid, I do believe, believe fervently, in those boxes, in seeking out the sturdiest ones available. In reading what I have written I am troubled to see the seals being loosened.

Big beaver marshes supposedly dominate the last miles of the stream. The Forest Rangers know little about these waters, their firsthand information limited to an occasional aerial view, but they speak dubiously of fishing much beyond the hatchery and warn of a long chain of ponds, unwadeable stretches of dead water. I realize my mistake. I had thought of this as a mountain stream, like the headwaters of the Missouri, where the river begins with clear springs breaking out of living rock, and a person can step from one solid bank to the other over a narrow brook already leaping with hope and promise toward the journey ahead. This is the illusion, always unstated but always assumed, that has led me to make the trip the hard way, to work against the current toward that fantasized source. But I have come to accept what I should have recognized from my own knowledge of this terrain, what I have looked at on the map without seeing. An uphill struggle does not necessarily, or even usually, mean a movement toward high ground. My path has been away from the bright waters paved with stones and fingerling trout that I found above Highway 16; from the start I have been headed toward waters that are swampy and stagnant, thick with silt and decay, and any fisherman—any psychiatrist—knows that turbulent waters are less to be feared than waters that are unmoving and unmoved.

Last night my parents telephoned, and in the course of the conversation I mentioned that I had remembered Joe Columbus last week and told my mother what I had recalled.

"He didn't die on the Woodville road," she said. "He died in Keokuk. The reason you made the Woodville connection is because that is where his widow moved after she married Joe's brother." She paused. "The brother she met at her husband's funeral."

I am confused and bewildered by the certainty of my misremembering, fear that all has been deformed in my recollection, know, of course, that it has been.

This morning halfway up the drive I pass the chunk of granite that Elizabeth found and had me carry yesterday, to the spot where, earlier in the summer, we buried Smeagol's collar. She was not especially sad, instead seemed rather pleased to have discovered a suitable marker. I turned the stone while she, a few steps away and face pinched in concentration, chose just the right angle. Her decision made, she brushed at her nose with the back of her hand, relaxed her gaze, and said, "There."

In the days after the clown had leaped from its box and provoked Elizabeth's laughter, nothing more happened. The surgeon declared her heart repaired and celebrated the technical success, but there was no more laughter, no further evidence that the spell had been broken. The neurologist had not witnessed the scene with the jack-in-the-box and was skeptical, doubtful that we had actually seen any reliable evidence of intellectual function, of mind. Karen berated him, said she knew what she had seen, but my doubts returned.

A week later, as I was feeding Elizabeth—she unable to sit, but strapped to a chair, head flopped to one side and resting on her shoulder—I talked to her, tried to tease some irrefutable sign from her, told her over and over what a big girl she was as I spooned the baby food into her half-open mouth. Her eyes opened widely, slowly, as though requiring great effort, and she started to shake, especially her arms, a rough jerking movement like that of the convulsions which had begun three days after surgery and had continued for twenty hours. I began to panic, my own hand shaking, and I tried to talk her back into composure, telling her once more, frantically now, what a big girl she was. The tremors only worsened.

A nurse who had been with Elizabeth from the beginning rushed over to see what was happening, stood behind me, and when I turned in appeal for help, she was weeping. "What is it?" I demanded angrily, assuming the worst. "She's doing 'So Big,'" she cried, as Elizabeth struggled, pushing against the tremendous weight of neurological short circuits and weeks of paralysis, until her arms were raised as high as she could lift them, acting out the game she had learned from her mother.

At 6:30 I park the car by the first pipeline and pull on my waders. To the east, against a slate-colored sky, the trees show the first tinges of fall, hints of yellow and red against the dark timber. Many of the ferns in the clearing have already turned.

A blue heron lumbers into the air as I approach the stream, head forward, legs back, its body a thin gray line against the gray sky, its wings large and ponderous in their heavy movement.

Sarah has been eager to see every appearance of the women's Olympic basketball team this summer and complains that the ghostly images which appear on our TV set make it impossible to identify particular players, even to tell the teams apart. She is convinced that Cheryl Miller will make a slam dunk sometime during these games and does not want to miss the big event. "They will show it on film," I told her, "later." But she wants to see the accomplishment the moment it occurs, wants to jump to her feet and drive her own fist down in triumph simultaneously with those players sitting on the bench or craning their heads upward from under the basket. Elizabeth, who normally cares little about basketball—her sister's sport—has grown excited too, and when we got the game on the screen she asked repeatedly and urgently, "Which one is Cheryl?" There was no way of telling as ten gray figures moved through a flickering blizzard.

"Those could be guys," Aaron muttered and started back to his room. "Call that a TV?" he said as he passed me, shaking his head in exaggerated disgust. "Real big spender, my dad."

"Cheryl will be the one who gets into the air," Sarah said, determined, ready to wait as long as it took, rushing over to fiddle with the dials whenever the picture broke up completely.

The announcers, reporting on other events, spoke constantly of Carl Lewis and the possibility of a new broad-jump record. During the Mexico City Olympics, when Bob Beamon cleared more than twenty-nine feet, soared far beyond the markers for all the previous jumps, jumped past the limits of the electronic measuring equipment, I thought for a moment, as he soared higher and farther than any jumper in history, that he had broken free and would never come back down. The accomplishment seemed all the more miraculous because it was so unexpected— Beamon lived in the shadow of greater jumpers who were either recently retired or past their prime—and even after the fact, in the endless replays, there came a moment in mid-flight, just before his body entered the slow, inevitable trajectory of descent, when I would come out of my chair, a tightness in my throat, and think, "By God, he'll do it," all the while knowing he wouldn't, that he would fall just as surely as the lesser of us. On the track, after that incredible jump, Beamon knelt, stunned, between two other American jumpers—one a laughing Ralph Boston, who, meet after meet, was clearly the greater athlete, but whose entire career had been eclipsed by this one leap. Beamon appeared to be weeping, surely aware that this was as far as he would ever get and unable to rise under the weight of that knowledge. "O gravity. O grave."

Suddenly, in the game against Spain, the picture cleared, and we watched Cheryl Miller, saw the intensity and pleasure of the game in the brown fineness of her face as she moved like a dancer around and over her opponents, blocking shots, taking passes, laying the ball easily over the rim. She did not dunk the ball but soared, again and again, over the other players, stretched long elegant fingers above the basket, toyed with the possibilities. Karen came to watch, standing behind her daughters. Elizabeth sat bent forward, enchanted. And Sarah leaped with every move to the basket, her face shining with each little triumph, unaware as she thrust her arms above her head, fists clinched in exultation, that she was making the same "So Big" gesture as her infant sister all those years before.

Past the point where I turned back on Friday, a grove of spruce and cedar leans heavily over the Run as though bent before an unrelenting wind. One spruce has fallen into the stream, and farther ahead a living cedar has completely crossed to the other bank, its trunk only a foot or two above the water and its branches growing straight up like little Christmas trees on a bridge.

The stream, narrow, overgrown with paper birch, and thick with gray boulders, has become a Durand painting. The bark uncurls from the birch trunks like old parchment, only whiter, and branches crisscross above center stream, creating a single aisled cathedral. There is no wind, no bird calls, only the mumbling water that runs darkly around my ankles.

In ninth grade, in the spring, I became an avid high jumper. Despite being an undersized ninety pounds, I had played football—at end—the previous fall, even managed on one drizzly November and against our biggest rival a game that after twenty-eight years I can still replay like some old black-and-white movie, tackle after tackle of a back, already one of the area's best—and largest—athletes. I can hear him on top of me muttering, "I'll kill you, you little shit, next time," and the next time, terrified, I crashed into him, and he fumbled, and somehow, wonderfully, the ball rolled under my body. I did not sleep all that night but lay awake engraving every play into memory, already suspecting that this was the game of my lifetime. The next morning and for days after, I could not raise my arms without pain, so great was the damage to tendons and joints.

I liked basketball, though I was neither tall nor fast, and made that team as well, barely, and it was basketball that revealed the spring growing into my legs. Then one day in gym class we jumped, broad-jumped, high-jumped, jumped over hurdles, went on a binge of levitation, jumping benches, garbage cans, and one another. In my first efforts I took the high-jump bar upright, scissoring one leg over and then the other and coming down stiffly and on my feet. Even with this crude style I placed fifth in the All City track meet, going against taller boys, boys who had hair on their chests and talked knowledgeably, or so it seemed to me, about girls, but more importantly, boys who rolled over the bar rather than jumping with head and torso erect like someone trying to sit on a very tall chair.

I built high-jump standards out of plaster lath, pegged them to support a bamboo pole, and then worked on the strange series of movements which would allow me to kick one foot up and throw my body parallel to the bar, then, outstretched, to twist downward while kicking my trailing leg over. The shock of hitting the ground quickly taught me to cut the roll short and land on my hands and knees rather than on back or side.

All through high school and college I spent my April Saturdays awaiting my turn, then taking the seven—two followed by a little hitch in my gait and five more—steps, springing upward with a quick look down at the bar, kicking, and then falling to the sand or sawdust below. When the timing was right, the last steps—not too fast and with a bounce, themselves barely contained jumps—were rich with promise, legs strong and held in check before the full leap upward. As the body, any body, rose past the bar, all the watching competitors in unison would lean to the right and lift their left legs as the jumper kicked high his own trailing leg. I never became particularly good, but I could jump higher than my own head even after I grew to six feet.

I always landed face down, not looking upward like the better jumpers. The cost, I discovered—when, in my last competition jumping into foam rubber rather than sawdust, I completed my roll—was four inches. My usual kick flattened my body into what was, at best, only a break-even proposition, whereas by dropping my shoulder and kicking over onto my back, I could lift considerably higher. Clearing six feet four inches meant my best-ever big meet finish, but still I could not bring myself fully to trust the cushioned pit, to avert my eyes from the inevitable.

Until high jumpers switched to the flop and started going over the bar back first, falling on their necks and shoulders in deep nests of foam, I, like all the other old jumpers watching from the stands or in front of a TV, would be compelled to rise to my feet as the athlete approached the bar, then, inevitably, I would lean with him, bend my knees in the conditioned kick that must provide the final upward surge if the standard is to be cleared. Watching the event in these Olympics, I found myself standing up as the jumpers moved into their leaps, but when they faced skyward I no longer knew what to do with my feet and shifted dumbly in place.

The stream branches again, the wider and swifter water coming from the right, and I turn to enter it. Tangles of logs and roots clog the current and, together with a large gravel bar that fans out to the left, indicate the path of heavy runoffs. But everything apart from the main channel is dry today.

I still play basketball, but it is a different game, against players half my age, players blissfully ignorant of how few years it will take to deaden the spring in their legs and bring them down, inescapably, to earth. Like all old ballplayers, I get position, make my opponent go over me or jump against my weight. Like all old ballplayers, I shoot more hook shots, not because it buys a little more room and time, but because it makes me feel like I am airborne, when in fact all I've done is stretch my body, lifting my right foot while grounded, tiptoe, with the left. Still, it feels *almost like a leap, even though I and the other players know the difference.*

Around another curve the water shallows beside a large open area on the bank. The flowers here are even more autumnal than the ones I saw earlier. Thistledown sticks up in ragged white tufts. The joe-pye weed is darker, more shriveled-looking, and its leaves are yellowed. Water skimmers cover the stream in a sheet of twitching legs, and I wonder why nothing is eating them. So near the hatchery—surely a refuge for castoffs and escapees, an aquatic Georgia or Australia—I expect trout.

The fly snags a thistle, and as I approach, I find the offending plant bound to another by an intricate web that glistens with drops of dew, its netting broken in one corner and the severed threads doubled back into the surviving pattern.

Rivers are themselves threads, lines that link us to whatever we have left behind. They were, for our exploring ancestors, that which anchored them somewhere even when they journeyed through what was not yet any place at all, lines leading back to some definitive point. They are the hope that we can somehow pursue the new without ever letting go of what we have abandoned, a way of not being anywhere and yet still not being lost.

Twice I have gotten lost while getting in and out of trout streams, both times on the Paint, both times at night. My second season of fishing I went upstream one evening after a heavy rain. I had never been in those waters, and about two hours into the wade I came to a deep beaver pond. By working my way slowly around the shallowest edge, I managed to get through, proud not to have been deterred. I fished for another twenty minutes and then started back downstream to the only exit route I knew, the place where I had entered, a spot just before the river curved away from the railroad track that I had followed from the road. Everywhere else a tangle of underbrush and treacherous marshes confined me to the Paint. It got late and dark, and as I retraced my steps I realized that the river had continued to rise throughout the evening.

The beaver pond, when I reached it, was four or five inches deeper than it had been earlier, and, having risen well above my wader tops, it forced me into the thicket along the western bank in search of an overland route back.

I could not hold a straight line, was compelled by alders and bog holes into a meandering course that would have done the most accomplished drunk proud. Wherever there was footing, and the slightest hint of an opening, I went, figuring somehow I could twist it all back to a westerly line, and trying to ignore the fact that in the nearly complete darkness I hadn't the vaguest idea where west was. As it grew later and darker I reassured myself that in one direction lay the railroad track, in another the river, and in another, though three or four miles removed from where I had left the Paint, the road. Only the fourth possibility meant real trouble, and surely I could make do with three-to-one odds even in the absence of any sense of direction.

Finally I broke through the undergrowth and scrub timber and once more faced the river. At first I felt frustration only at the lost time and hoped that I had at least gotten past the deep water. Then I realized I was on the wrong bank, that, incredibly, the current was flowing in the wrong direction. Somehow I had circled the entire Paint river without hitting either train tracks or road. Of course I knew the impossibility of such a feat, eventually overcame my dislocation, and forced myself to act on that knowledge, wading directly across what turned out to be a rain-swollen tributary and hitting the tracks a hundred feet beyond.

My most vivid impression from that experience is how easily entire rivers can get turned around, and how difficult, once the reversal has been accomplished, is putting them back where they belong.

The second time I lost my way I was fishing downstream to an abandoned logging trail where Joe had parked the Jeep before heading off in the opposite direction. I had moved slowly in the hope of picking up an early-feeding brown and, in the growing dark, was keeping watch for an ancient logging bridge's single surviving timber, the marker that would place me a football field's length from where I could find Joe. Misled by another log, I climbed out a quarter of a mile too soon, and wandered for half an hour in an irregular circle that finally brought me back to the river. Just as I reached the bank I felt a tug on the fishing rod and discovered that the fly had worked loose from the cork grip, snagged in the brush, and laced the line through the woods, mapping my erratic path. I cut the line, leaving it like the thread of some disordered spider, and waded to the correct log. Joe had turned on the headlights to guide me back. All he said was, "Getting late for a stroll." And all I said was "Seemed the evening for it," and hoped he would not notice the empty reel, would not know about the line I had let get out of control, a dangling modifier left hanging in the dark.

As I approach the spillway gates and the fork away from the hatchery, a gun booms as though in warning, and then, in quick succession, fires four more times. A dog begins to bark, a dog that sounds like the Doberman. The barking, to my regret, seems inspired neither by fear nor pain but is aggressive, confident, as though gunman and dog are on the same side. The thought is less than reassuring, and I wish that I had two functioning ears to help me locate the sound more precisely.

Birch mingles with spruce, and raspberry bushes, heavy with

fruit, cover the bank. I reach for my ball-point to note the contrast between white bark and red berries, but it is missing. Three steps later a sharp pain runs through my left ankle, and I stop, loosen my waders, and finally, crouched awkwardly, work my hand down to the pen.

It is 8:30, and in the distance another gunshot, muted, more the echo than the real thing, and the barking of the Doberman.

I heard Terry and Jan's dogs last night, the collective howl of a wolf pack. Aaron and I were in the garage, looking for material to make a bookcase for his room, shining the flashlight over the hoard of lumber I've collected, used, and recollected through the years, and pulling out the cleanest two-by-sixes, those that in their last incarnation had served as forms for the cabin's slab. I was yelling at Aaron because he had turned the light away from the stacked boards, leaving me in the dark while he tried to locate the source of scratching sounds somewhere on the far side of the boat trailer. He ignored me and caught a deer mouse in the light's beam. It froze, big ears erect like a comic-book character, its silhouette rising rabbit-sized on the garage wall. Aaron, delighted by the theatrical effect, laughed, and a mile away the dogs began to howl.

Terry and Jan have a log cabin in the woods on the other side of Highway 16 and keep fifteen or so dogs, each chained to its own post, each possessing its own hut, members of a team that runs in winter sled races in Minnesota and Wisconsin, even Alaska. Previous summers Terry kept them in shape by running them down our road, harnessed and pulling a wheeled platform where he sat, reins in hand, as the dogs barreled along. The pageant was hushed, the only sounds those of paws striking gravel, the clatter of wheels, and the rumble of the team's collective breathing. The animals surged with a strange intentness through the leaf-dappled light, and after they passed I would watch as they crested one hill, plunged out of sight, then rose again in full flight at the top of the next, as though desperately trying to escape the human burden hunched behind them, no closer and no farther away than when they began.

There are lots of rapids through here and, between waves of alder, frequent clearings, but the water is shallow and the sun has suddenly appeared in full force, casting the shadow of my line sharply across the stream whenever the surface of the water flattens. A big tamarack rises above the Run, its short, delicate needles—the annual replacements of a larch—holding the sunlight in bright little blossoms.

Aaron with the mouse was typical Aaron. There is an imperturbable quality about the boy. Though shy, he seems—generally—at ease with the world. Large for his age, but coordinated, even graceful, strong but unaggressive, he is a joy to be with, a calming presence in a house full of high-strung, anxious people. Whenever a sullen silence settles over the dinner table, he will look around intently, then, lowering his voice to adult depth, ask, "Do I detect a note of unspoken hostility here?" Sometimes he confuses popular song lyrics, changing lines like "It's so funny" to "Disco bunny" or "There's a bad moon on the rise" to "There's a bathroom on the right."

But he can also be easily embarrassed, rails regularly at the television for mention of "diarrhea" in Pepto-Bismol commercials or at ads for feminine-hygiene products.

Sometimes I look at him in wonder, so different is he from me, grateful for the two daughters who came between him and a first-time father's ego. He is nevertheless growing into my body, sharing already my shoulders and hips, though blonder, brighter than I could have ever hoped.

I cast to the base of a dead alder clump and catch a little brookie that attacks the fly as though he thought it about to take off, coming at it from the side and curling down on it hard with his entire body. Farther along, another brookie takes the fly, rising beside the trunk of a dead elm that stands a foot deep in water, leaping up where the current first strikes the tree.

The Run flows through more tamarack in a series of shallow bends that offer no casting room. I hurry along, scattering colonies of water skimmers that swarm like levitating spiders across the water. Again the brush falls away and trees return to the banks, and around the next bend the water flows through a dense stand of dead spruce, the work of spruce budworm. Naked limbs, stark and brittle, reach out above black-eyed Susans, as they await their fall.

When we picked up Sarah in June, after her trip to Providence, we came back through Chicago, looked quickly into the usual museums, went to the top of the Sears tower—like the other skyscrapers, added since we moved to St. Louis—then passed our old apartment building, Sarah's first home, and over to the University. Along the Midway everything seemed changed, so unfamiliar that I doubted we were on the right street. "It's the trees," Karen said. "The trees are different." The huge elms were gone and in their place puny locusts, a quick fix with scraggly limbs and tiny leaves, more like large weeds than trees, lined the sunken lawns of the Midway, swift-growing parodies of past grandeur.

Around the bend a cutoff stream for a beaver dam enters from the right, creating a large island complete with its own white pine. Several blowdowns and lots of beaver debris offer cover for trout, and I pull a six-and-three-quarter-inch brookie out from under a brush pile. I seem to be fishing well, or at least casting well, but with little more than illegal trout to show for my effort. What am I doing wrong? I think of Joe's ten trout on Friday and my sense of incompetence grows. I wonder if I could catch ten trout in a hatchery? In a fish market?

As I weave through the clutter, a high ridge of cedars and dead spruce fronts against the Run on the right, while alder backed by dead elm covers the lower bank to my left. I am moving through a catalog of modern tree blights and watch for white pines covered by rust to complete the collection.

The Midway at Chicago, the dry remains of Venetian-style canals created for the Columbian Exposition, was, when I was a gradu-ate student, a series of intramural fields, places where, if you waited and pulled the oversized ball peculiar to Chicago's glove-less version of softball, you could stroke a hit into the elms for extra bases. In the days after the King assassination, the two area street gangs—the Blackstone Rangers and the Englewood Disci-ples—met on the Midway to sign a peace treaty, an agreement to keep the neighborhood quiet while rioting was breaking out in other parts of the city. On a warm April day they marched onto the ball diamonds, scores of teenaged boys and young men, single file and taunting their rivals, until they stood facing each other in the bed of a canal whose origins were as meaningless to them as Egyptian hieroglyphics, and that had been dug to cele-brate a new world whose promise they had never shared. The taunting continued but the lines held as the leaders, officious as any other heads of state, struck their agreement. All the while, gang squad cops and nervous National Guardsmen looked on from the margin.

I watched from a reading-room window, behind leaded glass and Indiana limestone, watched from this Gothic fortress events less real to me than those I was reading about in The Tempest.

Out of view and to the west, pillars of smoke rose above other ghettos, and armored vehicles guarded overpasses along the Stevenson Expressway. Looking down from the library's third story, I watched, as I would shortly watch the riot in Grant Park and countless subsequent antiwar demonstrations, safe and aloof, and all the time thinking, "I must get all of this right, must hold it in memory for some future use." My memory of the event remains, or so it seems to me, relatively clear. What I find nearly impossible to recall is the person answering to my name who stood behind those windows.

Wading quickly through a series of catchpools held by fallen trees and piled debris, I watch for cabins—one on either side of the stream where private land briefly touches the Run—landmarks telling me to leave the water, backtrack and cut cross-country to the east. Somewhere in that direction the map shows a broken line weaving through the trees, the tortuous trail back to the hatchery.

After several yards the right bank opens on a meadow thick with lobelia and containing a tar-papered shack.

Somewhere nearby and to the right there should be a second camp belonging to someone named Deloria. I want to locate it, then see if I can reach the owner and get permission to enter from that side tomorrow. According to my map, shortly beyond Deloria's the Run forks, and I go to the left. But just past the tar-papered building the stream narrows abruptly and is so overgrown with alder limbs that I have to lift them above my head to pass.

I am hot and sweaty now, impatient to find the uncertain path toward the car. No camp appears on the right, but finally I see the fork and start back.

At 10:30 I get out of the stream, one hundred yards below the tar-papered cabin, on what the map identifies as public land. There is no evidence of a path, but I push my way up a steeply

rising hill toward what I hope will be a trail—toward the dotted
line that is a cartographer's promise of a way out. The going is
rough over fallen trees and through dense undergrowth, and out
of the water my jacket and waders insulate me like a thermos
bottle. Still, after several sweat-filled minutes, I reach the top of
the rise. There is, however, no sign of a trail. I crash deeper into
timber, zigzagging around the worst barriers, unsure of my directions because clouds have once more blocked the sun.

At last I strike a path of sorts and take it to the left. After half
a mile it forks, one branch swinging to the right, heading back
toward the tar-papered camp, while the other cuts sharply toward
where I think the hatchery must be. The road seems little used,
but I follow it, and two hundred yards later it comes to nothing
in an old gravel pit. Dogs bark in the distance, but I cannot get
a fix on their location. I turn around and try the other fork,
thinking it might curve back toward the hatchery, but instead it
veers sharply in the opposite direction. Thunder begins in long
rumbling surges, and I return to the gravel pit.

Just beyond where the trail seems to dead-end, hidden by trees
and high grass, it recovers, and after another quarter of a mile
reaches the upper gate of the hatchery. I call out to the house.
No one answers, but a dog appears at an upstairs window and
barks—not a Doberman but some kind of miniature sheepdog.
I yell again. Still no answer, and I begin the first hesitant steps
on the gravel road that curves around the cabin.

A u g u s t 16

When the alarm went off yesterday a light rain was falling,
and I was glad for the opportunity to sleep in. Late in the
morning the weather cleared, and I wheeled more gravel through
the spongy muck that lay under the old cabin, plowing my way
through the water and peat, then dumping the fill in the lowest

spots. Later my writing followed a similar slogging pattern; the words—like cement blocks, rigid, all corners and rough edges— refused to flow into sentences and paragraphs, but seemed instead only mortared together with conjunctions and lumpy transitions. And the redundancy which is a stream, is fly-fishing, is life, after all these pages threatens, like life, to become mind-killing. I can't exclude it and still write about the Run, about fishing, about whatever is in me this summer. The trick remains to make something supple of these unyielding words, to find something new, even unexpected, in these wearying repetitions.

Whatever caused Elizabeth's seizures and her coma returned her physically, at fifteen months, to infancy. While her eyes shone with awareness, her body refused all her commands, seemed to forget all the lessons it had so diligently learned before surgery. Her mouth could no longer shape words, her neck could not support her head, arms and legs that had propelled her across the floor and up onto kitchen cabinets only weeks earlier now could do nothing. In the months and years that followed—in a process that still goes on—she fought to regain control of all the disparate parts that are a person, struggled to hold her head erect, to sit upright, labored her way through the spastic stages of splayed hands and curved-back fingers, of feet that sprawled away from the line she wanted to follow, of slurred speech. And school has always been a battle, a battle largely misunderstood by the people who witnessed but did not recognize it—including, sometimes, her family—people who could not realize the neurological intricacy of holding a pencil or the death-defying feat that descending a flight of stairs can seem. And largely the heroic dimension of this work went unnoticed because Elizabeth kept it to herself, remained miraculously good-natured—"What a sweet child," people said, continually missing the point—as she fought to recompose herself.

Before I turn out the gaslight and end my day, I catalog my children, check that they are properly covered, even watch the rise and fall of their chests to be sure they are breathing. When Elizabeth sleeps on the top bunk, I wedge a blanket under the outer edge of her mattress to keep her from falling out of bed—even though we both know it is no longer necessary. This summer I have suddenly become aware of the beauty she is growing into, have been startled by the grace she has come to embody.

In the afternoon Billy Hager came by for the logs from the old cabin, the structure that predated D. F. Carlysle's work. They had been nailed upright, vertically, plated on the top and bottom and joined by triangular batten strips and chinking. When Aaron and I were tearing down this part of the building, I beat the walls with a sledgehammer, Aaron taunting me with the number of blows each section would absorb and laughing whenever a wall bounced back into position despite the fury of my assault, or when the logs sagged but would not fall. Once they were down, the two of us, working with crowbars, pulled the logs apart and stacked them at the end of the drive. Billy wanted them for his sauna. Because they are spruce, dried to the weight and consistency of balsa wood, they will catch fire quickly and heat the water and rocks for the sauna's steam.

The cutting was easy, "like going through butter," Billy said, except that we kept hitting nails, throwing out a string of sparks and dulling my chain and then his.

For the first time in all the years I've known him—more than sixteen now—Billy spoke of Viet Nam. The subject came up when we were talking about Kurt. Last year while cutting a hemlock that had blown down in his front yard, Kurt lost his footing, and ran the chain saw halfway through his palm.

We talked small talk, about how close Kurt came to losing his hand, about our own near misses, about trees one or the other of us has hung up. Billy, a recruiter for the National Guard, talks easily and well, most often the light banter of the bar or the hunting shack, an innocent grin on his face but a warning slyness through the eyes, the look of a confidence man. Sometimes, maybe half a dozen in all the years I have known him, the look and the talk change, not to the wariness that often seems the only male alternative to drinking banter, but direct and open as though some heavy curtain has been momentarily pulled aside.

"Still," I said, "I like cutting." I told him about the time Karen, filling in some magazine quiz, asked what would be the first thing I'd go back for—once she and the kids and the pets were safe—if the house caught fire, and I answered, "The chain saw."

Billy nodded, then the change came, and he started talking about Viet Nam. It had been several years since he had spoken in my presence as neither jokester nor con man, and that time, too, we were hauling wood, loading eight-foot lengths of hemlock that Billy was scavenging to cut into siding for his cabin. That time he told me he was getting a divorce and about his worry for his children. This time there was nothing so dramatic, just a few sentences about a guy he had known during the war and a little about what river patrol was like, but his tone made clear that something serious and difficult was beneath the surface, its shadow appearing briefly and indistinctly before we resumed our usual, safer talk.

I knew he had been there, but when you are my age and never went, you do not ask a vet about Viet Nam. There is too much to explain, too much that cannot be explained, about why he was there and you were not. Perhaps the two years between Billy and me provide the reason; maybe it was because I was old enough at the wrong time, married at the right time, in school for a long enough time. Certainly it was not for any act of conscience— only chance and something known solely, if known at all, to the draft board that left me 1A for two years, uncalled and untouched. For Billy's and my generation Viet Nam was the main event. I saw it, then, on television and read about it now in other

people's books, books in which something happened and goes on
happening, and in which I play no part.

*I met Billy the first summer I came to the lake. He and his father
were sitting in what had been Billy's grandfather's cabin, was
then his father's, and is now—the consequence of a trade—
Billy's. They had come out for a Sunday afternoon and offered
me a beer. Billy talked. I don't remember now what he talked
about, but Billy can always talk.*

*He was young then, sixteen years ago, and going to school
while working at whatever job he held at that particular moment.
I was also young, and so I suspect we talked about the future we
both still—though for different reasons—believed in. And Billy
would have had plans, or in their absence would have made some
up. Billy has always had interesting plans.*

*We have helped each other out from time to time. I gave him
a hand with the hemlock for his cabin siding; he helped me build
a new outhouse to replace the old structure, the one porcupine
had chewed up and that Karen and Sarah found so repulsive.*

*Sometimes, when the stakes are not too high, we work well
together, Billy's unflappable confidence overcoming my anxious
perfectionism. On those occasions it is often two or three days
before I notice all the mistakes we have made.*

This morning, as I come downstairs, the puppy crawls out
from under the stove, belly sprawled on the brick hearth, as she
pushes along like a swimmer. She has an old tennis shoe in her
mouth, and when she clears the stove, she leaps toward me,
shaking her head violently from side to side until the shoe slips
away and slides across the room.

Outside the air is chilly, and the sight of my breath and the
bright red leaves on the scrawny maple beside the house gives an

autumnal feel to the morning. This is always the first tree on our lot to turn, a fact that, together with the scraggly limbs, has convinced me for ten years that it is dying. The only reason I haven't cut it down—it lends no beauty to the place—is my growing curiosity as to how long it can hold out.

The loons begin to call, and in addition to the two familiar voices, two younger ones share in the laughter that rattles across the lake and bounces back off the trees on the distant shore.

I was twenty-five when the war in Viet Nam began in earnest. In school, but unprotected by any deferment, I tried at first to ignore the conflict, regarded it as a distraction from the liberal agenda to which I was committed—civil rights, the Peace Corps, the war on poverty. Later I was ambivalent. The draft board called my brother Jack back from Honduras to take a physical that Peace Corps doctors had already told them he would fail, pursued Jerry, who opposed the war, pursued him until he, too, failed their tests and was spared the trip to jail or to Canada. But me, who would have passed the physical and who, uncertain and lacking conviction, would not have left the country, me they ignored. Me they could have had for the asking, but not for less.

The evening before last Karen and Aaron and I drove along the township roads to the south of the Run looking for access to the stream. I had the map with the penciled-in logging trails, but the Forest Ranger had made it clear that these were rough approximations at best and in some instances might be completely misremembered.

Aaron had brought along a Buddy Holly tape that my youngest brother had given to me. It is the only music I own that Aaron has ever liked, and as Karen and I watched the woods for some sign of a road, he suddenly had "That'll Be the Day" booming through the car and was pounding out the beat on the dashboard: "You say you're going to leave me; you know it's a lie, cause that'll be the day when I die." Karen quickly reached over and turned the volume down, but Aaron continued slapping out the tempo. Softer, Holly's voice still cut through the shadowed quiet with the boyish drawl of the drawn-out "welllll," the hiccupping "day–eh–eh," the "when I die" clipped, incongruously joyous, as though the statement could be defeated by the bravado with which it was expressed.

"You like that?" I asked, taken aback by the thought of my son's keeping time to a song from my adolescence.

"It's pretty good," he conceded, "for back then."

I looked to see if the last had been said in innocence, but his face was unreadable.

"How come you don't hear him now? What happened to him?"

Under Aaron's voice I could hear the other one, nearly as young and, for all its claims to the contrary, nearly as innocent. "You say you're gonna leave me, you know it's a lie . . ." Buddy Holly bouncing, laughing, mocking the words with an infectious confidence, and, seated between his mother and me, Aaron bouncing and laughing with him.

"He's dead," I answered. "A plane crash twenty, twenty-five years ago," then to no apparent purpose, "He'd be older than me—" and I turned the tape deck off. Karen had spotted an opening ahead and to the north, and we pulled into a deeply rutted logging trail, recently used but so torn up I could only drive in a short distance before the way was blocked. Karen looked skeptical as I explained how this had to be the logging road the ranger had noted, had to connect with the lines he had drawn on my map parallel to the Run.

I want to start the next leg from Highway 2 and then finish up somewhere on this, the south side of the stream, near a place where I can meet Karen and the car. But there is no telling how long a wade will be required, nor is it clear just where the trail we found on yesterday's drive finally leads. It is all guesswork, some of it mine and some of it that of a very skeptical Forest Ranger. And, too, it requires that I find a way in. The idea of retracing my way to the tar-papered shack is unappealing, and I have considered, instead, finding my way into the camp that eluded me on Tuesday's wade—Deloria's. Last night I decided to ask Joe about the owner and the likelihood of getting permission to cross his land. Joe was out fishing, and I talked to Vi instead.

I asked awkwardly, rounding into my subject, embarrassed that I needed to cross private property. In the U.P., asking to go on someone else's land, someone you do not know, is no trivial thing, not because people are particularly unfriendly but because they value their privacy. And this is as true for the owners of tar-papered shacks as for those who have expensive cabins and trout ponds—even more true for owners of tar-papered shacks, since they have not built to impress others, have not overly presumed on the rights of ownership. So much changes so rapidly that your own land seems vulnerable, and the reluctance to have others disrupt, or even to enter, this place that has been set apart, reserved, is strong, especially for those who build their cabins farthest from primary thoroughfares. The intrusion of even a single fisherman, seeking nothing more than access to a stream, sets a precedent, threatens to open a path to your door which, once established, can never be erased. My reluctance to make such a request grows from the strength of my own territorial instincts. Better in my mind that someone cross unknown and not trespass on the symbolic place I inhabit than for me to know for certain that the intrusion has taken place. And yet another part of me insists on getting permission.

Vi did not take her eyes from the battery-powered television on the wall above the stove. In the darkened cabin the flickering image of Dan Rather dominated the room, his summary of the latest presidential poll a constant undertone to my reluctant question.

Vi sat at the table, a cigarette between the fingers of her right hand. The television's glow brought a translucence to her skin. Her hand shook slightly. She was watching the TV and hearing Dan Rather, but she heard me as well. There is little that Vi misses.

She did not answer at first, just inhaled on the cigarette and released the smoke while the President, her own age but tanned and fit, came on the screen. He was speaking before a roomful of people. He seemed jocular, confident, and the audience was delighted. They also looked tanned and fit. "You tell them, Ronnie," Vi crooned, shaking her head in irritation and despair. She emphasized the last syllable of "Ronnie," turning it into the "e" equivalent of the long "o" that comes at the end of so many U.P. Finnish first names. She fell back into silence, and a Chrysler commercial took over the screen.

Perhaps she was considering how Joe or I would react to such a request. "Stan Deloria was a classmate of mine," she said at last. "He's not young anymore." There was a weariness in her voice reserved for politicians and the subject of age. "And he's got heart trouble." She shook her head. "It might upset him."

"I don't want that," I said, relieved not to make the call. "If that's likely to be the way he'd take it, I'll find some other trail." I got up to go, but Vi did not respond, did not dismiss me, and I just stood in front of the chair.

Vi frets. She worries that Joe will get hurt in the river, that Karen or one of the kids will be injured on one of our projects. Perhaps because she is diabetic, she lives with a special sensitivity to the fragility of things. And, too, she thinks me irresponsible. She was convinced, when we were building our cabin, that I was endangering everyone in the family, and she kept her distance until the worst work was done. She thinks, I suspect, that I push Joe too far as well, encouraging him on adventures she believes seventy-five-year-old men should relinquish.

She shook her head, a slow deliberate shake this time. "Stan's a nice guy," she said. "Go ahead and call him." She turned from the TV to look directly at me. "Tell him you know Joe and me. Tell him you won't go in without his O.K."

Stanley Deloria didn't sound old or sick on the telephone. "Hell, yes," he said. "Nice of you to ask. Everyone else just plows the hell on in." He laughed. "Don't worry about the gate. Just a pole nailed to a couple of chunks of wood." He laughed again. "Supposed to look like posts, but you can pick the whole damned thing up like a sawhorse and move it aside." He pushed away my thanks. "There's a trail just below the camp that will take you close to the water, but watch it. Things get pretty swampy after that."

I thanked him again, but he was not ready to let me go. "It's O.K., O.K." He paused, then chuckled. "Some nice holes above my place." He paused again. "Used to be anyhow." He laughed at the memory. "Just park at my place, and you can fish upstream, then back. Make it easy on yourself."

I explained that I wouldn't be returning but would find my way out somewhere to the west, explained that I was trying to wade the length of the Run.

"Well, I'll be damned. Whatever made you think up a thing like that?" He didn't wait for an answer, or maybe he already knew the answer. "Hell of a crazy idea." But he said it with relish. "Good luck to you. Don't sink in one of those holes and drown." He laughed. "Don't know where the hell you're going to get out." He was still laughing when he hung up.

The road into Deloria's rises steadily, curving through the timber. The long grass rubs against my waders with a rasping sound and leaves them wet with dew. At the crest of the hill a big buck steps tentatively from the trees, its long, thin legs lifted and lowered with slow deliberation, until, seeing me, he freezes in mid-stride, right front hoof still raised. He watches me from under a broad rack of uplifted antlers, head high, carefully balancing his burden as we face each other in the gray light. I can see his nostrils, dark and flared, his large black eyes, can count the newly polished points: five on one antler, four on the other.

He drops the suspended hoof and turns without hesitation or hurry. Then, with a contemptuous gait, he ambles twenty feet away, flashes his white tail and lifts in one effortless leap over ruts and grass to the steep bank across the road. And he is gone.

Buddy Holly sang in Davenport, Iowa—just across the river from where we lived in Rock Island—a couple of nights before he died. A local radio station sponsored the show with Holly, the Big Bopper, and Ritchie Valens. I tried to get a job as an usher in order to see the performance for free, but the positions were already taken, and I never got inside the movie theater where Holly performed. I'm not sure why I wanted to go; I didn't date in high school, so it was not to impress a girl, and I didn't much like crowds even then. Perhaps it was because two winters earlier my family had taken the only vacation of my childhood, had gone to Texas to visit my aunt and uncle over Christmas, and there, out of the northern cold, I had driven around with Bob, a cousin one year older than I, and all the things I was not— witty, confident, popular—listening to the first Top Ten rock station I had ever heard. And mostly, driving along the bayous of east Texas, it was Buddy Holly, Buddy Holly and Sam Cooke ("Darling, you–ou–ou–ou send me") we heard. The Jeep and the warm night air, the freedom of it all, were what I thought growing up must be about, and drifting in and out, repeated hourly by a disk jockey with a generic disk-jockey name, was Buddy Holly's voice, bouncing like a high jumper's last strides through the lyrics of "Peggy Sue."

When, two winters later, his plane came down, I knew that no one could escape, not if Buddy Holly couldn't keep from crashing. Not long afterward Sam Cooke was also killed.

Deloria's camp, simple but well maintained, lies at the foot of the hill, and despite the apparent lack of traffic on the road in,

the clearing has been recently mowed. I know the cabin is unoc-
cupied, and yet I edge around next to the trees and as far from
the buildings as possible until reaching the alder thicket below
the camp.

I enter the Run somewhere below the bend where I stopped
on Tuesday, and walk downstream to find the tar-papered shack
and make sure of my location. The Run is completely overgrown
by alder branches, and, except for the improved footing the
gravel bottom provides, it is little different from the swamp
below Deloria's. But as I force my way east, I come to a familiar
set of rapids, and then the brush gives way for the camp on the
southern bank.

*Billy's camp is legendary. He has put considerable work into a
new building to house his tools and sauna. It is a large building
constructed on engineering principles that are not immediately
apparent, even from the inside where the rafters are exposed. It
is a place where he can lock up all the tools and machinery he
accumulates, but with typical generosity, he has told everyone
where the key is hidden so that we can use the sauna when he
isn't around. He built it on a slab, and when finished, he had a
good-sized batch of leftover concrete that he poured in front of
the cabin, an eight-inch-thick platform for his picnic table. It
looks like the top of a bunker, fully capable of withstanding a
nuclear attack.*

*Meanwhile his newly re-sided, repainted cabin—famous for
garter snakes that supposedly showed up in its bunk beds—has
a precariously slumping roof, badly in need of shingles as well
as reinforcement.*

*My first carpentering job came the summer between college
and graduate school when, with my father's help, I framed a
three-room apartment in an unfinished attic. It was a good expe-*

rience. Dad would come by in the evening after his own work to help me plan out the next day's labor, guiding me through the difficult stuff. Then during the day I would work by myself, putting in the studs and doorways for a bedroom, bath, and kitchen area.

Toward the end, however, I was not always alone. The apartment was for a woman, soon to be released from a state institution for the criminally insane, where she had been sent after shooting her husband to death while he watched television. Her daughters and grandson had, in the years of her confinement, become good friends with my family, which was part of the reason that the dead man's estate was paying me to make a place for the wife who had, downstairs in the same house, murdered him.

She came home before I finished the job, and sometimes in the afternoons would climb to the attic to watch me. My father and I had joked about what to do in case the mankiller didn't like my work, but she turned out to be simply a quiet, middle-aged lady with little to do, clearly lacking any enthusiasm for television.

Pushing hurriedly through low-hanging alder, I backtrack to the point above Deloria's where I began.

Fishing is impossible through here. Even when the brush opens briefly, there is no room for a backcast. Occasionally I try roll casting—something I've never seen done but once overheard a man who looked like a fisherman describe in a tackle shop—but as I swing the loop down the line, it grows increasingly sluggish until, at last, it either collapses under its own weight or barely nudges the fly beyond a limp leader.

Beneath a tall tamarack the stream widens into a large shallow pool. Sunlight gleams in the delicate needles of the tree, needles that will be sloughed off like leaves in the fall and that appear more fragile in midlife than the darker foliage of the evergreens.

In the tamarack's shade the water is dark, only the ripples reveal-ing the rocky bottom's presence. I roll cast to a cluster of rocks fifteen feet into the pool, and, amazingly, the loop runs down the line in a perfect O, sending the coachman smartly to the boulder on a fully extended leader. The fly barely touches against stone before it settles to the water and is immediately taken by a small trout. I release the fish and try another roll cast, but this time I throw the line too heavily and it staggers drunkenly, then col-lapses with the loop still four feet beyond the fly.

Writing up my notes for Tuesday the fourteenth, fighting the usual snarls of syntax, fighting to hook some life with every line, I realized how much digression has taken over my effort. And for all the self-consciousness I've brought to this work, all the commitment to composure, I am still unsure what exactly I hope to make. I started out intending to describe a place, a rather simple place at that—no Niagara or Yellowstone, just a run—to get it right and on its own terms. Of course I've seen the "I" in every line but wanted it to be a seeing I, an Emersonian I/eye that would deliver the subject to the pen, make of it, finally, a small "aye" of affirmation.

In the whaling industry a hunted whale was either a "fast fish" or a "loose fish." Any legal claim to that prey was based on being fast—fastened—to it. The whale at one end of the line belonged to the boat at the other, regardless of what party first saw or even harpooned the beast. A broken line meant loss of ownership perhaps for the whale as much as for the vessel that pursued it. Somehow my lines are holding—despite my complaining I can feel, at least some of the time, the play and tension of life—but I do not know to what I am fast. Surely every cast represents the desire to be hooked to something, but I still cannot say what is the object of that longing.

Perhaps this effort began as a sort of apology for not being better at killing trout, an offering of trees and flowers to replace the missing fish. But if memory first entered this account to break the routine, not just of fly-fishing but of the present tense as well, it has developed its own momentum and has grown in volume with a convergence of currents that must have been at work in me, unnoticed, for a very long time, currents that have carved channels and gouged out holes that I have never charted, and now stumble into with no more awareness than I have brought to much of the Run.

I am not at all sure this is a journey I am prepared for, not in these jury-rigged waders and with this inadequate gear. The original impulse behind my wade grew from the discipline of all those thin lines, the railroads and trails and pipelines and streams on my map, the narrow paths that lead forward and backward but to neither side, the narrow if not the straight which I promised to pursue. I am violating the discipline of the Run, and being tempted into the thicket that lies on either hand, an old vice that has frustrated my life and my career, and that I'd hoped in middle age to conquer. This wade was to focus rather than diffuse.

I have, in nearly all things, been unable to hold to the direct route and have drifted off course time and again, one project spilling into another endlessly. And more than my career. I am unable, have always been unable, to get my life in focus, to contain it in any meaningful way. I meant this venture to be different, to be orderly, one end to the other, from start to finish oriented on a specific goal. I intended to be the observer, not the observed, to be understood but not found out.

In Tuesday's rush upstream, during my search both for Deloria's camp and the fork above it, I must have come this far before heading back. Yet today the water is completely unfamiliar, and I still have not reached the Y. Upstream from the

tamarack pool, the Run widens even more. This must be where
I stopped on Saturday, the locating fork surely lies just above the
island. But things seem awry. I am in a washed-out beaver pond
(of which I've not the slightest recollection) with a narrow,
slow-moving channel entering from the north—the arm of the
fork which, on paper, continues for only a half mile or so before
giving way to a wash that is dry except after heavy rains and
spring thaws. The water to the south, the main branch according
to the map, is wider but motionless. I choose the stagnant water,
concluding that the other channel is merely a cutoff around a
still-concealed beaver dam. But there is no functioning dam, only
debris left from past flooding. In fact, this branch looks like some
old diversion, and not the main trunk of the Run at all. I turn
to the right, walking through a narrow cut that links the two
branches, and return to the thin trickle of water I had earlier
rejected.

*I should have recognized the risk of deflection, not just because
of a lifelong willingness to be diverted, but because nearly all
river books become, inevitably, books about memory. It was
Twain's capacity to remember the river that made him, in* Old
Times on the Mississippi, *a pilot, and years later those waters, two
decades removed, washed into his story with a power that disturbed even him. And Norman McLean's masterpiece,* A River
Runs Through It, *celebrates memory and above all its capacity
to re-member him with that which he had loved but had, temporarily at least, lost to time. Rivers always become memory.*

*But I am not sure what I want to remember or be re-membered
to. When, earlier in the summer, we took the kids to see the
University of Chicago, Elizabeth asked why we had not returned
before. In fact, Karen had often wanted to go back. The avoid-
ance had been mine. I tend to stay away from places once I have*

left them behind, and in the face of the question I recognized the uneasiness present in even this small return, the vague but haunting fear that I might somehow run into myself, the me I once must have been. It is not a fear of the person I might have become had I stayed in one of the old places—not the "other" self that haunts Henry James's "The Jolly Corner"—but of suddenly meeting the one I was, walking (ignorant of "my" existence) into a classroom or playing ball on the Midway. For some unexplainable reason it seems an encounter that must, at all costs, be avoided, one that would prove unbearably sad.

The map offers no satisfactory explanation of where I am. Either I've taken the wrong branch or have somehow missed the first fork altogether and reached a second where the runoff from a south-lying beaver pond flows into the mainstream. If it is the first case, then I should in another hour, at the most, lose the Run. If the latter, then all is well. The problem is, I've no idea which it might be. I hesitate and then continue north against the slight trickle that passes for a current.

I am not sure, given such a meeting, which of my selves I expect to be disappointed. Nor do I know the source of so strange a fear. Early on I developed a capacity to detach a part of me and in unpleasant moments let it stand aside and observe the pain from a distance. Perhaps that is a talent shared with everyone, but it is one at which I became proficient while still very young, so much so that in years of childhood dental work I hardly ever required novocaine. It was as though the work were being performed on someone else, and while I could hear the drill and smell the sick, sweet burning of pulverized tooth, unless my concentration were broken I need not feel the hurt. The same in fighting, another activity for which I had little talent; when the pain or the anxiety got too great, I reconstructed myself as the observer rather than the subject.

Maybe that duplicity lies behind my reluctance to go back to a place where I once belonged, and the suspicion that I could somehow, literally, be beside myself. Or maybe the real fear is not of redundancy but of the impossibility of ever being centered, something elusive enough in the singular, surely impossible in the plural.

Another turn and the water widens again as it cuts toward a ridge of popples. Even though the air seems motionless, distant leaves flutter gently, revealing their light undersides. Gradually the marsh narrows and the alders yield to higher banks of popple, tamarack, and white birch. I still doubt that I am on the main branch of the Run, but the higher ground, the lighter, almost festive, colors of the trees, are a welcome reprieve from the heavy atmosphere of the marsh. And as I move quickly through the shallow water, the current begins to pick up, the water slowly regains its voice, a low throaty gurgle as it breaks over stones.

The pattern in the vegetation continues, the thicket giving way on the steepest banks to timber, not defeated, only in a strategic retreat, waiting for the land to slip down once more, and with that loss of elevation the alder surges forward again in quick advance until, victorious, the ranks on one shore reach out in celebration to those on the other, completely shutting out the sky.

Beyond the alders the Run bends. And in the middle of the curve, water rushes in from another channel, this one creating a small island to the left. Then more water enters from the right, adding much to the stream's clamor if not to its volume. A few yards farther along, where the Run begins to straighten, the cause of these diversions appears: a three-and-a-half-foot-high beaver dam, itself a tangle of branches, that suggests the completion of an alder victory.

Above the dam a kingfisher perches five feet over the water on a broken elm. Its white throat and facial markings show clearly, and its crowning tuft sweeps back like an ineffectively combed cowlick. As I clamor clumsily onto the dam, he twists toward me, his eye a gleaming black pebble in an oversized head. He tilts his head to the side, then, chattering his aggravation, pushes off into flight. At his cry, three female mallards suddenly appear from the brush to add their protest and, thrashing their wings in aggravation, promenade upstream, rumps and heads held high like Victorian matrons passing a saloon.

On the way to Texas, in 1957, we stopped in Little Rock to see an army friend of my father's. Central High School had just been integrated and the National Guardsmen Eisenhower had called up to maintain order were still on the campus despite the fact that all the students were on Christmas break. The son of my father's friend was a year older than I, had his driver's license, and was eager to get away from the adults.

What I most remember is not the bizarre sight of uniformed troops patrolling the sidewalks around the vacant building, or the vehement attacks of my companion on the President and the few blacks who had entered his school, or the eerie play of spotlights on brick walls; mostly I remember the suede jacket, soft and supple, with knit cuffs and collar, that the boy had loaned me. At fifteen I coveted such a coat more than a class office or a varsity letter. In the bathroom, before we left the house and after I had carefully combed my hair back on the sides, as close to a ducktail as I could manage, I thought I looked grown up—at least like a senior.

In front of Central High School and in the presence of history, I listened to my companion's tirades, watched the uniformed figures, and wondered if my hair was still in place and thought it a great waste that there was really no one there to see me.

The beaver pond is huge compared to the narrow stream I've been wading. Here the ridges on both banks have fallen away, and in their valley water has been piled up a hundred feet wide and at least that far beyond the dam. Drowned alders and dead elm rise from the pool. No current is perceptible.

From the top of the dam there isn't any way to guess at depth. The water, black with silt, is unreadable, looks from this vantage point bottomless. I drop to a sitting position, then enter carefully, hips and legs pressed against the wall of tightly woven branches, feet pointed downward in search of solid footing. Just before the lower portion of my body disappears, I see that the largest patch on my waders is loosening, lifting around the edges like the perimeter of a frying egg, and I know it cannot hold much longer.

Next to the dam I find a sort of footing—though nothing to feel secure on—where, when I stand on tiptoe, the water stops its climb just below my wader tops; but as soon as I venture even inches away, the bottom drops quickly and the stream becomes unwadeable. Fly rod tucked under my right arm, and holding to the dam with my left hand, I work my way along its length in search of shallower water. Progress is slow because silt sucks at my feet, and without the leverage gained from my handhold I would be unable to wade even here.

The dam viewed from the less obstructed upstream side stretches like the Great Wall of China, wandering more than a hundred and fifty feet until it disappears in alders and high grass.

I work my way slowly to the brush on what looks to be the shallower end, then probe with the fly rod in an effort to gauge the depth of the water. Two feet from the dam there is a six-foot drop-off, and below that the bottom is soft with silt. I push my way into the alders and, clinging to their lower branches, make my way around the pool, shuffling my feet slowly along, continually testing the depth as I move through the silt, navigating chest-deep water beside a narrow ledge of dissolving bank. This is the only possible passage I can detect, and still there is no evidence of where the Run enters.

Absurdly, since I can barely keep the fly rod under my arm, I watch for a spot from which I can fish, even try a few feeble casts while hanging from the alders like a nervous child on a jungle gym (Sarah should be here to film this). All that breaks the surface is the swamp gas released with every step I take. Sometimes when my foot strikes a submerged branch, the sullen bubbles rise four or five yards away and sit, dark lumps held by the viscous surface, like grotesque toads protesting my passage. They are carriers of the stink that pervades this place, the cloying smell of rotting vegetation that I stir with every step. Where are the clean waters, the pure springs from which all good things are supposed to flow?

Always the issue is grace. But it is, for me, a confusing matter. This grace, the grace of line and language, is somehow earned, or at least follows discipline and labor. Granted, even then it seems miraculous when it comes—if it comes—but still it is somehow and to some degree the result of work. That other grace—that gift at once impossible to believe and yet the only thing worth believing—cannot be the reward of labor, must be undeserved and freely offered.

This is a notion very important to me, one which has dragged me through Martin Luther and Karl Barth, but one which I can only accept in the abstract, and then only for others. I cannot, for myself, distinguish cheap grace from any other kind. I cannot find a different hope, but neither can I wholly accept this one. So these other, less redemptive, lines, where the labor shows, represent all the hope of which I now am capable.

I momentarily give up on trout but realize that secretly I have been expecting a reward for this travail. Having left the usual fishing waters behind, I deserve some enormous brown, grown huge in isolation, to provide a fit conclusion, a moral for the story if not the life.

But perhaps trout do not matter anymore. No, that is sacrilege. Of course they do; they must. Rather I no longer know why they matter. Little time remains before I yield to fall and work, and there are enough fish in the freezer for one last meal. And while I talk about big trout, I am no trophy fisherman, can hardly imagine myself in a taxidermist's shop asking for some tarted-up replica to hang, perhaps with a barometer in its belly, a corpse on the wall. Maybe I want the fish that brings three wishes. But for what would I wish?

In the sixties a group of graduate students used to gather faithfully for the Miss America contest and wait especially for the climactic moment when the finalists, in testimony to intellectual and verbal dexterity, were interviewed.

"And what," asks a smiling master of ceremonies, looking like a cross between a kindly old uncle and a child molester, "would be your three wishes?"

"Oh," comes Miss Mississippi's breathless reply, "just world peace, religious toleration, and the conversion of the Jews. And"—this with a look of deep sincerity like that of the big-eyed children in dime store art—"if it's not asking for too much, a new bicycle for little cousin Bubba down at the orphanage."

Beads of water are working slowly but persistently inside my waders. *My* first wish is that we had let Korea go to the Communists. Then I'd be here with dry feet, and some Russian sewer worker would be bitching about his leaky overshoes.

The sky has darkened. More than just overcast, the air is heavy with the threat of rain. Forget the monster trout; forget longed-for epiphanies; it will be enough to get out dry, to stay above the surface, to get free of the silt, to keep out of the rain, to keep the patches on my waders. Little victories develop a sudden, wonderful appeal, and wishes get used up just in muddling through.

To make hiking easier when I eventually leave the Run, I am carrying a pair of old tennis shoes tucked inside my waders, the laces tied around the bottoms of the suspenders. A lace breaks and the shoes slip down into my right wader leg, making movement even more difficult. I try to pull them out, but every time I bend, no matter how slightly, water slips over the wader top. The thought of drowning while trying to catch up with a pair of runaway tennis shoes straightens me back up, and I leave them to burrow ever deeper, slow moving ferrets chewing at my leg.

The edge of the pond is erratic with alders jutting out in peninsulas, then giving way to fjords. When I try to cut across the narrow arms of water and grab at the next finger of humus, the bottom immediately drops away, and I lunge back to the precarious handrail provided by the last stand of alder and take the longer route. And because there are little islands of alder throughout the pond, I can never get a panoramic view, cannot see either width or length beyond a relatively small area. Only the distant ridges of timber locate me. Without them the maze would seem interminable. I'm not wading a stream but a god-damned metaphor, and somewhere God, borrowing John Wayne's voice, is saying, "Welcome, pilgrim, to the slough of despond."

At last, coming out of an isthmus and grabbing the next available bush, I think I see the inlet. Granted, it is indistinct and may be only another bulge in the pond, but in that direction the water does seem to narrow—and at a point where one might expect the Run to reappear. As I work closer, the slightest hint of a current becomes detectable. Not much. Nothing I can prove by looking at the water, but something subtle moving beneath the surface, felt rather than seen. And, too, the pool, which has been cold throughout, seems even colder now.

After hesitating a moment, still suspicious of the water's whimsy, I move ahead into the channel. The current remains invisible as the route between the alders continues to narrow, and I warn myself that this may only be one of many paths, part of an unpruned labyrinth. I am good at preparing for disappointment, but despite my best efforts I begin to feel like I am in a stream again.

Suddenly the alder falls back, revealing a wide marsh. The stream bottom rises, and big rocks break the water all around me. For a moment I am sure this is the dead end I've been approaching ever since the confusion above Deloria's, but then in the shallower water the current becomes undeniable, and, as I push on upstream, I hear rapids.

Something in this place reminds me of Kahlki's boatyard, more than twenty years and four hundred miles away, a family business dating back to the height of the riverboat industry but, by the time I was a boy, little more than a collection of rotting wrecks on the mud flats of the Mississippi flood plain, owned by the last, aged Kahlki. Old Fred used to come to church wearing a straight-brimmed hat and a rumpled brown suit, shoulders blanketed with dandruff and food stains down both lapels. His face was creased and pitted, blotched with huge blackheads and tufts of whiskers that popped up like water grass wherever he had lifted his razor prematurely. He never came into the sanctuary but sat in a hall off to the side, listening—or dozing—beneath a loudspeaker.

Fred loved old boats, paddle wheelers especially, loved calliopes and Texas decks and gingerbread trim, and for many years he ran a nickel ferry between Rock Island and Davenport, virtually in the shadow of a bridge, just to keep the business alive, just for the pleasure of it. The boatyard, overgrown and abandoned by all but the old man and the few boys who sneaked in to play among the relics, contained parts of old barges, rowboats, a broken-down keelboat, and, rising out of the weeds, ruling over the lesser wrecks, the W. C. Quinlan, *Fred's last paddle wheeler, its railings broken, decking rotted away, the great paddle wheel slumped to one side, but still majestic in its field of ragweed and Queen Anne's lace. My brother Jack loved the* Quinlan *almost as much as Fred, and he rushed down to photograph it when the big flood hit in 1965.*

I had always hoped the Quinlan *would someday, on a record-breaking crest of water, be lifted free, carried over the levee and into the river one last time. But even the '65 flood was not up to that, and not long afterward the* Quinlan *went up in flames, the fire set, it was rumored, by someone who had stolen the brass fittings and was eager to conceal the theft.*

The sky, though still clouded, has grown less threatening, and on that slight evidence I decide once again that I'm through the worst of it. Surely the difficult waters have been waded; surely good fishing and solid footing lie somewhere just ahead. Cabeza de Vaca, wandering in the sixteenth-century Texas wilderness, wrote later that he had held fast to the belief that if he continued on a western path, kept heading toward the setting sun, he would find the object of his desire. I do not remember his saying just what that object was, but in a sudden surge of enthusiasm I endorse his conviction, if not his example. There is no reason why this cannot still work out. I will bring Sarah to the stream after all. And Karen. One brief wade before it is over, and, though I expect the water will remain too deep for Elizabeth and Aaron, I can involve them some other way. They can all come to meet me at the headwaters, can take turns wading the trickle that will mark the stream's beginning. I am ignoring hard-won lessons, letting experience slide away in maudlin avalanches.

I know my tendency toward sentimental absurdity and, recognizing this one, try to turn it into parody before it gets away from me. I imagine the first Frenchman stepping over the Mississippi. Meriwether Lewis at the source of the Missouri. The mock heroic seems right. We will picnic on the headwaters of Cook's Run; a day to remember when the summer is gone. Even when the father is gone. It is out of control now, an airport paperback, a shameless "I Remember Papa." I imagine myself as I will appear to wife and children—a slit of eyes and nose between broken hat brim and grizzled beard; an old blue jacket with "Washington University" in small, cracked letters; and olive waders, sprouting lichenlike patches along the inseams—coming toward my waiting family as though I've emerged from beneath the surface. The ancient mariner, fearless challenger of creeks, at the end of his wandering.

I move ahead, sure after miles of uncertainty that this cannot be an intermittent stream but is in fact Cook's Run.

The stream runs lovely and straight through this valley, both banks now carrying flowers between the stands of alder, mostly drowned, and of elm, dead trunks slowly releasing their bark from long, silvered wounds. I cannot fix my location on the map because there is no evidence of the sun behind the gray clouds, and I do not know which direction I am facing. I swear to buy a compass before my next wade.

Fred Kahlki left a lot of money when he died. I heard, towards the end, he considered willing it to a waitress who used to serve him breakfast, but mostly it went to the church whose sanctuary he could never bring himself to enter. It was more money than the church had ever seen, and there were fights over how to spend it—conflicting wishes—and eventually the congregation split. The church kept running on Fred's money despite the loss of members.

God never intended Baptists to have money, intended for them, with the first arrival of wealth, to become Episcopalians.

I suspect the waitress would have done better with the inheri-
tance, being more properly trained in financial matters.
    I wonder what became of Buddy Holly's money. Who profits
whenever that dead voice sings "That'll Be the Day"?

Then it all seems over. Around the next turn I find another
dam, much taller than the last, if not so long. It rises like Grand
Coulee, and even without the bushes that grow from its top, it
is over my head. I cannot imagine how deep the water must be
on the other side, and, despairing, I stare at this latest obstruction.
How long, I wonder, will it take me to go back through the big
pond below. But, on closer inspection, the dam proves to be very
old and bears no evidence of recent maintenance. On this, the
downstream side is a gravel drift, the main channel swinging in
from the right through a break at the far end of the structure and
then paralleling the dam before straightening once more. At the
break the wall opens like a gate to an ancient city, both sides
decorated with raspberries and flowers as though for some trium-
phal entry. Beyond this opening the Run immediately doubles
back, paralleling the dam on the upstream side just as it had
below. All that is impounded is more sand and a meadow of dead
bushes and trees.
    Its tight loop completed, the Run climbs toward what I think
is the west, a high, timbered ridge on its left and a meadow,
sprouting from the ruins of a vast old beaver pond, on the right.
    Under a gray sky, I walk up an aisle of ruined saplings divided
by small clumps of alders and white flowers, the only color
provided by the appearance of an occasional goldenrod, rough
and dirty yellow.
    The water has deepened, but I can hear rapids ahead. I realize
that I am humming.

In our infancy my father used to rock each of his five children
to sleep, always with the same songs: "Yes We Shall Gather at

the River" with all of its schmaltzy nostalgia, but also, to keep things in perspective, "There Is a Fountain Filled with Blood" and "Birmingham Jail." I have been humming the first of these.

Wide but shallow and bottomed with fist-sized rocks, the Run curls back and forth, drifting close to the high southern bank and then away, coyly, toward the lower side of the valley. The water ahead glistens darkly where its rapids catch the light, but under-foot the stream is clear, revealing patches of water grass at the edges of each bend and little trout that dart from this shelter, tagging at the feathers of the fly, then following the retrieve all the way to my feet.

I forgot "Little Brown Jug"; my father also sang "Little Brown Jug," sang it in a breathy voice that bounced with the child riding astride his knee, or, if a baby were being serenaded, that slowed— "ho" (pause) "ho" (pause) "ho" (pause) "you and me"—paced by the breathing of an infant sliding into sleep.

I never sang much to my children, really only to Elizabeth in the days after her surgery, and then only folk songs inaccurately remembered. When I sang "The Riddle Song," I nearly always forgot how there could be a chicken without a bone and had to slur the words and rush on to the next line. Besides, they preferred the stereo to my rough voice, even to their mother's more disciplined and soothing music. Whenever Karen sang to him, Aaron would interrupt with "No sing, Mommy, no sing." And though she accepted the judgment without complaint, her feel-ings were always hurt by the rejection.

Somewhere among the spruce that have taken over the ridge, birds begin to sing, and at the same moment the sun breaks through, catching alike the dark needles high up the slope and the long, bent-over strands of yellow-green grass beneath the water.

Willows appear on the bank, their pale, fluttery branches positioned like curtains, cloaking the entrances to several of the animal trails. Fresh beaver cuttings line the shore beneath the willows, and a small inlet enters from the right. Noise from the rapids around me covers any sound from the spillways of a dam, but, after the past two, I grow apprehensive, convinced another lies ahead.

And I find it around the next bend, but a manageable one, no more than two and a half feet above the water, complete with a pool that is conveniently narrow and only about twenty feet long: a nice pool, fishable, but completely lit by the sun, which has broken free of all cover and shines directly, shadowing a man Emerson could have been proud of. Twenty feet upstream, this beaver, or some other, has begun construction on another dam, an insurance policy or, perhaps, a place for the children. The work is recent, the gnawed-off stumps still yellow, veined with red; and the leaves, still firmly in place, have only just begun to wilt.

Four years ago I taught, for the fall semester, at the University of Copenhagen. Sarah, fretful that she would slip behind her American classmates, enrolled in an international school across town, but Elizabeth and Aaron went to the neighborhood school a short distance from our apartment on the harbor and within the shadow of a church with a tall spiral tower. Aaron was seven, the age Danish children begin their education, and Elizabeth was nine.

Often on my way to the University I'd walk them across the canal and down the cobblestone street to school. Japanese tourists, from the buses that parked in front of the Church of Our Saviour, often stopped us to ask permission, politely and in carefully worded English, to photograph Aaron. In contrast to his sister and father, very blond and very shy, he seemed—at least to these other foreigners—the image of Danishness. He never objected but stood serenely with his back to the church or to one of the boats on the canal, and as they crouched before him, focusing their visit on this one child, let them picture him as Scandinavian, a character perhaps from an Andersen tale.

Above the dam the water, waist-deep along the banks, divides either for another fork or an island. Ahead is the noise of more and grander-sounding rapids. I choose the branch to the right and find another dam. This, too, is a recent creation but larger, longer than the last, at least forty feet. Its impounded water is slowly submerging a meadow, and because the alders have not yet drowned, this seems more the site of a flood than a pond. Still relatively free of silt, still relatively shaded, the pool should be a good trout hole, but the brush, which makes it so, also makes fishing difficult. Repeatedly I cast and snag, working my way upstream among clumps of half-submerged alder and dying marsh grass, untangling my leader first from one and then the other.

Aaron played on the local soccer team, a comic arrangement where his coach, one of the few Copenhagen Danes who did not speak English, would call instructions to him in Danish, always pronouncing his name "Herren." Since this was September, shortly after our arrival, Aaron never had any idea what he was being told to do. And so he would look to the sideline and to me, who knew nothing either of soccer or of Danish. The coach then would address us both, speeding up his words and adding elaborate hand gestures.

"Do something," I would instruct my son.

"But what?" he would mouth in embarrassment.

"Something you are not doing now," I would reply. Sometimes those strange instructions would satisfy him, and he would do something different. His coach, pleased with all our progress, would smile happily and clap his hands in approval of both the father and the son.

But the close of soccer season did not end Aaron's language worries. Sometime in November he became troubled and, when questioned by Karen and me, informed us that he had forgotten how to speak English.

"But," I reassured him, "you are speaking English now."

"No," he insisted, "I am not. This is Denmark, and I am speaking Danish."

We continued to offer reassurance, pointed out that we too were living in Denmark, and we were speaking English.

"But see—" his exasperation with our thickheadedness growing stronger by the minute—"you are older! You can still remember."

Behind me a beaver enters the pool with all the grace of a belly-flopping fat man. I turn in hope of glimpsing him before, seeing me, he dives. But he does not dive. Instead he slaps his tail angrily and paddles across the pool toward me, his huge head splitting the water like the prow of a tug. I am surprised, as I am every time this happens, by the animal's size, and I watch his approach warily, his dull black eyes staring at me, his fur glistening as the water beads off head and back. He must know I am a wrecker of houses.

When I first started wading and encountered a beaver like this, I was always intimidated. The unswerving path of approach, the unblinking eyes, the great teeth which, even concealed, are evident from the very structure of the head, all this made me increasingly nervous until, at last, the beaver would dive. Each time there came a momentary surge of relief, satisfaction that the animal had finally made out what I was and had been properly put in his place. But then I would think of those jaws beneath the surface, moving freely in the pool's murk, somewhere in the vicinity of my legs. It did not lessen the dis-ease of such moments when Joe told me, with barely contained glee, that beaver deal with trespassing kin by castrating them with their teeth.

As this one draws to within ten feet of me, he at last dives, slapping his tail in one final show of protest and authority, a judge's gavel against a watery bench.

There are, amidst the alder clumps and not yet submerged by the deepening pond, stands of joe-pye weed and daisies, blossoms just above the surface so that they seem to be sinking, drawn into their own liquid images—except that when I look more closely, what I had thought reflections are real joe-pye weeds, real daisies that have already been covered by the fast-rising pool.

The children were drawn to different aspects of Copenhagen. Sarah liked the freedom, the fact that she could take trains and buses or walk in the city with a classmate. Aaron liked the castles and churches, was most pleased by a night in the cathedral at Roskilde, the burial church for Danish royalty, where we were taken round by a limping sexton who led us in lantern light over the vaulted ceiling of the vast sanctuary, pointing out roofing timbers blackened by a centuries-old fire.

But for Elizabeth the great attraction was the mummified remains of a young girl on exhibit at the National Museum just a few blocks from our apartment building. Cut from a fen by peat gatherers, there was a delicacy to her preserved clothing, her surviving hair, even her leathery skin. Unlike Egyptian remains with their museum vagueness—a humanity expressed only, at least to the layman, in a generic manner—this was clearly a person with an individuality that had outlived her, some Iron Age princess sacrificed to the greater good and the Danish bog, but who would still be recognizable were there friends to remember features that had retained their fineness over the centuries.

Elizabeth made up stories about her, returned to her the life she'd lost so long ago, and visited her regularly. Despite our fears of bad dreams and morbid thoughts, her visits seemed always happy, oddly reassuring.

The depth here threatens to submerge more than daisies, is already great enough that I must stay on tiptoe, and, even then, an irregular trickle of water breaks over my wader tops, joining the Korean contribution. The pond has grown darker, siltier, and flecks of tiny debris mar the submerged blossoms like motes of dust on old photographs. And minnows are everywhere, swirling around my waders, swimming through the daisy fields.

The ridge on my left, beyond which my hoped-for logging road is supposed to lie, has begun to drop. It is not supposed to. Rather, it should be rising, eventually to support a stand of jack pine. But it declines this honor, and I cannot tell by the map where I am or how far away my exit point lies.

A plane appears to the south, a line of silver against the sky. It is not a fighter or a bomber, is apparently a passenger plane, though I cannot imagine the destination that would bring it along this route. Perhaps it is bound for Minneapolis to the south and west, but what could have brought it this far north? It seems hardly to move, rather to hang like a plane in a dream or an old movie, one waiting for the drama to build before it begins its final descent.

I have contradictory reactions to planes, am often reluctant to fly, fret for hours before departure, and yet am drawn to that moment of expectancy when the plane rounds over some strange city,

drifts down slowly filled with the promise of arrival. When I was
young and doing the greater part of my flying, planes seemed to
take their landings more seriously than now, brought to that
moment a proper hesitancy rather than hurtling to the pavement
with the impatience of an attacking hawk. I remember, as though
from a dream, hanging in the dawn air, already hot and heavy,
over Delhi, the weary descent into a Tehran dusk, the palpable
Aegean light over Athens. The planes lingered, allowed the im-
port of the moment to settle in, as I approached some new place
with fear and expectation—Mexico City, Rome, Bangkok,
Hong Kong, Tokyo—places no longer real to me, the settings
only for books or other people's lives. Subsequently, as revolu-
tions or earthquakes or terrorist attacks brought such cities onto
the television screen, I have wondered at all the anguish that in
my egocentric youth I must have ignored and that in egocentric
middle age I try to set aside. And not just the grand tragedies of
flood and famine, but all the dreary little disappointments that
build like coral wherever there are human beings.

In the worst stages of my flying phobia, I could not give up
my fear, so convinced was I that that my anxiety alone kept the
plane suspended and that even a momentary lapse would allow
the craft to plummet beyond hope. Now I suspect it was the pain
somewhere below, rising to meet our wings, that held us aloft
and slowed the descent to every city.

This plane, banking to the north, is not an airliner but an Air
Force transport, its star now visible in the morning sun.

Now, with every cast, the fly returns, followed only by chubs,
sometimes seven or eight inches long. The little trout have disappeared, and above a sort of wing dam the beaver has constructed,
the Run narrows further. Still waist-deep, its bottom is paved
with irregular-sized rocks, basket-big and larger, that make the

walking difficult. In many ways it has taken on the aspect of the old Run, the one near Basswood.

I was nineteen when I went to Delhi. The all-night flight began in Iran. A British businessman who sat across from me in the terminal kept saying, "Ah, Tehran, dusty jewel of the Orient," whenever he caught sight of another English speaker, and at the time I thought that a fairly impressive phrase to have turned, though one that perhaps did not require so many repetitions— and continued nonstop through an incredible span of darkness. The British Overseas Airlines flight also carried the mail, two bags of which had been stowed on the seats separating me from the aisle, and after the cabin lights had been extinguished, I leaned against other people's messages and watched the unbroken dark below.

We arrived in Delhi at dawn, and while it was nearly Novem-ber, the air we entered was hot, heavy with strange, thick smells. In time I became used to the place, no longer wondered how many of the bodies lying at dusk around the Red Fort were still living, and I walked a good deal in Old Delhi, always by myself but never alone. The children picking up cow manure, the narrow-gauge trains with bulging smokestacks, the sari-clad women perched like medieval maidens on the backs of motor scooters, the shimmer of flames at the burning ghats—these all seem like photographs to me, not events that happened, but things I saw in some old magazine. My memories slow with time until, at last, they freeze. I wish I could reanimate them, give them some semblance of life, but no matter how I try, the boy bent over his strange harvest never straightens, the toylike train always approaches but never arrives, the silk sari stretches backward but is not moved by any breeze, the flames forever hold position around their dead.

The ridge disappears completely as the land flattens on both sides of the Run. A few brown butterflies appear, and then, past a small inlet and a series of riffles, the marshy ground on the right becomes a daisy-flecked meadow, occasionally showing the colors of the season's last black-eyed Susans. Three more inlets break into the stream, as bright and noisy as truant kindergartners, but around the next bend, I find their source behind yet another dam, one considerably higher than the last.

On the Paint this time of year, I fish below all dams with special care, hoping to catch the trout that wait among the branches for a sudden rise of water and passage over the obstruction into the shallow breeding grounds upstream. Here, too, I cast the fly close to the dam, trying to provoke some response from any life hidden in those dead limbs. No large trout appears, but the pool is thick with three-inch minnows that glitter as they catch the light.

We drove from Copenhagen to the end of Jutland in late November, on our way to tour Norway and Sweden. The car ferry took four hours to cross to Kristiansand, and shortly after leaving port—and alas, eating dinner—we were hit by a winter storm raging in off the North Sea. Sarah, during the early stages of turbulence, had wandered off, had, I discovered, climbed to the upper deck despite the growing wind and dark. She had gone outside in hopes of walking off a growing queasiness and sense of claustrophobia which I too felt by the time I found her. Within minutes of our return to the passenger salon, the storm worsened, as did the physical discomfort until we and nearly everyone else were thoroughly sick.

Two hours into the crossing, an ordeal of violent dizziness and recurrent, gut-wrenching vomiting, and with the ferry lurching and groaning, for all apparent purposes out of control, Aaron asked fearfully if we were going to sink. Sicker than I had ever been before, so sick I had lost interest in everyone and everything but my own discomfort, I said, "Oh, God, I hope so." Later, warned away from the high pass east of Bergen, we contemplated returning the way we came, but the kids refused even to consider another ferry crossing, preferring, they unanimously declared, falling off a mountain to four more hours of seasickness.

As the Run swings back to the south, the ridge begins, much to my relief, to assert itself once more. If I am making the right calculations, an increasingly difficult task due to the lack of any discernible pattern in my watch's more recent improvisations, it is now 10:30, two hours before I'm to meet Karen, and I want to allow an hour for the hike out. But the land to the left continues to rise encouragingly. Instead of flattening, as I had feared, the ridge had only swung farther south and out of view. Now it closes quickly, and spruce begin to appear on the bank, some of them touching water with the base of their trunks. Deep pools have gathered in their shade. I cast into the shadow of the timber, and trout break the water, sometimes taking the fly, but they are uniformly small. Even next to the bank in the favored places, little fish are in command.

The scent here, after the sour smell of the beaver ponds and the contradictory aromas of decay and flowers drifting through the flooded meadows, comes fresh and clean with a crisp sweetness that tingles in my nose. I linger in the shadow of the ridge, casting lazily, changing flies, then back again. I assume that I am close to my exit, assume even that I can at any time climb the ridge and walk south until I strike the logging road. To be sure, on a whim, I climb onto the bank, lean my net, creel, and fly rod against a spruce, and start up the hill.

At the crest, I face what seems to be the ultimate dam—longer, higher, thicker than all the others. For a moment, coming out of the timber into a clearing, dazzled by the bright light, and dislocated by this huge dam, I am confused. The wall of limbs twists along the ridge in both directions as far as I can see, separating the spruce on the hillside from raspberry bushes and seedling popples on the summit: a fortress, the wall for some unbuilt city. These are, I finally realize, the tailings left by loggers, bulldozed into this long rampart and left behind to face out over the Run and the marshes beyond.

When the logging contractor that Terry Schreiber had been working for—Terry had subcontracted the logging and skidding—fouled up the Forestry permits, the Government sealed everything Terry had cut, cordoned it off, and would not allow it to be sold. He was worried about his equipment, newly purchased and requiring huge payments, worried that if he did not move it quickly, it too would be held by the officials. Late one evening we drove his truck to the logging site and picked up the skidder.

Terry is quiet, intense, and sees and hears everything that goes on around him, then keeps it to himself. Some evenings he would come by our place and wait at the back of the lot, leaning against his truck, until I walked out with a couple of beers. Sometimes we talked, often we just stood there and drank. Like many loggers, Terry reads a lot, and sometimes we talked about books. Sometimes we talked about trout or game. His is not so much a sportsman's interest as that of a naturalist. He studies trout or deer or bear or partridge or mosquitoes because they interest him, thinks about them as though they are part of a great puzzle whose pieces are strewn around him, and he in his lifetime has to get them all assembled in the proper arrangement.

In the truck, on the way to the skidder, he hinted that with the collapse of the pulpwood market and the high interest on his equipment loan we might be retrieving the machine for his creditors rather than himself. He let it out casually, then went on to something else, quickly and before another long silence.

"Somebody will be buying soon," I said but without conviction.

"Yeah," he agreed, "but everything is changing. Nothing's what I thought it would be." Another silence. "Why," he asked, "did you become a professor?" He made it two words—"pro fessor."

"I don't know," I answered, "it just happened."

"To tell the truth," he went on, "you never seemed like a professor to me." He laughed. "Who would ask a professor to help you steal your own skidder out of the woods in the dark?"

"I don't seem like a 'pro fessor' to most of the people I work with either." Another silence. "To tell the truth," I added, "you've always seemed a more likely 'pro fessor' to me, a biologist maybe."

He laughed again. "Maybe I could teach those city kids over at the forestry camp." He said it self-consciously, as though both pleased and embarrassed by the thought. Then, "Not me. Not me at the beck and call of every little bastard who can afford tuition." He paused a long time, then added, "But odd that it's you either."

A short time later, unable to keep up with the payments, he lost the skidder, and eventually he went to Alaska to take a job on a road crew. That winter, before he left, he sent me a card. There was a short sentence asking me to watch for a book he wanted. Then, "More than five feet of snow on the ground at Houghton. The grocery stores are all cleaned out, but don't worry, the National Guard is airlifting beer by helicopter."

Reassured that a trail must lead from these clearings to the road sketched on my map, I decide to continue wading for another

forty-five minutes, perhaps to the stand of jack pine that report-
edly marks both the end of the ridge and the termination of the
logging trail. It is now 11:10, Fields Adjusted Time.

I scramble back down the ridge and, after a brief search, find
my fishing gear. It is a relief to get back into the water after the
sweaty climb, but I don't delay, am eager now to cover as much
ground as possible before quitting for the day

*I cannot say why I became a college teacher, or why, now that
I am one, I don't work harder at being successful. Joe once told
me, after two martinis and a couple of brandies, self-pitying and
yet self-mocking too, "If I hadn't become a fly-fisherman, I
would be somebody today." He shook his head slowly. "The
river can wash your life right by you. Everybody else keeping
their eye on what's ahead, and you looking down into the water."
I had just started fly-fishing, and, I suppose, the speech was
something of a warning, but it also sounded like an invitation.*

*I think I may have become a teacher because I was afraid of
my own ambition, an all-consuming need to be important that
drove me throughout my late teens and early twenties until,
terrified by my capacity for manipulation and demagoguery, I
slipped into the classroom, an English teacher, harmless. I exhausted my old obsession—now a kind of wrath—on the basketball court or by cutting brush or building and demolishing cabins.
Sometimes I think I've defeated it, that the unfinished manuscripts, the stunted career, represent a victory, and then I feel it
rise, lazily, in my gut and chest like an animal stretching after
a winter's hibernation, and the old fears return.*

*But probably not that at all. I probably became a "pro fessor"
because it represented steady employment in contrast to what my
father labored at, or because it leaves so much free time on my
hands. Or more probably because there was a fellowship and*

nothing better to do, and then a job and no need to consider alternatives. Why did Terry become a logger, and now a construction worker? I think he knows how easily we might have exchanged places.

When Sarah's third-grade teacher asked her class to declare their vocational plans, she was troubled by Sarah's answer, troubled enough to call Karen and me with her concern. Our daughter it seemed, surrounded by prospective surgeons, engineers, and astronauts, wanted to be a shoe salesman, and when asked why, explained, "It seems like easy enough work."

There is always that possibility as well.

Around the next bend—a swing away from the ridge—I strike another dam, and when I stand on its back another dam is visible thirty yards ahead, and above that one, yet another. They rise like liquid terraces or a series of locks, each holding water whose surface level rises impressively above the water preceding it. On the banks all the alders and willows have been stripped and killed. Sharpened sticks jut out threateningly where bushes once grew. Nothing offers shade. So much for the idea that the worst is all behind me; so much for cheap grace. Above yet a fourth dam, a beaver paddles out from the shore. He seems lopsided, swims unevenly with the right side of his body slightly lower than his left, and even his head bulges oddly. I try to account for his strange look—has he been struck by a limb or caught in the twist of his own cut?—but give up. There are too many possible explanations with a creature that chews down trees for a living.

In the years after the war the great anguish of my father's life was the lack of regular work. It was hard for the rest of us, the constant uncertainty about money, the frequent moves as we looked for a place and a job. But the greatest burden fell on him. He and my mother are proud to a fault and expected a good deal more of themselves. Like Billy, like Terry, they had plans. They also had a growing family, a family more demanding than their pride.

It was not so difficult for me and my younger brothers and sister, there were others like us in the towns and housing projects in which we spent those years, but the pain was evident in our young parents, the pain of insecurity and of humbling circumstances.

For a time my father worked seasonally on a road crew, moving along the blacktop highways of Iowa. As the road moved so did we, and at each new town he would take Sunday morning off to relocate, taking us all to the local Baptist churches, small, unaffluent congregations. At the end of the service he would stand, clear his throat for attention, and ask if anyone had a spare room to rent.

Usually, after a season of other people's second floors, we would return to my grandparents for the winter, but one year, my first in school, we—my mother, Jack, and I—remained in a little house at the edge of New London, Iowa, while Dad hitch-hiked west, looking for work in Nebraska and Utah. All he found were brief stints, usually selling things, that paid little more than enough to get him to another place and to send a few dollars home. He was gone for what seemed to me a long while, and I worried about him, used to think each day on my way back from school that this time he would be there when I got home. When he did come back he seemed to me very tired and much older. He was, I think, twenty-nine.

Halfway through this pool I hear the roar of water from the next dam, a deeper, throatier call than that emitted by any of the four behind me. I walk cautiously, intent only upon getting to the next hurdle, convinced it will be followed by yet another. There is a slight turn, and then the fifth dam, the biggest in the series and holding more water than all four of its predecessors combined. Even on the downstream side the water is chest-high. I fish here both for the delay and in the halfhearted hope of big trout from water so deep and yet so thoroughly areated by the dam's turbulence. On my first cast I snag a loose stick and tow it back, dragging water like a sideways canoe. I try again in the other direction. Once more the line snags, and this time I am forced to wade over and free the fly by hand.

Giving up, I mount the dam, dig in with fingers and knees as though climbing a sandstone bluff. At the top my foot breaks through the limbs, and I have to work it back and forth to get loose, all the time concerned about the damage I may be doing to the waders and their constantly weeping patches. Once freed from the dam's clutches, I attempt to measure the pool's depth in my usual way, but the fly rod will not touch bottom even when I grasp it at the very end like a baseball captain winning first choice. The water is dark, but I ease in, holding to a large limb thrusting out from the dam.

I stop, still not touching bottom, just as the water threatens to pour into my waders, then feel my way along the dam until I strike a ledge of branches with my feet. But when I let my weight down, this foothold gives way to a soft, sucking mire, and before I can check my descent, water rushes over the wader tops with a smug slurp. I pull myself back up and, face and body pressed tight against the dam, slide along, hand over hand, edging left toward the higher ground that still lingers behind the once more departed ridge. I tow a creel filled with water and shoes, a millstone around my neck and shoulder, and adding to my discomfort, a cramp seizes the hand in which I grasp the fly rod. I clamp the rod between my teeth and flex my fingers in an attempt to undo the knotting muscles. Now my teeth hurt, too.

The jagged remains of a willow serve for a handhold as, at last, I venture gingerly away from the dam. Even here on the pool's high side, I take in water, but if I move steadily, not allowing my feet to settle too deeply into the muck, and cling to the growth that remains on this edge of the pond, I can make a kind of progress upstream.

I think it was in the New London house that I got in the habit of staying awake and checking on everyone before I went to sleep. In the small houses in which we then lived, sleeping in adjoining rooms or even the same room, I could tell by the sounds of their breathing who was asleep and who awake, could tell by the degree of raspiness in Jack's low snore when he was coming down with another bronchitis attack. My parents worried about my late hours and once took me to a doctor who thought the problem had originated with my dog and so wormed the both of us with a foul-tasting tonic.

It is a habit, though nearly broken by the worm medicine, that has stayed with me.

Slowly, as the Run turns back toward the ridge, the shore rises, becomes an impenetrable wall of undergrowth but one that offers plenty of things to grab onto. There is, briefly, a slope steep enough that I am moving along a cut-away bank, wading in chest-deep water, balancing on mud, and hanging to branches that stretch out above my head so that at times my feet are completely suspended and all my weight is carried by my arms. Despite the compromised position, I occasionally clutch a limb with one hand and toss short, looping casts with the other. No matter that this is absurd—how could I land anything that did take the fly?—the water looks perfect here, shaded by spruce branches and deep enough for big browns. If there is a God with a single ounce of American Middle Class blood in His veins, something worthy will come of this. I do catch two trout, but neither is a brown and neither is big. I manage their release by jamming the fly rod into my waders, grasping the hook in the same hand that clutches the branches, and removing the fish with the other. But these waters belong mostly to chubs, and, when not yielding the prize to a three-inch brookie, they tug at the fly in their stupid way.

When she was twelve and on spring break, Sarah asked to attend one of my classes. I was teaching a Twain course that semester and told her she could come if she read Life on the Mississippi, *the work we were scheduled to discuss that week, and one that, after a brilliant beginning, is long and often tedious.*

On the day of the class she came to breakfast dressed for her outing. I quizzed her and confirmed that she had actually read the entire book. At eleven o'clock she biked to campus, entered the classroom, and wearing an expression of unrelenting seriousness sat quietly for the next hour.

The class, both large and vocal, performed well, and when the students filed from the room, I asked Sarah if she would like to go to the Student Union for lunch. "I think I'd better go home," she replied. "We could talk about the class," I suggested, but she insisted on returning to the house.

All afternoon I fretted about her judgment of my work, wondered how I had disappointed her, and that evening I brought up the subject once more, asking her what she thought of the experience. "You were pretty interesting," she said, "but do you know you repeat yourself a lot?" I swallowed and composed a look of fatherly understanding, then explained how important repetition is in teaching. "Oh," she said. And then, "There is one other thing." "What?" I asked eagerly. "Do you—" she shaped the question with great care—"do you think you ought to be teaching a book in college that a twelve-year-old can read?"

The ridge backs off once more, and the shore I've been clutching grows increasingly uneven. I move toward the center of the pool, picking my way along the highest, firmest ground I can locate but, even so, take in little dribbles of water with every step. Another bend, this one easing back toward the ridge, and once more a dam and, to the north, a huge beaver meadow. Bleached-out huts are scattered through the marsh grass, and I can see the ruins of more dams ahead. The dam I face is also broken, but the water level in its pond remains high, and the bottom has the consistency of pudding. It is like walking in a dream, sinking slowly, unavoidably. The Run enters my waders in gulps now, and I pull myself from the edge of the stream onto a dry, uncluttered point at the base of the ridge.

I cannot guess what lies ahead. For a while at least, the ridge offers support, and as long as the Run parallels it I have something to cling to. But the marsh, the deteriorating stream bottom, even the little upheavals on the mud bars visible ahead, seem ominous. I look at the yellow flowers growing where the higher ground breaks briefly into the beaver swamp, then upward at the sky, as bright and clear and blue as a June morning.

But it is nearly over.

There are no butterflies. I hear no birds. Only the heavy smell of mud and rotting grass comes across the marsh that awaits me.

Yesterday I agreed to return to St. Louis two days earlier than planned, promised to be back in the office on the twenty-third.

On the map the ridge dies in less than half a mile; the Run turns north, then, with a big elbow, enters its last couple of miles in an area covered by the blue, bristly symbol of marshlands. Even before the elbow there are far more of these prickly lines than on any of the stream I've walked today. And not just along the stream; they appear rank on rank as the valley broadens, like a drawerful of false eyelashes dumped on the paper.

A college friend, one who wanted very much to please his father, a father who wanted very much to have a doctor for a son, discovered in his third year that he had lymph cancer. As a sophomore he had changed his major from chemistry to English, dropping from the premed program in the process, but had not told his family. Now, directed by his doctors to avoid exposure to chemical fumes, he was relieved not to lie anymore about his college courses. "Not such a bad deal," he said, "no worse than having to become a doctor."

He finished college after another change in majors, this time to psychology and, with the disease in remission, married and went to graduate school. He had, during all of this, discovered his vocation and hurried through his academic program in record time in order to begin his life's work. The year he finished his Ph.D. his holiday letter joyously announced that he had been cured, referred to his new life with eager anticipation, something neither he nor his wife had dared express in the past.

Two years later we got word of his death, of how the disease or the medication or something else had attacked his lungs, made breathing difficult, at times nearly impossible, and of how in a particularly bad attack he had panicked, rushed to the airport, and begun a southwest journey, getting off one flight and, when breath came no more easily in this place than in the last, rushing to another, kept on until, in the end, he collapsed in an Arizona airport and died, alone in a strange place, never finding the relief he so desperately sought.

When I first heard that he was dead, Simon and Garfunkel's "Bridge Over Troubled Water" was playing. Just as it had played on the morning I carried a jack-in-the-box to a comatose daughter.

Beside the bank leopard frogs show their eyes and snouts above the water, their bodies colored like camouflage. Chub minnows swirl mindlessly at my feet. I look for something more amusing, thinking perhaps the dowager mallards will be in this pool, but there is nothing, the only sound that of the wind as it comes upstream, sweeping everything toward the wide waters ahead.

One of the best books about memory is Thomas De Quincey's Confessions of an English Opium-Eater, *where the narrator learns to fear his waking experiences because of the oppressive power these take on when they return to him in an opium dream. The thought of the terrible implications the present may have when so remembered becomes maddening. As an artist he gains a significant victory—gains it in the very crafting of his story—over the awful forces at work in his life, but the darker lesson should not be forgotten, the price of that victory not be ignored.*

I don't know that P. J. Martin ever read De Quincey, but he once tried to deliver a similar message to me. P. J. came into my life when I was in ninth grade, came from the high school where he coached debate to find someone for a speech contest. He found me, helped me write an "oration," rehearsed me, and sent me off on my first plane flight and to my first hotel. In my turn I stood before a roomful of middle-aged men and repeated the words and gestures I had learned. When it was over they gave me a silver trophy and put me on another plane.

P. J. kept me on the debate team through high school. He was a small man, neat and balding, a man of almost quaint dignity and manners—a kind of reserved old uncle who seemed simultaneously fond of and exasperated by his adopted nephew. He had no family that I knew of and lived at the YMCA.

Once—I don't now remember the occasion, but I can see the look of seriousness, the hand brushing the carefully groomed remains of hair back against the sides of his head, and hear the gently formal tone of voice, each word precisely enunciated—he

told me something that had been told to him half a century earlier
by another old man offering advice to the young. The man had
said that memory could become, as one got older, a terrible thing,
that bad things done in the security of youth, things that seemed
negligible at the time, grew in significance over the years. P. J.'s
face filled with melancholy, and he continued, describing a
frightening paralysis that would come, sometime in the middle
of the night, sometime in middle age, when the ghost of an
ancient sin would rise from the dark pool of sleep and self. He
shook his head sadly, perhaps aware of the inevitable futility of
the warning, and said, "Nothing ever goes away. Everything,
sooner or later, finds you out."

Out of the Run, I pull off my waders and take the wet sneakers
from my creel. The shoelaces are rotten and one of them breaks.
I tie it back together. It breaks again and I tie another knot,
relacing the left shoe so that the lowest eyelets are empty. I've
not worn them for two or three years, and even wet they feel
stiff and scratchy.

A faint trail climbs the ridge, and when I reach the top and
turn, I can see out over the entire meadow. The water looks
unmoving, the huts abandoned, the mud upheavals evidence of
munition fire. Yet there is fresh evidence of beaver all along the
ridge: big popple felled and stripped so recently that the wood
still shines.

A quarter mile past the fortress of logging debris the rutted
trail forks, and I turn into a grove of maples, tall trees with
foot-thick trunks, the air beneath them less sticky, less burdened
with resin than that under spruce and pine. The trail divides
sharply here, a branch entering from the woods on the left,
another, the one I choose, swerving abruptly to the north into
a stand of infant popples, then forks again. And since it is a toss-up
as to which is the less traveled, I go to the right past mounds of
pulpwood, abandoned to decay after the last forest was cut. Away

from the heavy timber, the day grows hot, drenching my shirt in sweat. The waders hang awkwardly over one shoulder, held in place by my left hand while my right carries the fly rod, butt first. With every step, the net and creel slap away at either side. It is like a scene from a children's book or maybe an old movie—a bedraggled figure trudging through an open field along an overgrown road somewhere between two forests in the middle of nowhere.

I try to check directions by the sun. But it is too close to noon, and I cannot decide which is the east-west line. Once again I swear to buy a compass and try to remember how far to the south the sun falls in August.

I do not have a compass because I find it nearly impossible to spend money on anything that can be done without. I have at my parents' house a perfectly good—or so I remember—Boy Scout compass, a gift from thirty years ago. It would be wasteful to duplicate it just because it is four hundred miles away.

Of course this is absurd, but where money is concerned I am inclined toward absurdity. I carried a homemade wooden creel slung from a piece of clothesline my first five years of trout fishing, lugged around five pounds of extra weight that within minutes was cutting deeply into my shoulder, rather than add to the expense of a self-indulgent hobby which could never pay for itself. Eventually Karen found a wicker creel on sale and brought it home, but even then I delayed until the next year spending the additional four dollars for the harness to hang it on. The same logic leads me to put new clothes away for months or years (usually until they are no longer in style) so as not to wear them out before I truly need them. In stores I bypass the checkout line, finding an excuse to go somewhere else while Karen pays for the groceries. I do not think of myself as miserly. I do not find pleasure in accumulating money, but there is something deeply troubling to me about the act of spending, about all financial transactions, including those from which I benefit.

An incredible blast shakes the trees, shakes the ground, shakes me. Caught by surprise, I am as thoroughly startled as if I had been fired upon. Heart pounding, I realize I've jumped off the trail and am crouched in the high weeds beside a log pile. It was a sonic boom—one of the fighters based at Marquette. I've heard them several times, but in the woods or on the river they always catch me more by surprise than at the lake or on the road. I rise up and, surrounded by infant popples, curse a nameless pilot and—with little rhyme or reason to the litany—a catalog of offenders who have no obvious connection with sonic booms. But mostly I curse the end of summer and all the other endings and my confusion in the face of them. I have exhausted my three wishes. Nothing is changed.

The path is fading and in a while is gone completely. Ahead the three-foot popples are undivided by anything so obvious as a trail. All right, Mr. goddamned Frost, which road should I have taken?

I double back to the last fork. Goldfinches flit around the woodpiles, catching up the sun in dazzling displays of yellow.

At the next dead end I return to the first branch I bypassed and turn again into tall timber. I do not know the alternative should this trail die out, and try to remember the map, to impose my path on that green surface, and guess where I've gone awry. I tell myself that one of these paths must connect with something; whoever was here had to come from somewhere. It's just a matter of exhausting the possibilities, and this is the last of the possibilities.

In the taller grass burrs collect on my pants legs and on my jacket, whole colonies of prickly seedpods. They snare the net, tugging weakly like bedraggled children at a mother's skirt, then tear from their stems and add to my burden.

Then I hear a voice. Karen is calling, first to me, though I'm still concealed by the curving road, and then to Aaron, who trails somewhere behind her. She is clearly exasperated with us both, and yet amused. Aaron is singing "That'll be the day," mimicking the playful lament of Buddy Holly's stilled voice. I am laughing when, lurching wildly down the trail, I meet them in the high grass.

A u g u s t   1 9

It is Sunday morning, and I am lying on the bed in the loft. While I was at the stream on Thursday, Charlie came by with his rubber-tired earth-moving rig and finished filling the hole where the Carlysle cabin had stood. He was loading the machine to leave when I got home. Of course he wouldn't take any pay, and I felt doubly guilty because he had run over a nail and punctured a tire. "In the neighborhood," he laughed, waving away my thanks. Then, "I get depressed thinking about all the shovel salesmen you make rich." He is sturdy, built like a lineman—from a time when football players had more human dimensions—and he radiates strength, strength and goodwill.

He stood by the truck, ready to rush off to another job, but instead of leaving he launched into a series of stories about projects he and the boys had worked on this past winter, laughing his way through accounts of minor disasters. Lawrence came by looking for him and was, as always, eager to get to work, but he likes listening to his father talk—perhaps because he himself is so shy—and hung back, grinning the Wiegand grin behind the older man, the son a thinner, blonder counterpart to the stocky, reddish father.

I still have more shoveling to do, repairing the road and leveling the fill, but I am reluctant to get up and do it. There are other chores too—the usual rush before closing up the cabin.

The chimney pipe needs caulking, and the garage roof has to be swept free of sticks and other debris, the worst pockets of moss scraped away. And I've set posts to close off the drive next door and need to stretch cable for a gate. There is much to finish if we are to leave Tuesday evening and make the all-night trip to St. Louis.

Today is sunny and warm. Karen has gone to Joe and Vi's, and Sarah is reading downstairs. Outside, Elizabeth is calling "Marco, Marco" in a voice that sounds more and more like a woman's, and, amidst laughter and splashing, Aaron calls back, "Polo, Polo."

Last night friends telephoned from St. Louis. They were leaving to take their daughter to college for her freshman year. The daughter is a friend of Sarah's. Sarah talked knowingly on the phone, talked about schools and how lucky the daughter was to be going away, and how Sarah had liked Brown when she had been there earlier this summer. I felt like an intruder and went next door to shovel gravel.

Elizabeth runs into the house calling giggly warnings back to Aaron before she slams the door between them. I can hear her wet feet slapping on the floor. Then Aaron slams the door and she cries out, "This is not your towel. You left yours on the line last night, and it blew into the bushes." Her bedroom door slams.

Now Aaron is talking to the puppy, who is apparently trying to sleep under the stove. I picture the puddles forming on the floor.

"Have you dried off?" I call down.

"No, he hasn't," Elizabeth volunteers, her words muffled behind the bedroom door.

"She's got my towel," he says. She laughs in her room. "Anyway, I'm almost dry now."

"Well, get dressed," I say. "We've still got to carry the lumber to the garage and cut up that maple for firewood."

He doesn't answer. Saturday the girls cleaned the best of the boards we saved from the old cabin, but they are unplaned and splintery, unpleasant to handle even with the nails removed. And tree cutting is hardly a more attractive alternative, since Aaron dislikes the chain saw's noise.

In a few minutes he leaves the dog and goes to his room. He begins to play a halting version of "Scarborough Fair" on his saxophone.

When I look toward my feet, I can see, through the high front window, over the trees and to the far end of the lake where the old logging camp used to be. There remains only an uneven clearing, a lumpy yellowish break in the tree line.

Overhead is a skylight, and when I look up I can see the tops of our two tallest evergreens. One, a balsam, is crowded with grayish-green cones that point skyward from their branches. The other, taller and with downward-hanging cones, is a spruce, ragged with layers of dead limbs broken by an occasional green bough, until there is a sudden flourishing of living branches at the very top. Between the highest of these branches hangs a half-moon, white and ghostly against the blue morning sky.

Friday I did not go fishing. I drove to the Forestry office and they told me the waters beyond my last wade were impassable, but, apart from checking a few hunting trails they maintain in this area, they repeated that they rarely enter the Run above the hatchery. I headed on east and talked to the DNR officer in Crystal Falls. He said to give it up. "Too many beaver dams. Too swampy. Maybe you could float some of it, drifting downstream, but I wouldn't even bet on that." He paused and then, as if offering a concession, added, "Nobody from our office has seen much above Deloria's except from the air."

I complained about the fishing, and he told me that in the best stretches—around the hatchery and in the meadows—they, too, had been doing a count, due to a mix-up, shocking the same fish the Forestry people had hit a day or two earlier. "Bad timing for you," he said flippantly.

"Typical," I said, and for a moment old antagonisms, unmentioned in the earlier part of my visit, rose in my throat, and I leaned toward him. "I remember," I began, then, surprised at how quickly and strongly the anger returned after so many years, just looked at him, saw my anger mirrored in his eyes, turned and left.

More than a decade ago, the DNR decided to improve our lake. Their first step in that effort was to poison all the fish. There had been angry exchanges between Karen and me and the officer in charge of the project, this officer, the same one who had decided to stun trout a day after the Forestry Service had done their damage—and a day before I waded the best fishing waters on Cook's Run.

Driving back to the lake and nursing my anger, I decided to stop again in Iron River and see if I could learn anything reliable about the history of the Run. I went to the newspaper office and was directed to the sports editor, a big, burly man with blond-white hair and a droopy mustache. He motioned me to a chair, then toward a coffeepot, while he continued on the phone— something about a trappers' convention, then a question of someone caught selling fisher pelts. I've grown accustomed to city sports reporters, ex-jocks, TV personalities with blow-dried hair and gold chains around their necks. Ericksson, in contrast, looked like a bouncer for a less than reputable tavern. The big game here is in the woods; football and baseball are high school sports or something reported over the wire.

He hung up the phone and asked how he could help me, knowing instinctively that I had nothing to offer him. I inquired about files on logging history, stories on the Run, asked how I could find articles on the Cook brothers, and if the paper was that old.

"Oh, it's old enough," he said, his voice pleasant, his manner indicating a willingness to talk, and yet suggesting a kind of formality in the exchange: friendliness and reserve. "More than a hundred years old, but you won't find the files." He looked bemused by my confusion, but there was irritation in his voice.

"We had an editor who thought we needed space more than old papers, so he destroyed the first fifty years. You won't find anything there."

But he himself knew a great deal, recent stuff, told me about the court case over the illegal dam, told me how the culprit—the owner of the fancy house—had built partially on federal land, then maneuvered a trade that gave him the best frontage on the stream, told me all of this cautiously in terms of the official complaint, in terms of the court record, with lots of "allegedlys" spoken in a sardonic tone. He said the timbers in the Meadows weren't from bridges but early DNR efforts at trout cover, and told me about the dam sites he was sure of: one above the railroad bridge, and another by the sedimentation pool.

Next I went to the bank and asked the president about the Cooks. He is a dapper man, nearly always dressed in a three-piece suit, a man who smiles easily if not always convincingly and likes to talk about a famous wildlife painter whose work the bank exhibits. He is not a man to play poker with, not one who often loses, not one to bluff. He holds our mortgage, and both his handshake and his indulgent smile somehow reminded me of that fact.

He leaned back in his chair, pulling away from me to consider the question. "Some of the family," he began, templing his fingers in front of his lips, eyes cast upward ("Here is the church," I thought, "here is the steeple"), "descendants, of course, were involved in a sawmill and some land." He did not open his hands to see all the people. "We helped them with the sale." The corners of his mouth pulled up briefly into a fuller smile, then dropped back into their officially friendly position, the reassurance universally offered by bankers and undertakers to the uninitiated. "We helped with the arrangements." He leaned forward, picked up a pen, and wrote down two names. Turning to a filing cabinet, he leafed through papers, locating almost at once what he was looking for, and added addresses to the names, one in California, the other in Minnesota. He shrugged as though in apology. "It's been some time, maybe twenty years (how, then, could he have had the names so close at hand?), and one of them was old even then, but you might find someone who could help."

I thanked him and rose, dismissed. He stood too, shook my hand again, then with an unbankerly grin, that of a mischievous schoolboy, said, "Your banker knows lots of things," and, as though completing the joke, released that look, replaced it with one of innocence, and pointed to the oil mallard taking flight behind his desk. "Like art," he added.

I went to see Joe on Friday afternoon. Bill, Billy's father, was there, and they were already talking about the Run, reminiscing. Bill is a retired mining engineer, Swedish with perhaps some Finnish blood, one of those Swede families who lived in Finland, or Finns who spoke Swedish, depending on the local preference. He is a big man with a large, balding head, and he talks like he moves, deliberately, a wariness in his tone and in his eyes, a man of strong convictions but ones that he expects to come under attack.

"When I was a boy," Bill said, "we used to row to the logging camp at the end of the lake, then walk through the woods to Cook's Run." He was looking somewhere up in the trees. "Let's see. That's forty-five minutes—an hour maybe—rowing the lake. Then at least two hours over the logging road to the headwaters of Cook's Run. That's four miles or more. We'd catch our limit, fifteen trout then, hide them in the bushes and catch another fifteen."

"You'll never see fishing like that," Joe said to me, remorse and glee mixed in his voice. "All that water ran free then. Hell, we'd dynamite out any beaver that clogged the stream. Water so cold you thought your legs were gone." He rubbed his hands together as though for warmth. "Remember that big pool?"

Bill blinked slowly. It was like watching window shades closing over blue glass.

"The big pool," Joe repeated. "The headwaters pool."

Bill still looked uncomprehending. His eyelids slid down again, and Joe bounded to his feet.

"You know," Joe said, impatience making his voice aggressive, "off the township road."

"The spring hole," Bill said, nodding slightly.

"Yes," Joe continued, shaking his head in irritation, "the spring hole off the township road. You could catch a trout with every cast, sometimes two if you ran an extra leader and fly. Trout going every which way." His hands struck out in opposite directions, and his flattened palms cut the air with little darting movements. "All you could do was hang on. Never kept anything under a foot. That was a hell of a pool."

"Is it gone?" I asked stupidly. Both men looked at me for a moment as though I'd just walked into the middle of something.

"Nothing's the same," Joe said contemptuously. "You can't find trout like that in the freezer section at the grocery store." He shrugged, "Oh, maybe in Montana or Idaho, up on the forks of the Madison, but I'll never fish those waters." He looked at me accusingly. "You might. You're young."

"Then we'd walk back." Bill's uninflected voice acknowledged no interruption. "Stop at the lumber camp for some cookies and row home." He looked away toward the empty meadow and beyond. "Couldn't even find the logging road now, I suppose."

"Did you ever see where the big dam was?" Joe asked. "The big dam right at the elbow where the Run cuts south."

"No," Bill said. "We never went that far downstream."

"Oh, was that something," Joe exulted. "They must have had a lake there nearly big as this one. Big dam, and it backed water to the north and then upstream to the west." He looked at me, and there was wonder in his voice. "I've not been there for fifty years. I couldn't have been twenty-five when I floated down to that elbow. I wonder what's there now." He turned back to Bill. "Wouldn't it be something to see that again?" Bill didn't speak.

"Probably nothing left," Joe said to me. "People set fire to dams just to see the blaze." He paused, forehead creased, fingers rubbing through his bristly gray hair. "I don't remember if any of the dam was there then." He suddenly seemed troubled.

Later, on the map, I found the pool which, along with two intermittent streams, forms, on paper, the headwaters of Cook's Run. Close by, dotted lines mark a rough township road that cuts through national forest until it hits the corner of a privately owned forty, white on the map. Joe gave me the owner's name.

I called the owner. He sounded angry just saying hello—a man, I'd guess, in his early sixties, suspicious. I told him what I was doing. "Don't come into my place," he interrupted. No, I explained, I was wading the Run and wanted to know if it was manageable by his land. I would either get out on one of the hunting trails below his camp or catch the township road. It was clear by his "humph" that he regarded the township road as his private drive, but his tone grew slightly less hostile.

"Wade it! Shit," he chortled. "You couldn't get through there in a boat. And if you could, there's no trout." At that he was off, railing against the Forestry department and the DNR.

His accent was thick Upper Peninsula, far thicker than either Joe's or Bill's, and it got thicker as his anger grew. "Growing up, we caught fifteen- to sixteen-inch trout all through there. Took 'em for granted. All without the goddamned DNR."

"Thanks," I told him, more depressed by my prospects than ever. His voice remained a growl, but a lower one. "O.K., and if you could manage the water there, which you can't, you could use my road."

"Thanks," I said, genuinely appreciative of the uncollectable favor.

"But stay away from my camp." And he banged down the phone.

That night Karen and I took Joe and Vi to Iron River for a fish fry. After dinner, when we approached the cemetery at the edge of town, Vi asked to stop so that we could see her brother's grave. He died last winter and though the grief has crusted over, it remains painful, unhealed below the surface. He was younger than Vi, always in better health, and recently retired; there is anger at that wrong mixed in her mourning.

We found his stone, and, instead of the heavy religious engravings of the other monuments, this piece of granite bore a small cabin beside a lake, a deer beneath tall pines, and overhead the Big Dipper, the North Star, larger than the rest.

As we drove back toward the cemetery gates, we passed a man and woman in their mid-fifties, walking briskly along the road. Joe saw them and grabbed at my arm. "Stop," he shouted. "That's Tommy. Tommy, Vi."

She was in the back seat with Karen, silent since leaving her brother's grave, but she smiled and said, "It is Tommy."

Joe rolled down his window and, in an uncharacteristic show of friendliness, called out. The couple hurried to the car. The man grasped Joe's hand, and the two talked, vaguely including Vi and the other woman, and with occasional words to Karen and me, but otherwise completely absorbed in one another.

Joe asked about his health. Tommy said, "Oh, you know, you've been there."

"Cancer's rough." Joe shook his head knowingly. "But you look good. Keep fighting."

And then they talked about old times—a party with another couple at Joe and Vi's years ago. The other couple, fat and drunk, began to dance and shook the small cabin to its log foundation. Tommy's wife joined the laughter, and Vi, smiling, nodded her head at the memory.

At last the men parted, but reluctantly, holding on to each other's hands until the car began to roll, promising to visit each other. They live a few miles apart but had not seen each other for years, clearly did not expect to see each other again despite the promises. Joe was deeply moved. "Poor devil," he said to Vi. "You can see it. His color, his eyes." She nodded her agreement. And then, softly, "Tommy's a good man. I hope he makes it."

It was already after 7:00 but the light of a northern evening still hung on. Suddenly Joe said, "Turn down sixteen."

"Don't be crazy," Vi said. "It's late and you're not dragging us back in there."

"Where?" Karen asked.

Joe sighed, "We'll just take a look. If it's bad we'll come right out."

"Jesus Crump," Vi exclaimed. She was angry. "You never get too old to be a fool."

"Where does he want to go?" Karen asked again.

"The headwaters," Joe said. "Where Cook's Run begins." Then, conciliatorily to Vi, "I just want to show Wayne where he'll have to turn in if he ever wants to see this part of the Run. Wayne said the road was good through here." He looked at me quickly, warning me not to contradict him.

I turned south onto 16 and then, two miles later, onto a gravel road. On the left a very professional-looking chain-link fence ran beside us, a barrier which had puzzled me ever since Karen, Aaron, and I had passed it last week. "What the hell is inside that?" I asked Joe.

He snorted, sneaking a conspiratorial glance at Vi. "He wants to know what the hell that is." Vi ignored his effort at reconciliation. "That," he went on, "is a private club. A game reserve for rich men who like to kill animals that come trotting toward them expecting to be fed. A place for real sportsmen, not amateurs like us."

I checked the odometer: the fence continued for four miles, unwaveringly straight in this country of meanders and bends.

Joe started talking about the owner of the preserve, how he'd inherited the land and his father's mill and lumber company. There is throughout his history an anger at the fence, at so much land closed to him, and yet an awe at the arrogance of such possession, at the blatant absurdity of the arrangement. "A tax writeoff," he declared. "Just a tax writeoff for all the money he inherited." He paused. "The old man was a real hellion. He saw what he wanted, and he took it." Joe's hand jerked forward and clenched tightly. "There were some real men then," he said wistfully. "Not just the kids who got it all handed to them by Daddy."

"Oh, real men all right," Vi muttered in the back seat.

The road left the fence and swung back north. The dark had deepened, and Joe leaned forward, face close to the glass, watching for a turnoff.

"Watch now," he demanded. "It's right in here someplace."

I switched on the headlights, catching the ragged trunks of birch, the rough darkness of hemlock, but no divergent track.

A woodcock ran down the road ahead of us, lifted briefly in heavy, looping flight, then settled just in front of the car, barely beyond the headlight's beam. We caught up to it, and the bird took flight again, this time settling in the ditch to the left of the road.

Joe rolled down his window and seemed about to thrust his head through the opening, so intense was his search.

"Why don't we just put the top down while we're at it?" Vi complained as the wind caught her hair.

Joe ignored her. "It's got to be around here someplace," he said. "There's still a camp in there." He looked at me. "You call him?" he asked. I nodded, and he looked back at the road. "It'll be soon," he said.

It was an overgrown track running east. I stopped, and we got out in the growing darkness to inspect the deep ruts and the bent grass, indication that someone had recently driven in, though clearly in a truck, riding high above the ground. Joe bent over, walked a short way down the road, then straightened and, excited, declared, "We can make it. I'll direct you here at the start. Keep you out of trouble."

Karen tried to treat it like an adventure, but Vi would have none of that. She shook her head as I guided the car toward Joe. Then to no one in particular, "I've been down this road before."

We drove for a quarter of a mile—slow, painstaking driving, with the constant clicking of weeds on the car's undercarriage and the occasional clang of a stick or a big rock. I waited for the roar that would declare the destruction of yet another muffler as I steered between the ruts and around the largest rocks. We passed what looked like another track—a trail that, at the top of a little rise, ended almost as soon as it had begun—then descended through a deep cut until we came to a water-filled hole that blocked further passage.

"It's not far," Joe called, still keeping his distance from the car and its occupants. "Leave it here."

"Not here," I said. "I'll back up and park it."

I forced the car up, onto the edge of the track, just as headlights broke over the hill ahead of us. Vi called Joe back, and he climbed through the door, reluctantly but protectively.

The truck, on oversized tires and elevated frame, scrambled easily through the wash below us, and then took the hill like a bear, accelerating with the incline, slowing only as it reached us. The narrowness of the cut forced the driver high on the bank as he pulled alongside the car. Tree limbs shrieked against metal, but above us in the dark cab he pushed on insistently until his door was only inches from mine.

"Mind if I ask just where you think you are?" There was in his low voice contempt for flatlanders and automobiles. I looked up toward his window and could see a white T-shirt and above that a dark face and a darker mustache. A deer rifle was silhouetted against the rear window.

"Tell him you're looking for Stambaugh Hill," Joe said, referring to the big hill that rises in the center of town twenty miles away. Karen laughed. Even Vi let escape a half-smothered chuckle.

"Headwaters of Cook's Run," I replied.

He shook his dark head. His glower seemed practiced, as though developed especially to go with the disheveled hair and drooping mustache. He looked down at me in my restaurant clothes and my compact station wagon. He revved his engine pointlessly. "Private property," he said.

"Township seems to think this road belongs to them," I answered, trying a dark grin against his glare.

"Couldn't tell by the work they do on it," he said, a note of caution slipping into his voice for the first time. I laughed, but the humor was unintentional, and he seemed offended by my response.

"It's private land off the road ahead." Then, "Just who are you?"

Joe leaned across me and peered up at the dark man. "I know the owner of this land, and you don't look much like him or any of his family." There was authority in his voice, and the man in the truck seemed taken aback. He did not expect this knowledge in a car with Missouri license plates. "Fact is," Joe continued, "you look more like one of the people who works in the Post Office."

The face moved forward out of the darkness into the frame of the truck window. "I got permission. I'm a friend," he said, the bluster lessened if not completely gone. He stared intently, trying to see Joe more clearly.

"Then you'll know how far we are from the headwaters," I said.

"Not far," he answered, his eyes still trying to make out Joe. "There's a pump by the road. The spring hole's just beyond that." He had, in a sullen way, become more cooperative. "But you can't get there in that."

"That's why we were backing up," I said.

The man in the truck revved the engine belligerently.

"Thanks," Joe said. "See you at the Post Office." I eased the car to the top of the hill and off to the side of the track. The truck rushed by with a roar of power and the clatter of slapping branches.

Joe led the way down the road until the two of us reached a break in the trees and a rusty pump, its handle raised parallel to the ground, and beyond the pump, the black, still waters of the spring hole. A few stars had come out and the pond reflected their light back at the sky.

"Here is where it begins," he said. "Wouldn't think anything could move out of this, all choked like it is." Thick weeds, barely visible in the dark, curled in the water before us like animals rubbing against the surface. I thought of old lab specimens, eels, snakes—whatever—suspended in formaldehyde-filled jars and grown slightly fuzzy with age.

"Where's the outlet?" I asked.

Joe pointed to a dark corner backed by tamarack and spruce. "Over there someplace," he said. "Can't be more than a trickle." He shook his head in despair. "You could never wade through such a mess." He looked off into the night. "Not now. Not like this."

On the way back to the car, Joe swung suddenly toward me. "The canoe," he said triumphantly. "Go down from here in a canoe."

I had counted on wading. The whole point somehow was to walk the stream, and even as I saw that possibility disappearing I was reluctant to give it up. "I'll go with you," he declared as we reached the car.

"Where?" Vi asked suspiciously.

"Down the Run." Joe's enthusiasm grew, even in the presence of the women. "You know how long it's been since I've seen any of this?" His eyes were on me. I eased the car back up the road. "Twenty-five years maybe."

"When you were fifty?" Vi asked. She seemed caught between sarcasm and sympathy.

"Must of been thirty-five or forty years," he said. "We put in up here and drifted all the way to where the big dam used to be."

"How will you get there?" Karen asked, Joe's enthusiasm carrying into her tone.

"Canoe," he answered defiantly, as though expecting contradiction.

"Ours is too big," I warned. "Too clumsy to lift over beaver dams." I spoke cautiously. This was not what I'd planned, and, too, while Joe seems strong as a man twenty-five years younger, I was worried about him. The exchange at the cemetery remained with me, was troubling though I could not read its significance.

"Better yet, my rubber raft," he said. "Easier to lift, and then we could carry it out when we get to one of the logging trails."

I didn't answer. His scenario had its appeal. While not the ending I had planned, not my triumphant, mock-heroic exit from the headwaters, not the weary explorer, slogging out at last to wife and children complete with picnic basket and holiday gaiety—"Father, husband, we presume"—it had possibilities. What better alternative than accompanying a seventy-five-year-old man, a kind of homecoming where the present stream is viewed through the memory of what once was here. This seemed, all things considered, almost preferable to my original scheme, which was, after all, only another twist on an old cliché. This, perhaps, made for more satisfying conclusion both to the river and to the essay.

That was yesterday. Today Joe has become doubtful. Karen talked to Vi, and Vi said, now protective of her husband, that he is not sure we can get through, even by floating, and that, if we could, the rubber raft is old and leaks.

When I saw Joe later, he looked tired. "What you heard was right," he said. "It's too choked and dammed to float." He looked across the lake. "You've seen most of it. Give it up. All that's left is muck."

We sat for a while. "I'd like to go till it actually stops me," I said at last. "And I'd like to see where the big dam was."

"You better take my doughnut then." His doughnut is a floating device, an inner tube with a canvas seat that fits around waders and buoys up the wearer in deep water. "And my fins to get you through the pools."

I laughed. Joe looked at me, then he laughed too. "We'll have you looking like the Loch Ness monster," he said. "Hell of a boost for Michigan tourism." After a while, "Well, what are you going to do?"

"The usual," I answered. "Think about it."

Downstairs Aaron has quit playing "Scarborough Fair" and is laughing. He is telling Elizabeth that the puppy has fallen asleep with its feet in the air. The boards still wait to be carried to the garage; the moon remains in the top branches of the big spruce, and a loon calls from the far end of the lake, a light crackling call rather than the mournful cry of evening and early morning.

"Let's go to work," I say as I get up and start for the stairs, but Aaron is already rushing out the door, carrying Elizabeth's towel as she shrieks at him from her room.

A u g u s t 20

I did not set the alarm, but it is 5:45 and the dog is dropping a golf ball on the downstairs floor. Each time the ball stops bouncing I wait, undecided, before going down to take it away from her, and each time, after the bouncing has stopped, there is a silence that suggests she has tired of the game. Then, as I begin to slip back into sleep, she drops the ball again. Finally I give up, get out of bed, and dress. These mornings I go down the stairs sideways, one step at a time, stiff in hips and knees. Today, I sidle toward the landing, muttering at the dog, who takes my complaints as encouragement and, more eager than ever, accelerates the pace with which she picks up and drops the golf ball.

The dog has mushroomed in size over the past three weeks, and today, in her pleasure at seeing me, she bounds around awkwardly on big feet and lengthening legs, falling and rolling in a shapeless mass of white. Her ears bounce with every step, lifting and falling like fat, fluffy wings, and her rear end seems constantly out of control, like an unattended ladder section in some slapstick fire truck routine.

Outside the morning is cool but already sunny. Dew glistens in the light, both on the grass and in the dog's coat.

Karen drives to where I met her and Aaron last Thursday, down the Forest Highway and onto the gravel road that fronts against the high fence of the game preserve. We will be leaving for St. Louis in two days, and she talks eagerly, happily, of our return. I stare out the window, watching the unyielding fence as we drive through the timber's shadow. On the tape deck someone sings, "They said I would shine like a light in the city; I hoped it would be like the moon on the sea."

When we stop at the logging track, I unfold the section of Forestry map I now carry, no longer trusting the freehand copies I sketched in my notebook.

"Where should I pick you up?" Karen asks. "And when?"

I can't answer with certainty, can only list the alternatives. "If I can, I'll make it as far as the big elbow. Meet me here," I say, pointing to the outlet on Highway 2, "at noon."

Karen looks at the map skeptically, at the dotted line I plan to follow. "You'll never find your way through that maze." The hunting trails tangle halfway between highway and stream in a nest of intersecting lines. "You should have a compass."

"I can use the sun," I say. "And besides, if I stay on the high land moving north, I'll have to hit the highway eventually."

She shakes her head but does not mention all the work that remains to be done before we leave. "If you're not there by one, I'll call the Forestry office," she says. It seems as much warning as reassurance.

"Jesus!" I say and she flinches at the blasphemy. I start again, this time attempting a tone of compromise. "Give me until five," I say, "and first come back here in case I get hung up and have to backtrack."

"Two," she says. It is my turn to shake my head. "What do you think they will do?" I ask. "Come in with bloodhounds, or maybe helicopters?"

"Yes," she answers.

"Wait," I say, "until you see what they charge by the hour for a helicopter. Or even a pack of hounds. Better let me find my own way out. It'll be cheaper." She is not amused.

The pool where I got out four days ago looks this morning like a scene from a forties horror movie, someone's idea of a blasted heath. The sky has clouded again, and steam rolls along the surface of the water in large ragged rifts. Skeletons of elm and alder jut from the fog and, like the hummocks of mud that break the pool's surface, suggest some old violence. Nothing moves, and a pale scum films the water, an enormous milky cataract. The beaver is out of sight, but he is here, splashing someplace near the dam.

It is, according to my unreliable reckoning, 7:10, and I am tired. Last night I had my annual back-to-teaching nightmare and slept fitfully in its wake. In the dream I discover late in the semester that I have never met with one of my classes, and when, guilt-stricken, I rush to the room, the students are waiting for me even after all these weeks. But the course is calculus, a subject about which I know nothing, and so, as in each year's version, I merely stand before them in despair. The despair always lingers long after I awaken. Today it blends with my awareness that, no matter how far upstream I manage to wade, I will still fall short of the headwaters. As I slide over the edge of the bank into the dark water, the whole venture seems childish. The academic book, the long-overdue proof of my professional seriousness, remains where it has been all summer: in rough draft in a suitcase under my desk in the loft. Perhaps it is, as I sometimes think, a good book, but I expect in the end, if I get to the end, to be disappointed by it, too.

How in hell did I become an "academic" leading an "academic" life? I don't mean the teaching but the hypothetical nature of it all, a sort of experiment, a line of inquiry that in all likelihood will lead nowhere but which bears watching, and manipulating, on the outside possibility that it will prove to be of some slight importance. To say I am an academic has become for me—as with an academic question—like saying, "Let's pretend for the moment, just for the sake of argument, that I am." It is the superfluous briefly taken seriously before slipping back to the periphery. "But this," I tell myself, "is what I wanted, what I want."

I have waded all summer in the shallows of self-pity, done it wittingly, ironically, but all the while I've been moving into greater and less manageable depths. I've read enough stories to know the ending toward which they all must tend, know the longing that this time it might be different and the satisfaction— when, at last, it is not—of having old knowledge once more confirmed. As a reader, if not as a writer, I know where I am headed, have watched the metaphors emerge precisely at the moment I had hoped to escape metaphor, have recognized what, inevitably, was informing my unsuspecting hand. And I am torn, torn between the need to keep the secret a bit longer and the urge to be the first to offer explication, between a need to deny the course I've long been settled on and the temptation to give away my own meaning, the one I had hoped, this time, to avoid.

Behind me, hidden by clouds of steam, the beaver crosses back and forth like a sentry, slapping its tail again and again.

Once, when Smeagol was only a year old, I took him with me as I tried to find a shortcut into the Paint. Somehow we walked into a swamp that looked much like the Run does here, and before I knew where we were I was knee-deep in silt, unable at first to overcome the suction and pull free. I worked my way out, but it took more than fifteen minutes in waist-high water, and all the while the dog, bewildered, paddled around me in circles. What today reminds me of that time, I suspect, is the way in which the low banks here, like those in that place, are thick with sharpened limbs, some of them two and three inches in diameter. With their bark stripped away and whitened by exposure they look like gnawed bones. Beyond this ominous hedge and on both sides of the now-narrowed channel stretches a wide floodplain, a wasteland of silt and swamp grass and the stubbled limbs of dead bushes bound together with spiderwebs; the kind of place where Ezekiel might have seen his wheeling vision. Somewhere behind me the beaver continues to smack the water.

The channel shallows to my knees and the silt becomes less threatening as the stream begins to move again, winding into the marshy meadow. And the sun reappears, burning the steam into ribbons and then the ribbons into nothing at all. Thigh-high banks of mud rise straight up beside the Run, and green and brown leopard frogs line the margin, blunt noses pushed above the water, legs splayed out behind. They watch me, bobbing with the waves that mark my passage.

A long time ago I was much taken by amphibians and reptiles; I collected and observed them. At first, when my family was constantly on the move, and at a time when I was always the new kid, coming to school for a few weeks, then disappearing again, I kept a single cage made from orange-crate slats and scavenged screen wire. Sometimes it housed a salamander, sometimes a toad or a snake or a newt, usually for just a few days before I released the captive and rebuilt the cage for a different occupant.

Later, when we had settled in Rock Island, I talked another boy, Calvin, into a joint turtle-capturing venture: if the little dime-store variety could sell for forty cents, what wouldn't people spend for a more substantial specimen? We waded the swampy regions just above where the Rock River gives way to the Mississippi, netting everything we could reach with contraptions we had constructed of old mop handles, coat-hanger wire, and discarded kitchen curtains. The turtles—mostly the painted variety but a few nasty-dispositioned snappers, and even one soft-shell we had cornered in the shallows off a sandbar—we kept in washtubs in Calvin's basement until the scraping of claws against zinc upset his otherwise tolerant mother, and we had to release our livestock before we had ever gotten them to market.

At last, living in a government housing project, I kept two big bullfrogs, not just the usual day or two, but weeks, and became, in time, increasingly negligent about their feeding. They both died. Like any boy who has spent time around a Missouri farm, I had killed lots of frogs, had amputated their legs while they watched with bulging eyes, accepting my knife with a resignation terrifying in the remembering, if not at the moment. But these later deaths were the result of laziness and self-preoccupation, and afterward I tore up the cage that I had rebuilt so many times and had carried to so many nondescript towns. Even in those days I gathered guilt the way a cheap sweater collects lint, gifted even then with a sort of spiritual static cling.

Walking has become easier, more pleasant. I begin, despite the absence of any visible trout, to cast, flicking the fly away from the persistent chubs, chasing away the ghosts of ancient victims, and trying to recover old hopes and ambitions. The stream falls into a regular pattern of shallow straightaways and deeper bends, the footing consistent, firm. Perhaps the warnings about impossible headwaters were wrong. Perhaps if I had simply gotten on with it, I could have managed the entire Run without difficulty.

Then the terrain abruptly changes, the Run rises suddenly to my waist, and simultaneously I hear water falling in the distance. Still the stream winds sedately through its swampy valley, unchanging, until the dams, a succession of three, begin once more, and with them the sucking silt. To the left popple continue to dominate, offering no evidence of the jackpine which the ranger said will become visible before the Run makes its big swing north. Past the third dam I scan my map once more but nothing falls in place.

I cannot account for my persistent fear that I will lose the "right" track, will miss the way. Every fork has brought its own doubt, though rarely with any justifiable cause for concern. And even if I were to get diverted, what would be the harm? The fear at work in all of this is not exactly a fear of getting lost—I don't really know where I am anyway, only that I am somewhere between an arbitrary point of entry and an anticipated, and inevitable, exit. It is something more subtle, something to do with failing to pay attention, of missing the point.

On car trips I tend to fluctuate between anxiety and obliviousness, one moment fretful that I have missed a turnoff or have misread the highway signs, and the next inattentive to all the locating information around me, absorbed in some inner narrative. Sometimes it is a mixture of the two; I will be aware of an oddly twisted tree or a half-painted house or a peculiar cloud formation but unable to name any of the last three towns I have driven through. I just never seem completely sure of where I am, and in moments when I am made conscious of that fact, I find my tenuous hold on location troubling.

Once, when I was eleven or twelve, I was sent with out-of-town relatives to direct them to my grandparents' house, a twenty-minute drive I had taken scores of times. After two hours of wandering, my exasperated aunt parked the car, called my father, and waited for a reliable guide. I never could explain the problem, but somehow, when I was responsible for finding the way, everything had rearranged itself, had become totally un-

*familiar. It wasn't so much that I was lost; more that things were
not where they should have been: the world asserting its whimsy.*

While I watch for the pine, vaguely convinced that despite all
reason, I have let the Run get away from me, missed its departure
the way I have missed, in southern Wisconsin, the turnoff for
Interstate 94 more times than I'd care to count, I step into a deep
silt hole, my feet sliding out from under me as they break through
a thin sand crust and settle into the debris below. Before I can
grab hold of the closest hummock of grass and pull myself erect
once more, water sloshes into my waders. The silt does not
willingly release me, and I twist and pull for five minutes before
finally breaking its grip. Inside my boots the water is cold, the
soaked socks lumpy under my feet. This bears no resemblance to
the Run of five minutes ago.

Clinging to a bank of grass, I struggle on ahead, but it is
merely a bank—not *the* bank—since this whole area is cut by
chutes that divide the old ground into islands, each with its own
grassy plateau. The only evidence that I am on the main channel
comes from the fact that the drop-off here is abrupt and nearly
straight down. I make my way now by hanging on to the grass
with one hand and digging my toes into the decaying bank like
a rock climber. But the hummocks are shaky, barely anchored,
and I stagger from one to another, lunging over the intervening
gaps to grab the next stand of vegetation. The drop-off is, arm's
length away, more than the rod's seven-foot length, and the silt
at my feet, when I slip down into it, comes higher than my knees
and without any evidence of a solid underlayment. The dark
debris stirs all around me, catching on my waders in dirty ribbons
and stinking of rot.

My passage through this maze seems endless. Nothing indicates
change; nothing suggests progress. My left arm aches from the
effort of clutching at grass and carrying the weight of my body.

Everything else complains of the strain of pressing tight against the unstable islands.

The revivalists of my youth—the itinerant beseechers who came with the August heat to little country churches and tent meetings, bringing with them the fear of the Lord to stir us from our dog days' lethargy, came to convince bored farmers that even they were part of a bigger game—painted apocalyptic visions of the Rapture when the faithful would be lifted up and the rest of us abandoned to the lurid nightmare of rivers running with blood, the sky raining fire, and the heavens rolling up like a scroll. Their colors were those of the old Evangelist, the old Revelation— garish violets, unnatural purples, everything the color of an angry bruise. They said we would all be grouped in twos, the ark undone; two men in the field, one taken, one left behind; two working at the mill, one taken, one left behind; two driving down the road, one taken, one left behind.

Their hell was a terrible place to me, not because of the flames but because of the overcrowding. Always, in their depictions, teeming throngs pushed and shoved against the horror, and I, who found the crush of a county fair terrifying, feared hell as the ultimate embodiment of claustrophobia.

At the time any particularly striking sunset or the pre-tornado green of a midwestern sky would fill me with an awful dread, and I watched for the heavens to be rent and the host to stream down in chariots—God's army of accountants—to stop the clocks, balance the books, and wreak havoc on the landscape with their terrible colors. In such moments I avoided being alone with anyone, especially in a car, convinced that safety lay only in groups of three or more and as frightened by that ultimate abandonment as by hell's swarming masses. The choice between

*loneliness and the crush of desperate bodies has always been one
I've resisted, wanting neither to be lost in the crowd nor the only
one left behind. And I was, even then, willing to forgo heaven
as long as there were others who would remain on earth, the place
that despite the preachers' exhortations retained my deepest loy-
alty.*

After twenty minutes among channels and hummocks, I hear
falling water. Such undeniable evidence of change would be
reassuring except for the threat of yet another dam, of an even
more difficult wade.

But the stream before me narrows and, defying the map's
configurations, cuts directly south. I look at the scrap of green
paper and then back at the fork in front of me with a nagging
uncertainty and a growing despair at the remoteness of any exit
to the north and at the thought of having to return the way I
have come. Then I look to my left where the ridge is visible once
again, and on its crest the ungainly limbs of jack pine thrust up
against the sky.

*The Evangelist's ending blended, in time, with another scenario,
the nuclear holocaust for which fifties children were as carefully
prepared as fundamentalists for the Second Coming: "Crawl
under your desk; cover your eyes; don't look up at the deep
purple rose of Charon sky blossoming overhead." Day after day
we knelt, heads bowed in undoubting anticipation.*

*Eventually, sitting on the floor in a St. Louis den, I settled for
the fall of Saigon, the constant rain of artillery and flares, the
rising columns of smoke tinted by searchlights, and then, at long
last, the descending chariots, their uniformed attendants lifting up
the elect and thrusting aside the others. Desperate crowds pulled
down the gates of the American embassy, struggled with ma-*

chine-gun-carrying marines—their own young faces lined with anxiety and doubt—in one last effort to reach the helicopters and claim their salvation before the breaking of that final seal.

The Run's turning is only a diversion, a feint to the south before it bends emphatically in the opposite direction. The water remains deep, the bottom silty, but the valley narrows, and on the banks the pink, grainy blossoms of knotweed encourage the hope that I've left the marshes behind. Still, I hold to the stream's margin and slog along as though I am walking in wet cement.

Suddenly the water shallows to three and a half feet, and the bottom becomes firm, paved with sand and gravel. Which of these is the Run? Why can't it make up its mind?

The old dilemma: I want something to happen but nothing to change.

I crawl around an uprooted spruce that reaches all the way from one bank to the other, and beyond that I find another dam. Still there is little change in depth, but past the next bend I enter a silt marsh, more muck and tall weeds, and only the distant funnel of trees suggests that this too shall pass.

The marsh grass rises on both sides higher than my head, and the stream yields to a sandbar covered by no more than four inches of water. A plover squeaks nearby, then flies off. Froth has piled against the bank, and, to the left, the current becomes visible once more. The sand here and there gives way suddenly, in pockets that open like trapdoors beneath me, but the drops are shallow, no deeper than my knees, malicious little jokes that I fall for every time.

Ahead the plover reappears, teetering on spindly, sharply an-gled legs, delicately picking its way through a mound of foam. Taking flight, the bird lifts a line of froth, then sets it adrift on the air.

For the first time today I hear the wind in the trees. A female mallard cruises the twenty-foot-wide pond behind a small dam, warily extending her neck, then pulling it back as she watches my approach. When I enter the pool, she takes off with much complaint, beating the water loudly before she gains the air.

Thirty feet upstream the dams return in earnest, the first one small—only about eight feet across—then a double-tiered affair, the lower section holding a calf-deep pool, the upper, twenty feet upstream, raising the level another three feet. Willows line the banks, a lighter, more refined replacement for the coarse alders. Their slender leaves turn easily, gracefully, in the air.

It takes me three attempts to mount the higher dam. Twice my feet break through the shallow toeholds I force into its side, and twice I slide down the steep wicker wall. The third time I pick a spot with large limbs that offer better climbing, and I make my way to the top, where I can look out across the valley. The high ground has fallen back, leaving a marsh to the west but ahead I can see where trees once more approach the Run.

My one small gesture toward protesting the war grew not from my conviction but from the conviction of one of my students. Five years older and a father, I felt somehow responsible for him after he told me of his low draft number and of his pacifist beliefs. He had been denied conscientious objector status because his appeal was secular. I liked him. He was my best student, bright, yet unassuming and good-natured. I was not a very good teacher and felt badly about that fact, but his ability to learn—even in my classroom—made me seem less fraudulent. So I did what I could. I called a doctors' group I had heard about and arranged for an examination, one in which he would be checked for any medical condition, no matter how slight, that could justify reclassification. And they did find something, some small abnormality of the spine, made a case, and forwarded it to his draft board.

He came to tell me as soon as word arrived that his appeal had been successful. We congratulated each other, and I encouraged him to go home for the weekend and tell his parents. He hesitated—there was a paper due in my class and his relationship with his father had been troubled in recent months—but at my urging and in his own eagerness for reconciliation he decided to make the trip.

After he left my office, I told myself that small acts could also be significant, that while I had taken no dramatic stand, I had, perhaps, helped save one decent and vulnerable kid from the brutality of the war. It was an easy answer, but I settled for it.

Driving home that night, the object of my small effort had a flat tire—the left rear tire—and as he bent to his work on the dark shoulder of the Interstate, he was struck by a semi and killed.

When I return to the water, moving away from the dam, the stream deepens quickly, and again I find myself clutching at the bank's meager offering while the water flirts with the top of my waders.

I try estimating the distance to what Joe thinks to be the old logging-dam location and guess it at less than half a mile. I am making good time, and if I allow forty-five minutes to get to the highway, I have nearly an hour and a half of wading before I need to leave the Run.

Perhaps if this kind of water continues, and if I get a very early start, I could cover the remaining distance tomorrow, could make it to the end after all. Why should the wade ahead be more difficult than what has gone before? Perhaps completing the journey is not so unthinkable, requires only an extra day to close the cabin and an all-night drive to get to St. Louis in time for my first duties of the fall semester. The foolishness of this hope is obvious, and yet, each time I've thought my way stymied, the Run has let me pass. Why shouldn't that pattern persist for one more day? Even as I argue the point, I see Karen's unpersuaded face.

When I look down, I find that the large patch on my left thigh has loosened, its entire perimeter lifting and falling with my every move as though it is breathing—has developed a life of its own.

Then comes yet another barrier, an ancient dam, its water filled with grass that reaches above the surface, jutting up to form a wet, bristly lawn. And the series of obstructions does not end. Beyond the pool, a big log, at least twenty-five feet long and three and a half feet in diameter, crosses the stream. It is backed in turn by another pair of logs—the first, two feet thick, the other, two and a half. They are bleached with age and deeply grooved, and in these grooves, and any other pockets where they can find rooting, grow delicate grasses and ferns that shiver in the breeze.

Can this be left from the brothers' business? Nothing here suggests the enormous lake a logging dam would have created, and surely, even after seventy-five years, that much water would have left its mark. The valley, despite the marsh on my left, seems too narrow, doesn't open for a lake site, but these timbers were clearly man-cut.

I hope to see, if I reach its location, some irrefutable evidence of the old dam, timbers, chains perhaps. The Cooks came to this enterprise late, the first of this century, when most of the area's "corkwood" had been cut, and heavier logs, maple and basswood, were being taken out by rail. Winters they would have cut the pine from the ridges around the Run and dragged it onto the frozen lake behind their dam. In spring they would release the impounded water, sending the logs downstream on that wild surge to the Paint and, farther, into Wisconsin. This, then, must have been one of the last logging dams, and perhaps because it is removed from easy access, some remnant of it will have endured. But perhaps, too, this is one more misunderstanding, one more misrepresentation of a past faded beyond recall.

The impulse to make sense of things, regardless of what those things are or how resistant to sense they may be, simply will not go away. I rarely wait for sufficient evidence but jump quickly to conclusions, anticipate the story after the first line. This cease- less knitting, and the constant unraveling that attends it, is irresist- ible to me but it makes me—despite my good intentions—an unreliable witness. Rather than accepting the thread, I anticipate a tapestry. This is not because I believe there is an order in all things—my impulse is in fact just the opposite—but because I seem to assume that there should be, and that it is my obligation to act as though there were.

This means, too, the persistent metaphors, the refusal to let things simply be. Rivers and memory and narrative all mirror one another; and logging runs, more than forests flung adrift on an unleashed flood, become as well—terrifyingly, exhilarat- ingly—the soul's own run, its deadly confusion and its violent crests.

I never called the Cook descendants identified for me by the banker, never went to the historical society to research the Run. Even in this I have been no scholar, but have settled for a kind of muddling through, discontented but accepting a misremem- bered past and an inaccurately recorded present.

The next obstruction is yet another abandoned beaver dam, this one broken in the middle so that it gapes open, giving way, stick by stick, before the current. I wade through its rough mouth and find the inevitable next dam. And beside it, the high ground on the right ends in a point of spruce and white birch. The trees against a blue sky, broken with scattered cumulus clouds, have the familiar attractiveness of a Sierra Club calendar, an easy wildness, a comfortable scene for a kitchen wall, but ahead, beyond this clear pool and the birch that fly their loosened bark like yachting pennants, the Run enters a great marsh, a wide valley just visible from where I stand beneath the trees.

On this failing bank, beneath the timber, grass grows in a parklike glade. The pool is filled with minnows, and I fish it, delaying, holding back, even when all I catch are the sluggish chubs that, once hooked, hang helpless as cabbages while I drag them in.

The pool continues, waist-deep and with solid gravel footing, around a sharp bend. Big logs, some flat-cut, man-worked, line the bank. One I pace off at over fifty feet and with little appreciable change in diameter. Grooved and hollowed with age, its old knots point inward, accusingly, to an empty center.

My grandfather St. Clair was in most respects a stern man. He could be hard in his judgment of others and demanding of his children. He was a pious, hardworking farmer who did not care much for farming but never found any other vocation he liked better. Grandpa was proud that he had never tasted alcohol, had never smoked a cigarette, and had never gone to a movie on the Sabbath. Once when he was traveling to Texas with my Uncle David, he lost track of the date and was talked by his son into a movie theater. Inside, David announced that the day was Sunday. I was never told whether Grandpa actually sat through the film or, warned at the last moment, escaped sin in the nick of time and kept his record intact.

This is not to suggest that he was in any way a silly man—he was not—but he could be irritatingly difficult, and I doubt that many of the people who loved him—a sizable group—actually liked him. I loved and liked him, was so devoted that my grand-

mother Fields, jealous that anyone should receive more of my attention than she, said that I'd follow Loyd St. Clair over a cliff. After careful consideration I said, "No, I wouldn't do that." But I followed him nearly everywhere else and did whatever he asked of me. And, in turn, he loved me in his hard way, telling me as much about those things that mattered to him as he told anyone; he took me with him when he went to the field or to town; and he learned to forgive the small acts of foolishness to which even the most obedient grandson falls prey. The time that, dared by my older cousin, I jumped from the back of the moving pickup, missed my footing, and got chewed up by the gravel, Grandpa retrieved me, and I, more afraid of his rebuke than of the stinging cuts that covered my body, felt only relief when he helped me into the truck's cab and drove home in silence.

The year after his cancer surgery, when he had gotten back as much of his strength as he would ever recover, he returned impatiently to the work of his farm and tried to carry on as though nothing had changed. But he knew the difference and fought it as he fought all weakness, treated it as sin that was to be redeemed, like all sin, through self-discipline and toughness of will. The cancer, however, was already navigating through his bones, spreading pain and debilitation in its wake.

Sometimes in the evening, while my youngest uncle was in the barn milking—an uncle who was waiting for his army induction and his own imminent departure—and Grandma was in the kitchen cleaning up after dinner, Grandpa would go off without me to the pasture west of the house. One time, when I saw him heading away on the tractor, I ran behind, concealed by the cloud of dust that rose between us. When at last I came within earshot, I heard the noise of erratic movement and nervous lowing and, mingled with the more familiar sounds, a terrible cry I did not recognize. Cresting the hill, I looked down to where the cattle,

*drawn by the prospect of being watered, milled around the stock
tank, looking confused and fearful, and in the middle of the herd
stood my grandfather, he of unfailing discipline and sternness,
head thrown back, howling in anguish like a wolf caught by the
realization that this trap's jaws would never be released.*

The valley above the clear pool expands to a width of at least
three football fields and reaches ahead nearly an equal distance
before the land ascends and carries trees once more. This must be
the big elbow where Joe located the last dam, the site of the Cook
brothers' big lake. Now high marsh grass bends before a breeze
that is coming from the south, murmuring constantly—not the
haunted sound of needles moaning or the rainlike whisper of
leaves, but a lower, more constant sigh. The water is waist-deep,
and the bottom once more unreliable. Both banks are rotten
mounds of grass so shaky they seem totally detached from earth,
cut away from one another by crevices of muck, treacherous and
unpromising. Unable to see beyond the immediate hummocks of
weeds and only able to guess from my memory of the map the
actual path the Run follows, I have no choice but to hold to the
main stream until I can get to the far-off timber somewhere
beyond the elbow's curve. Nor can I see through the water, dark
with silt, to the bottom of all this.

Except for the constant drone of the wind-moved grass, there
is no sound. No bird calls; no splash of frogs. Beneath my feet
and all around me, suspended and afloat, is the broken-down stuff
of old trees and weeds, an enormous wet compost heap through
which I make my way. Even the air carries the thick, cloying
stench of rot. And I can see now that the living trees ahead are
beyond reach, separated from my path, as the Run makes its
right-angle turn, by more than a hundred unpassable yards.

*There is a strange and wonderful poem by Christopher Smart, a
sort of hymn to both his cat, Jeoffry, and his God (the distinction*

is far from certain), something written, as I recall, during a
prolonged residence in Bedlam. The only line I can remember
comes in the midst of all his praise: *"Poor Jeoffry! poor Jeoffry!
the rat has bit thy throat."*

Odd the way something so peculiar gets tucked away, then,
for no apparent reason, shows itself in the least expected of
circumstances.

The stream bottom grows increasingly treacherous, not the
sucking stuff of the earlier ponds, though there are pockets of that
and of what feels like quicksand, but a deep silt crusted over, only
slightly more congealed than the frustrating solution through
which I walk. I feel as though I am moving on thin ice and that
if I break through the barely frozen surface I will sink indefi-
nitely. Sometimes the grass hummocks are too far apart, too far
removed, and with nothing to hold on to I must move slowly,
gingerly, through the high water, easing over the treacherous silt
with the fly rod held out in my right hand, left hand lifted for
balance, trying to keep my weight from falling heavily in any
one place, a bear on a tightrope.

*On this frail crust I remember going once, when I was very
young, to visit an aunt and uncle in their recently acquired house.
They were settling in and boxes were still being unpacked, walls
being repainted. In my exploring I found my way into the attic,
the first time I had ever been in an attic that had no floor, and,
after a short walk on the joists, I stepped down onto the ceiling
tile that was stapled in place from below. I plummeted through,
more amazed by the insubstantiality of things than by the fall.
Incredibly I landed on a sofa that had been pulled into the middle
of the living room while the walls were being replastered, landed
between my startled uncle, sitting on one end of the couch and*

my father—no longer amazed by his children's peculiar en-
trances—on the other.

As I step forward toward a four-foot-long, crescent-shaped island, the crust gives away. I drop suddenly, waders overrun by water as I fall in an abbreviated belly-flop, right hand still clutching the fly rod as I lunge to my left, grasping for the grass on the quarter-moon hummock. The grass breaks free in my left hand, and I claw my fingers into dirt and roots. The sliver of ground shakes but holds, and I pull forward, dragging the water's weight with me. Carefully, pulling one foot and then the other out of the silt, I feel for some grip on the bottom, eventually finding an old log buried in the debris. Around my body the water, slowed perhaps by the strands of rotten vegetation it holds in suspension, responds sluggishly—gravylike—to my desperate efforts, and the marsh stink rises thickly, sulphurously through new faults in the broken crust.

I cling to my small piece of sod as the invading water gurgles down my legs, and when everything has at last settled into place, my boots are filled to my knees. After catching my breath, I pull completely upright, then wait for my shaky legs to regain their strength.

I feel old, very tired, and the liquid weight I have taken on both pulls me down and makes the feet of the waders uncomfortable, causes the twisted rubber to chafe my anklebones, and my socks to ball up hopelessly under my feet. The irritation is out of all proportion to the damage.

While in college I was active in the ecumenical youth movement. It was an era of grandiose organizations of the young, a time when even the President of the United States fueled his boldest schemes with our energy and our bodies, a time of mass gatherings and solemn assemblies. During the early sixties we conducted a series of meetings, one on each continent, with thousands in attendance, meetings at which we passed pious proclamations, exulted in our numbers and our youth. We found ourselves irresistible. Older church leaders, always more preoccupied with the niceties of doctrine and polity than were we, watched skeptically, troubled by our limited regard for tradition—for them— and yet impressed by our enthusiasm and daring. Never before had there been so many of us; never before had we seemed so likely to take matters into our own hands. We came from capitalist countries and communist countries, from America and Europe and from the third world, most of us leaving our homes openly and with official approval, but some slipping out under false pretenses or without any approval at all.

The Lausanne meeting established the anthem for all the assemblies that followed, the clarion call that sounded again and again, sounded in an odd assortment of tongues but always with enormous fervor and absolute confidence: "Thine is the glory risen conquering son, endless is the victory thou o'er death hast won." Our elders, observing from the wings, took this as a sign of religious commitment and were themselves moved by our fervor. I've come to understand, and suspected even then, that our declaration had little to do with religion, had to do rather with power, the sons declaring their time, their victory, elbowing aside the fathers and their tired formulas in order to get on with it, to change the world after our own vigorous image.

In the years that followed—years in which such movements virtually disappeared, fell away before black power and the new left and our own inadequacies, died before the aged bishops and executive secretaries who reigned at the time of Lausanne—our youth did not prove invincible any more than did our exuberant fellowship.

Near the end of that decade, at a funeral service for a fellow

graduate student—a bright and tormented young man who, at
last, had stilled the inner turmoil by stepping in front of a
train—the soloist sang "Sheep May Safely Graze," not, I think,
with confidence but with longing. In time the claims of endless
victory, of the son's triumph, yielded to the frail hope not for
power but for a refuge in our powerlessness, not to lead but to
be shepherded.

Despite the revulsion I came to feel for the war, I wish now,
now that it is safe to do so, that I had not waited to be called
but had volunteered for Viet Nam, if only as a show of solidarity
with my generation. There rather than Lausanne was our place,
our time.

I make it to an old beaver dam that, nearly hidden by vines,
seems to stretch only from water to water. It is easy to climb,
and from its top I get my fullest view of the marsh. Two
abandoned beaver huts loom from the waters ahead, both old
gray ruins in a wilderness of channels and hummocks. I look
behind me, but the last pool, the one edged by spruce and birch,
is lost to sight. All I can see in that direction and to either side
is the marsh. Ahead of me and to the west, timber, dark evergreens and bright popples, edge back toward the stream, but even
from here it is apparent that the trees will make only brief
contact, if they make any at all, before retreating once again.
There I must find my way.

*The first semester I taught I was given a course consisting of all
the important texts I had never read. One of these was* Antony
and Cleopatra, *a play I was too young to understand at the time
but which I have grown into. At that time I found middle-age
desperation an embarrassment, found Antony a sad parody of the*

appropriately youthful lover Romeo, and led the discussion to other matters. One line, however, stuck, in part because it came after the humiliating botch of a suicide, a scene which stirs deep-rooted sympathies in me, but mostly because it represents a comic bathos to which I am particularly susceptible. It comes when the dying Antony discovers that Cleopatra, whom he had thought dead, the source of his despair, is alive, that it was all a ruse. "I am dying, Egypt," he tells her, "dying." In particularly black moods, I find the line irresistible. It is there today, welling up with each soggy step, the taunt of middle age.

Poor Antony! The rat has bit thy throat.

I would like to remove the waders, drain them before going farther, but the dam is narrow and rickety, and the task, at best, an awkward one. Instead I edge to the north end and reluctantly crawl back into water that rises to the tops of my boots, and ease forward onto the silt.

A sandpiper flies by, squeaking at me as it passes.

Again, today, the midday sun refuses to locate me, but I think I am heading due west, perhaps moving slightly to the south. The stream bends more sharply, more southerly, and I hit a huge dam, painstakingly maintained, and impounding a lake that is more than seventy-five yards long. I climb to the top, toeing into the sticks until I stand crouched and unsteady, looking into a pond that is surely deep as well as wide. Since the dark water conceals everything beneath its surface, I cannot say how I know it is deeper than any pool I've yet encountered, but I do know, and the impact of that knowledge is greater than I have anticipated. Without question I am out of my depth, have reached a point where all my improvisation will fail. No more tiptoeing or pulling myself along while clinging to the branches that grow along the margins.

For days I have known this was inevitable, but now that the

defeat is at hand, I feel a tremendous sadness along with the weariness. I tell myself this was a lark, an amusement not to be taken seriously, but the weight of the failure is not lessened.

The defeat lies in more than just not getting to the Run's headwaters. It has to do with the indeterminacy of this ending, of having come so far on—despite my reluctance to use the word—faith without at last knowing where I have arrived or what it all comes to. The headwaters, that dark pool I saw with Joe, at least contained a conclusion, but here on my last dam, looking ahead to other dams, I cannot see the anticipated end.

After all these miles of keeping to my narrow path, all these days of undersized trout, I have come at last to just another swamp. With what will I fill the last pages of my notebook? I feel as though I am reeling in all those lines, the ones on all the sheets of paper in the loft, and though the bait has been taken, nothing has been hooked. At the end of my leader, pinned to the cork butt of the fly rod, are the red body and white wings of a royal coachman, but now I see only feathers and tinsel, and am amazed that I ever thought to fool a big trout with so small an illusion, am amazed that it has taken me so long to see the inadequacy of what I've been casting on this stream.

Much has been misread, much misremembered. It is time to be sure. I have mistaken shallows for depth before.

I lay down the rod, the creel, the net, and the notebook and tie the waders tight around my waist, then, belly pressed against the corduroy of limbs, slide into the still waters on the dam's far side. My feet catch on a thin layer of sticks that sags beneath my weight, yet holds me high enough for my wader top to remain half an inch above the surface. I release my hold, turn from the dam, and step into the pool. Twigs and silt collapse, and I plummet downward, blinded by water the color of strong tea.

"I am dying, Egypt, goddammit, dying." Eyes open, I watch the flotsam drift upward, passing my face like ungainly birds against a brown sky. The weight I have gathered takes me deeper into these tannic waters, deeper until, arms flailing, I turn, catch the dam and begin the slow climb back to the surface. Finally I thrust my head above the water, retrieve my floating hat, and pull myself free of the Run.

Twenty feet away, and looking directly at me, is the hen mallard. She says nothing, merely watches knowingly and waits.

I look at the map, damp at the folds but otherwise undamaged, and guess that the trail out must be somewhere just ahead. I put map and notebook into my hat, then pull it once more into place.

Belatedly using the fly rod for a depth gauge, I check the water above the dam, and even beside the alder cannot strike bottom although I use the rod's entire seven-foot length. The pool is unwadeable.

The mallard paddles closer to me, effortlessly, calmly.

There is no hope of passage, and I retreat to the north, continuing on until I crash into living alder and scramble onto the lower slope of the ridge.

In "Big Two Hearted River," a river north and east of Cook's Run, Hemingway has Nick fish across from a great swamp, a swamp whose cover is home for huge trout. But Nick, who in the aftermath of his generation's war, is trying to get control over his life and mind, does not enter that part of the stream. He realizes, we are told, that fishing in a swamp is a tragedy. Still, though cautious now, he anticipates a time when, stronger, healthier, he will take on that risk, will try out for a grander role.

But weary as he is, Nick is not middle-aged. I will never enter the upper waters of the Run, in all likelihood will never return even to this place. Today's decision, like so many more significant ones made during half a lifetime, will be irrevocable.

In a small clearing I flop down and fight my way out of the waders. My pants are soaked to the waist, and my socks, reduced to greenish-brown mush, hang loosely, barely covering my heels and drooping seven inches below my toes. I pour three or four gallons of water from the boots, and after wringing out my socks, pull everything back on.

After a hundred yards and no sign of a path, I arrive at an opening that faces out over the valley. To the left I can see the far end of the dam on which I made my undistinguished exit, and I wonder if the mallard still waits or if she realizes her victory. To the right the valley opens into marshlands that continue until everything blurs in the midday haze. But I can see another dam, and beyond that the Run flows, a dark river winding through acres of yellow-green grass, grass broken again and again by beaver huts and dark hummocks of mud. Sunlight glances from water that looks denser than water—more like molten lead—flashing a metallic gleam as it cuts through the marsh. It is, from this height, beautiful, and again the ever returning temptation, and I think, somehow, I can continue—that if I get back in, perhaps at the second dam, I can go farther. In a final surge of energy and frustration I even start back down into the alder and muck, then stop, admitting once and for all that I cannot do it, not today, not this year, not ever.

The wall panels from Nineveh, huge slab reliefs done in limestone and now housed in the British Museum, portray a lion hunt—or a series of lion hunts. I wish my grandfather St. Clair could have seen them. The king, riding in a chariot, fires arrows at the pursuing beasts—not a hunt conducted in the wild, but one in which the prey are released from cages, captives goaded into one final rush at their captor. Behind the lions, warriors, armed with spears, drive them toward the lord, who stands, imperious and unmoved on his wheeled platform and there rains anguish on his victims, while other captives, his horses, bound by traces and by harness, keep him beyond the reach of tooth and claw.

In one panel a lioness, her spine severed by two arrows through her back, pulls forward on erect forelegs, dragging the paralyzed hindquarters, her jaws spread wide in one last cry.

The human forms seem lifeless, formulaic, devoid of personality, neither requesting nor requiring our sympathy. The lions provide the dramatic center; the lions we can understand, we can mourn. Their agony is the heroic subject of the panels. It is their story—not the king's—that is told here, and its ending seems as apparent and inevitable to them as to us.

Another panel—this one in alabaster, not quite so old but with the same deadly sovereign identified by the same name, though followed by a different number—and this time the king, sure of his triumph, has turned to aim upon some prey ahead. From a field littered with dead beasts, one long-maned male, his body already penetrated by arrows, seizes the moment and lunges nearly within jaw's reach of the royal archer. Two warriors riding beside their king have seen him and meet his charge with spears.

The lion strains against his fate, awesome in pain and rage and will. If somehow, despite the terrible wounds he already bears, he can make that ultimate leap, he will annihilate the kingly prerogative and end this horror. But the stone does not yield. The story, beautifully figured, exquisitely composed, demands its only end. Twenty-six hundred years after his emergence from the rock, the beast remains as far from deliverance as in the beginning. His body will carry him no farther, has already passed its zenith, and only the ennobling power of his inadequacy remains.

I return to the clearing and look once more at the Run as it flows down out of the beaver ponds, the marshes and bogs, less than two miles old, and yet wider and deeper than it ever will be in its maturity. Those beginnings will be concealed from me, the knowledge of the Run in all its simultaneity, its mouth and

its source always present—always beginning, always ending—
that is what I have been denied, that and the big trout that must
lurk somewhere ahead in the dark waters to the west.

*Perhaps the Evangelist, he of Revelation, was right. Perhaps at
the end the heavens will curl up like a scroll, fire will rain down
on the earth, and the rivers will run with blood. But perhaps,
when the last seal has been broken, the light will not prove so
unlike this bright haze, the landscape not be consumed by other-
worldly theatrics, the rivers run no redder than the Paint after
a more conventional rain. Perhaps the end will come with unmoving waters, thick with the world's sloughed-off skin, and in
colors and circumstances not so different from those before me
now. Perhaps.*

*And in the end, as with Beamon and Holly and the king's lion
and all the rest of us, it will be gravity that prevails, regardless
of the appointed few who may be snatched up by helicopters or
angels. We belong to gravity and the earth it weds us to.*

I surrender, sit down and remove my battered waders, pull on
the wet sneakers, then strike out cross-country in what I hope is
a northern direction. It is a little after eleven o'clock.

After twenty minutes without sign of any trail, pushing
through spruce and then spruce mixed with maple and pine, like
a straggler in a fairy tale, I happen upon a small flat-roofed
building, tar-papered with a long, eyelike slit staring at me three
feet above ground level. In a moment I recognize it as a deer
blind, but it troubles me, and I circle warily looking for the
inevitable path. There is no path, no way cut in by hunters, and
when I've completely circled the building and found nothing, I
approach it carefully from one of its blind sides, then peer in
through the slit designed for rifles. Inside is an overstuffed chair,
its corners chewed and its stuffing pulled out in big gray mounds.

The room is in disarray, musty, claustrophobic. How can there not be a trail? How did they bring in the chair? The lumber to make the blind? On one wall of the building a locust husk, neatly split down the back, shows amber and translucent on the decaying wood. Its thin legs still cling tightly, hanging on even as the creature's strange new life was departing. I flick at it with my finger. It hangs on still.

I move into the timber, but when after several minutes I stop to look at the map, it is missing. The soggy notebook is still in my hat but the map is gone. I think of finding my way through the maze of trails—if I ever hit a trail—unguided, and I backtrack. When I reach the blind once more, I circle it and, feeling watched, move quietly, keeping as best I can to the concealment of the trees. I find the map beneath a big hemlock, as though unconsciously I had, before, reconnoitered the building in this same secretive way.

When I was ten, I began to worry that I had not been baptized. Perhaps it was something some itinerant preacher had said in one of his more sulphurous moments, or perhaps it was only the pressure that all Baptist kids begin to feel at that age, a not so subtle push to answer the call, heard or unheard, and to go forward toward church membership. I was torn between my fear of damnation—an event that I knew would greatly disappoint my mother—and my reluctance to misrepresent things. To pretend assurance in issues of faith I knew was also a matter of considerable risk.

Eventually I revealed some of this to my father, and he took me to see Uncle Ivan. When the two of us were alone I finally, shyly, poured out my fears, described the two wrongs I was torn between. Uncle Ivan took me out to the barn to show me a new colt he had bought and, while I stroked the animal's head and mane, said for me not to worry, said that the God he tried to serve did not put a great emphasis on a person's saying the right words at the right moment, said that God, unlike some of His more enthusiastic preachers, did not spend his time looking for excuses to punish people. He said he thought any god worth his salt must respect honest doubt, and he thought the biblical God had a history of getting along better with doubters than with the most fervent of true believers. "I couldn't preach if I believed otherwise."

We walked back toward the house. "It's a funny thing about people," he said, "the way we imagine God to have the same weaknesses that we have; how we give Him our meanness, then think it all the other way around." We sat on the porch. My father drove up the road toward us, the cloud of dust rising behind his car visible nearly a mile away.

Then Uncle Ivan, speaking slowly and carefully, looking directly at me, said, "If it will put your mind at rest, I give you my word that God doesn't care one way or the other whether or not you get baptized. Do it when it feels right, but for now it is not something to worry about."

It had worried me, more even than I had realized, and the relief that came with Uncle Ivan's reprieve was both instantaneous and complete. This was a man who could be believed, and I trusted his words wholly, no matter how limited my understanding of them.

He put his hand on my shoulder: it was remarkably light given its size. "God's not something any of us ever comprehends, not at any age, and, because we can't understand God, there is a lot in ourselves that we never quite get hold of. In a year or two or ten, you won't know much more about all of this than you do now, but eventually you'll choose the way you think of God. It's a choice you make based on what you come to see in your-

self—the part of yourself you can figure out—and in the world around you. In a way it's all there waiting for you to imagine— you, the world, God."

He paused as my father pulled the old Mercury coupe, white with gravel dust, up to the gate. Suddenly it became very important to me to look at Uncle Ivan's face, as if, in the future, remembering how he had appeared I would be better able to remember what he had said, thinking already in the past tense about what was happening in the moment. He was, I thought— and it was a thought that surprised me, so odd and out of character, but I thought it just the same—beautiful, beautiful the way a tree is beautiful, or a river.

"There is enough that is terrible, enough to feed all those brimstone-breathing preachers, enough fire and filth for the meanest god imaginable. I don't doubt there is reason for the worst versions we come up with, but when I choose to imagine God, it's as the god of that colt out in the barn. I know that isn't the whole story, but when it's time to choose, that's the choice I make. It seems to me, wherever there is meanness, it is our duty to fight it rather than give in, even if it is God Himself we are reforming."

He rose, and we began the walk toward the car and my waiting father. After a couple of steps he stopped and looked down at me, "I've made my choice," he said, "and I live with it the best I can. In time you'll make yours." He smiled—not the condescending smile so many adults lavish on children, but the small, barely perceptible smile he sometimes gave my grandfather when they talked—then added, "And you'll do the best you can with what you come to. That's the way of things."

Perhaps mine is the god of rivers, one of immersions in tannic, dark waters and upcurrent wades that never arrive at proper destinations, the god of small trout and anxious loons. I suppose

I, too, have chosen but without fully accepting the choice I have made. What I had in mind at ten—some getting to the other side, some ultimate homecoming—I still have in mind. I suppose that, too, is the way of things in this thicket I call the world, that I call my self.

Ten minutes farther into the woods I hit a trail. It is overgrown with weeds and an occasional young maple, and though I am unsure if it is the path I am seeking, I follow it unquestioningly as it meanders along. In time I come to a fork, or rather the lower branch of a fork, and turn instinctively to the right.

Shortly after one o'clock I break into the opening of the second gas line—the first must have already crossed the highway—and almost immediately hear the whine of a truck passing a short distance ahead. And then I am on the asphalt.

I've no idea how far away from our agreed pickup point I have come out, but I start east, along the shoulder. I will call the cabin from the trailer camp on Golden Lake.

A car pulling a boat comes over the hill behind me, and I stick out my thumb. The woman on the passenger side has a worried look on her face, and the driver speeds up. Other cars pass, as well as a lumber truck, but none seems to regard me as a good risk. I am sweating; beads of water drip from my beard. I smell of marsh muck, and burrs bristle on my jeans, jeans that have—perhaps from their immersion in these waters—bleached out in stripes that parallel their seams.

I hear another car behind me and turn only when it slows. "Want a ride?" Karen asks, and Aaron laughs as he opens the door to take me back.

Always in my life there have been rivers, veins and capillaries that have nourished it and held it together in some loose fashion. Drowning rivers; baptizing rivers; rivers just to look at; rivers to stay away from; rivers that curl next to the town park, bordering a manicured lawn—backdrop for a white bandstand; rivers that wind through thick timber, where cottonmouths sun on low-hanging limbs; rivers I have watched with my grandfathers, and those I have been warned against by my parents, and those I have canoed with my brothers and friends, and those I have crossed with my wife, and those I have waded with my children. I have never wholly known any of them and have, in time, yielded each to its own inscrutability. So I let this one go, along with the others.

Then, again, perhaps waters, once entered, are never relinquished, and we continue in their presence as long as there is mind and memory.

Karen asks me what I am thinking. Aaron asks me what I have caught. And ahead the highway curves like the Run through hemlock and maple and pine.

A f t e r w o r d

A forest, viewed from above, becomes a vast, lumpy blanket of green, a quilting of textures as hardwoods join conifers, and of colors whenever spruce fronts against maple or hemlock against birch. From this perspective, spiring pines are diminished, become part of the subtle rise and fall of the timber, and lose the majestic advantage of their height. There are no trees, only the woods, only the larger, living thing, more beautiful in its fullness than one could have guessed from the closer view.

Kurt's brother Alan has flown the three of us in his small plane to see our lake from the air. We crossed many lakes on the flight from Iron Mountain but easily pick out the idiosyncrasies, even from this height, of the one we know best. At the center it is a deep blue—bluer even than that, a layering of blues, all still visible and yet submerged in some more complete version of themselves, and that great jewel encircled by shallows, a wide, brown band stretching twenty feet out from the shore.

The cabins are reduced to roofs, the Olssons' barely visible among the trees, ours a broad, rusty span, backed by the tan scar of a newly installed drain field—this summer's project. Small figures move in the yard, follow an ivory-yellow Brandywine, who bounds toward the dock. They wave and Alan waggles the plane in reply. Next door, where Carlysle's cabin used to stand, the grass is thick and sprinkled with popple shoots.

Sarah is not among the watchers. Having completed her second year of college, she has taken a summer job in Maine. But I can still see Elizabeth, who has recently begun talking about schools for the year after next. Karen would like her to stay close to home, but she, with her older sister's support, is insistent upon moving away. Aaron, already the tallest of the three, stands beside his mother. He does not wave, seems rather to have his hands in his pockets, and his shoulders are slouched as though he has just been awakened. His ritual this summer—he has a different one every summer—is to hold his breath whenever we drive past a cemetery, out of consideration, he says, for those no longer able to breathe. Brandywine leaps into the water, her splash a surge of white, clearly visible, like those left by the waves breaking against the far shore.

Alan swings the plane to the east, curling around until we reach the Paint just beyond Cook's Run. Two does stand below the fork. One bends to drink, the other's neck arches up, her head lifted toward us.

It is three years since my attempt at wading the Run. I have thought several times of returning. Most often the temptation is to put a canoe in at the headwaters and float downstream to the place where, then, I was forced out. Sometimes, in a drier season, I think of trying another wade, this time with the current. But I've left it alone, have never gone to the trouble of finishing that old business.

Below, the Run's first turbulence appears only as a change of color, a band of light on a ribbon of dark. Here and there evidence can be seen of a rough passage, an unevenness of the surface, a dancing of reflected sunshine, but—from above—the Run is static, an elaborate and wonderful design woven into the landscape, a subtle figure in this green carpet. Occasionally it disappears, but only to return in exactly the right place, the pattern sustained even in disruption.

In the meadows the meanders, the intricacy of curls, are breathtaking. The evening light burnishes the broad sweep of grass and tints the stream so that all seems, at one moment, a kind of tapestry, ancient and familiar, yet glimpsed for the first time, and in another, the work of some exquisite metalsmith. There remains some secret in those waters, some rich promise that is both reassuring and puzzling.

Below the plane the great elbow beyond the fish hatchery, beyond Deloria's, has lost its threat, looks a little like the Meadows though without the beauty of the river's turning or the careful symmetry of grasslands, seems just a stream strung across a yellow field broken by thin lines of brown. Then it widens, the marsh more obviously a marsh, the beaver ponds broader, more ominous. Perhaps because of the lowering light, the loss of the sun's alchemy, the water has darkened and seems, even from this perspective, to have deepened immeasurably. For the first time there is a chill in the plane's cockpit.

The changing perspective also applies to my wade, and what I have written about it. All that seems far away now, and I sometimes find it difficult to know why I took the business so seriously. Reading back over things, I am not always sure I recognize the author with all his self-absorption; and in retrospect I am amused that so much of what I thought I had remembered, other witnesses—children, neighbors—suggest I have invented, and how much of what I thought I had invented—a turn of phrase, a metaphor—I have since discovered to be the subtle work of memory, echoes of other texts and other lives. But there are passages, a glimpse of a river's grace or of the subtle spell a child has cast, for which I am grateful no matter who the author. What was, then, is not the same as what now is; that day's stream is not the one below me, its children not the ones who stand upon my dock or call at night from other places. But then my subject was always the reality of memory and not historical truth.

Sometime between Copernicus and Newton, Kepler suggested that what lies between the planets and the sun is not space but that other great something that appears in its invisibility to be nothing, the Holy Ghost. It is a dazzling leap, one which makes of gravity a work of grace, one which perhaps can reconcile us to other separations, other vacancies, a physics of the soul's longing.

Joe fishes more regularly this summer and speaks of dying only rarely, and two nights ago Aaron reeled in a three-foot pike from our once-dead lake. Things go on, not as I anticipated, but, like most of life, in ways that are both better and worse than any of us could have guessed.

About the
Author

Wayne Fields

was born in 1942 on his grandparents' farm near Wyaconda, Missouri. He is professor of English and dean of the University College at Washington University in St. Louis. His publications include *James Fenimore Cooper: A Collection of Critical Essays* (editor), *The Past Leads a Life of Its Own: Stories* and *Union of Words: A History of Presidential Eloquence*.